DISCARD

TO HEAL AND TO SERVE
Women Army Doctors in World War Two
©2013 Mercedes Graf

Published by Hellgate Press
(An imprint of L&R Publishing, LLC)

Hellgate Press
PO Box 3531
Ashland, OR 97520
email: sales@hellgatepress.com

Editor: Harley B. Patrick
Interior design: Michael Campbell
Cover design: L. Redding

ISBN: 978-1-55571-744-5

Library of Congress Cataloging-in-Publication Data

Graf, Mercedes.
To heal and to serve : Army women doctors in WWII / Mercedes Graf.
     pages cm
Includes index.
   ISBN 978-1-55571-744-5
1. World War, 1939-1945—Medical care—United States 2. Women physicians—United States—Biography. 3. United States. Army. Women's Army Corps—Biography. 4. United States. Army—Medical personnel—Biography. 5. United States. Army—Medical care—History—20th century. 6. Women physicians—United States—History—20th century. 7. World War, 1939-1945—Women—United States. I. Title. II. Title: Army women doctors in WWII.
D807.U6G73 2013
940.54'7573--dc23
     2013044628

Printed and bound in the United States of America
First edition 10 9 8 7 6 5 4 3 2 1

TO HEAL

AND

TO SERVE

*Women Army Doctors in
World War Two*

MERCEDES GRAF

Contents

Foreword

A little known fact about the women in America's Armed Forces is that they are only permitted to serve by law. Further, they have never been subject to the draft. Legislation established the first women's component, the Army Nurse Corps, in February 1901, authorizing the first servicewomen "in" the Armed Forces. The Navy Nurse Corps followed in 1908. Its important to note, however, that a few women prior to this time are credited with military service, including those who disguised themselves as men or those who were given credit or recognition as servicemembers because of work they were performing. While nurses were already authorized during World Wars I and II, the law was used to permit the service of non-nurses for the duration plus a short period thereafter. In the case of World War I, a standing law was invoked, while specific legislation actually permitted women's military service during World War II. Starting in World War I, a handful of women doctors were permitted to serve as civilian contract physicians.

Ironically, the only female recipient of the Medal of Honor, Dr. Mary E. Walker—a woman who tried desperately and unceasingly to join the Army as a doctor or surgeon and who cared for wounded and dying soldiers whether authorized to do so or not—was at the very best employed as a civilian contract surgeon but never as a military surgeon as she so desired.

From the standpoint of neglected or forgotten contributions of military women, women doctors probably lead the list. For example, concurrent with the dedication of the Women In Military Service Memorial, the Women's Memorial Foundation published *In Defense*

of a Nation, Servicewomen in World War II. Included in the book were
the non-medical officers and enlisted women in the then four service
branches, women in the Nurse Corps, the Dieticians, Occupational
Therapists and Physical Therapists, Women Airforce Service Pilots,
American Red Cross women serving in support of the military, the
United Service Organization (USO), and the Public Health Service
Cadet Nurse Corps. Regrettably women doctors, although small in
number, were overlooked. So it has also been in virtually every book
about war or conflicts, even in those rare times when the contributions of the medical team are included

Thankfully, Mercedes Graf, a most eloquent historian who previously has focused her research talents on women whose contribution
had been overlooked, has taken a look at the contribution of World
War II Army women doctors. This was a critical time in American
history, particularly from the standpoint of military medicine and
the massive recruitment of medical personnel. Graf has addressed
women doctor's status in the medical profession before entering the
Army, their assessment of the experience, and their subsequent career activity.

As I read the comments of the World War II women doctors,
and noted their frustration at the limitations frequently placed on
their work, I thought about an event I witnessed in the early 1980s.
A female doctor, a Captain, was assigned to our base as the flight
surgeon. General officers were supposed to have their physicals done
by the flight surgeon. One of the male major generals stopped me
in the hall to express his concern and embarrassment about going
to her for his physical. It happened that I, a female general, had just
gone to her and found her to be most competent. My response was
how wonderful it was, after 23 years in the service, to finally be examined by a female doctor. He said, "I never thought about it from
that point of view. I'll go as scheduled." Some years later, I presided
at her retirement as a colonel. The auditorium was filled with male

generals from one to four stars and their spouses, all expressing great regret that she was retiring. She had overcome!

The book addresses the medical skills and insights the World War II women physicians could have brought to the table, and sometimes were permitted to do. It makes clear, however, the barriers and obstacles under which they had to operate and which negatively impacted their ability to contribute. Sadly, many left service with a sense of frustration. Importantly, the book also speaks to the achievements and, for many, the effect their military service had on their careers after discharge from the Army. It leaves the reader with a hope that the utilization of women doctors in the service today has progressed far, far beyond the challenges these women faced in World War II. These are stories and a time in history that needed to be documented—that, Graf has done, and done well. We should be exceedingly grateful.

Wilma L. Vaught
Brigadier General, USAF (Ret.)
President, Women in Military Service for America Memorial Foundation, Inc.

Preface and Acknowledgments

Several medical historians have treated the work of women physicians since their entry into medicine. In the book, *Sympathy and Science: Women Physicians in American Medicine*, Morantz-Sanchez presented a picture of nineteenth century medicine and the experiences of several pioneers and researchers in the field who believed they had unique contributions to make because they were women. Abram, in *"Send Us a lady Physician": Women Doctors in America 1835-1920*, held that the stereotype of women as gentle souls and creatures who were natural healers worked in their favor, and she focused on the class of 1879 at the Woman's Medical College of Pennsylvania (WMCP). In her book, *Women Doctors in Gilded-Age Washington: Race, Gender, and Professionalization*, Moldow documented the careers of some of the outstanding women who were drawn to practice in the nation's capital during the 1880s and 1890s. Walsh, in *"Doctors Wanted: No Women Need Apply," Sexual Barriers in the Medical Profession, 1935-1975*, discussed the sexual barriers in the medical profession from 1835-1975 and she explored why women have not been given an equal chance in medicine. She also touched briefly on the subject of women physicians in both world wars. Finally, in *Restoring the Balance: Women Physicians and the Profession of Medicine, 1850-1995*, More demonstrated that "the insistent effort of women in medicine today" is to seek an inner balance in integrating public and private as well as civic and professional interests for themselves and their patients. Unlike the other medical historians, however, More considered in some detail how the issue of getting commissions for women doctors in WWI gave the Medical Women's National Association, later the American Medical Women's Association (AMWA), the opportunity to prove its usefulness by recruiting the services of women doctors with the American Women's Hospitals (AWH). In the next war, the AMWA's campaign on the exclusion of women doctors from the military reserves in WWII revitalized the activism of American women physicians.[1]

Not concerned solely with the history and progress of women in medicine, other writers focused on the role of various women's groups in war, and they included a brief treatment of female physicians. Lettie Gavin provided a comprehensive overview of various groups of volunteers in *American Women in World War I: They also Served,* but her treatment of women physicians in the Great War was limited to one chapter where she, like More, considered their work with AMWA and AWH. In her work, *Mobilizing Minerva: Women in the First World War,* Kimberly Jensen, like Gavin, devoted one chapter to the work of women doctors, mostly with the AWH, although she mentioned a few women who volunteered as contract surgeons. Jensen's intent, however, was not to pursue individual women, but rather to provide a thoughtful and provocative analysis of the intersection of war, gender, citizenship, and violence as it related to WWI women.[2] Graf's book, *On the Field of Mercy: Women Medical Volunteers from the Civil War to the First World War,* differed from other books on women in war because it identified individual women physicians in the Civil War and the Spanish-American War who had been invisible previously because they had to volunteer as nurses given the constraints of the time; or, by the time of World War I, served as physicians on contract without the benefits accorded to their male colleagues in terms of benefits, pay, and rank.[3]

Three works stand out in their treatment of Army women in WWII, although a discussion of women physicians was absent in all of them: Mattie E Treadwell's definitive account of the Women's Army Corps in World War II written in 1954 chronicled the efforts to establish the WAAC/WAC along with the reactions of the women of the Corps to Army life; Bettie J. Morden's account of the Women's Army Corps expanded the story of the WAC from 1945-1978; and Jeanne Holm's story of women in the military described their fight for the right of women to serve their country.[4] Only one book by Bellafaire and Graf, *Women Doctors in War*, dwelt on the experiences of women doctors in the Army from the Civil War up to the present time, but it contained only one chapter about WWII— and that was more an overview than anything else.[5]

Since the experiences of WWII women doctors have never been treated in depth before, I feel that the telling of their stories is long overdue. As commissioning was not granted until April of 1943, their Army service was relatively short, and for the majority of the women medical officers, it was only an interlude in their professional lives. This brings up several questions. What were their lives like before they volunteered? What motivated them to become medical officers? What did they do when they were in the Army and did crossing gender lines affect their wartime military experiences? What career paths did they follow in postwar years? I have tried to weave answers to these questions in various chapters throughout the book. In doing so, I have uncovered stories that testified both to the character and the convictions of these women as individuals, as doctors, and as pioneer medical officers. And the stories are as varied and sometimes as incredible as the women themselves: From a Chinese psychiatrist to a Jewish plastic surgeon who fled Nazi Germany; from the author of the first important German textbook in anesthesiology to a pioneer in the research of Sudden Infant Death Syndrome (SIDS); from a medical missionary to an expert in the Manhattan Project; from a pathologist who was married to a member of the French Resistance to a sculptor turned physician, and so forth.

Thus, the intent of this book is to delve into the background, lives, and career paths of WWII women Army doctors in as much detail as possible since it has never been undertaken before. In the interest of clarity, Army abbreviations herein are capitalized as is current usage e.g., WAC for Wac except in quotations where the original spelling is used. At the same time, there was little or no information that could be found for some of the women, and there is still much more information to be gathered for others than has been done here. I leave that task to other researchers behind me. Finally, like any good history, it is my hope that this is a true picture of the experiences and lives of these uncommon women—all Army doctors and all volunteers who proved that combat is not the sum total of war.

In gathering materials for this book, I have many acknowledgments and deep thanks to offer to so many people that it would be impossible to list them all. It goes without saying that this work would not have been possible, however, except for the generous help in locating materials and pictures from the archivists and staff members of the many medical schools, universities, and colleges across the country that these women doctors attended. This is just as true for the many librarians who assisted me with research in public and private institutions.

Of course, there are also many individuals who have offered me assistance and help to such a degree that I feel I owe them special thanks. At the U. S. Army Military History Institute, Carlisle Barracks, Pennsylvania, I had the assistance of Army archivist, Melissa Wiford who helped guide me in this process as she had spent months putting together Dr. Margaret D. Craighill's Collection which is cited throughout this book. Also, she and Jessica Sheets read the original book proposal and made suggestions on how to focus the manuscript in terms of the women doctors' specialties. Their contributions were invaluable when it came to locating information about the women doctors and their assignments and classifications in the Army.

At Governors State University where I was formerly a tenured professor, I had the help of Lydia Morrow, Eric Nicholson, Terry Rickhoff, and Lynn Dimaggio—and without Lydia's dogged determination to identify sources in the early phases of this process, the book would probably never have gotten off the ground. At Drexel University College of Medicine (DUCM) Special Collections, Legacy Center, I had the help of director of archives Joanne Murray, and archivist Barbara Williams, as well as former staff, Alex Miller. Of course, no book on Army women could be undertaken without the assistance of the staff at the Women in the Military Society of America (WIMSA) and especially to foundation president, Brig. Gen. Wilma I. Vaught, USAF (Ret.) and to curator of collections, Britta Granrud. I am also appreciative of the ongoing help of archivists at the National Archives and Records Administration (NARA) in Washington D.C. as well as to staff at the Library of Congress.

Several families and friends of these women Army doctors also offered materials and pictures that were used in this book. I am especially grateful to the families (mentioned separately in end notes) of Margaret Lynn Bryant, Eleanor Hayden, Clara Raven, Mila Pierce Rhoads, Genia Sakin, Josephine Stephens, Elvira Seno, anad Grace Fern Thomas for materials and pictures. I also give special thanks to the Lutheran Society for providing materials related to Agnes Hoeger and her missionary work.

I am especially appreciative of the rare opportunity I had to interview Dr. Theresa McNeel by phone; and in particular, for her patience with me in our numerous contacts—as well as her reading and rereading the transcript to see that I got it "right". If I have forgotten to mention others, I hope they will forgive me, and know their efforts were just as well appreciated.

~ NOTES ~

1. Morantz-Sanchez, Regina, *Sympathy and Science: Women Physicians in American Medicine* (New York: Oxford University Press, 1985); Abram, Ruth J. *"Send Us a Lady Physician": Women Doctors in America 1835-1920,* (New York: W. W. Norton & Company, 1985); Moldow, Gloria. *Women Doctors in Gilded-Age Washington: Race, Gender, and Professionalization* (Urbana: University of Illinois Press, 1987); Walsh, Mary Roth, *"Doctors Wanted: No Women Need Apply," Sexual Barriers in the Medical Profession, 1835-1975* (New Haven: Yale University Press, 1977); More, Ellen S. *Restoring the Balance: Women Physicians and the Profession of Medicine, 1850-1995,* (Cambridge, Massachusetts: Harvard University Press, 1999). Quote, More, 12.

2. Gavin, Lettie, *American Women in World War I: They Also Served* (Niwot, Colorado: The University Press of Colorado, 1997); Jensen, Kimberly, *Mobilizing Minerva: Women in the First World War* (Champaign, IL: University Press of Illinois, 2008). Too many books have been written about nurses to be listed here.

3. Graf, Mercedes, *On the Field of Mercy: Women Medical Volunteers from the Civil War to the First World War* (Amherst, NY: Humanity Books, 2010). This was the first time a separate group of women physicians was identified as serving in the Spanish-American War; and it was achieved by scanning roughly 1500 personal data cards of the contract nurses which asked the question: From what nursing school did you graduate? By purest chance, it was noted that some women physicians struck out nursing school and wrote medical school in its place.

4. Three books: Treadwell, Mattie E., *United States Army in World War II, Special Studies: The Women's Army Corps* (Washington DC: Center of Military History United States Army, 1954); Morden, Betty J., *The Women's Army Corps 1945-1978* (Washington, DC: Center for Military History, 2000); Holm, Jeanne, *Women in the Military: An Unfinished Revolution* (Novato, CA: Presidio Press, 1982). Two other recent books on WACs talk about them in the context of social issues that surrounded them in the 1940s: Jean Bethke Elshtain and Sheila Tobias, eds., *Women, Militarism, and War* (Savage: MD: Rowman & Littlefield Publishers, Inc., 1990); and Meyer, Leisa D., *Creating G.I. Jane: Sexuality and Power in the Women's Army Corps* (New York: Columbia University Press, 1996). For women in the Navy, see Godson, Susan H. Serving *Proudly: A History of Women in the U.S. Navy* (Annapolis, MD: Naval Institute Press, 2001); but women Navy physicians are not discussed. There is, however, a chapter about them in *Women Doctors in War.*

5. Bellafaire, Judith and Graf, Mercedes, *Women Doctors in War* (College Station, TX: Texas A & M Press, 2009).

MERCEDES GRAF

Introduction: Pioneer Women Doctors Campaign for Wartime Service

Throughout history, women have participated in war. They went as camp followers, cooks, and laundresses, assumed nursing duties, and when they could not bear arms, they sometimes disguised themselves as men. In the American Civil War, it has been documented that more than two hundred women assumed male disguises and enlisted in the armies of the Union and the Confederacy since they could not do so as females. At war's end, however, women soldiers demonstrated that they were effective in combat and they bore all of the same hardships and dire consequences as their male counterparts suffering "wounds, disease, and internment as prisoners of war" and even died for their country.[1]

Also serving on the Civil War battlefield were a handful of women doctors who have been mostly overlooked because they had to work as nurses given the gender constraints of the time.[2] Like the females who adopted male disguises, pioneer women doctors faced enormous obstacles in their quests to serve their country during wartime—a situation that did not change even as late as World War II. Thus, they had to overcome the barriers erected against them by a society that placed specific demands upon its females, they needed to learn how to cope with a medical establishment that was dominated by men, and they had to storm an all-male military hierarchy that held women did not belong.

The relation between gender and professionalism is an issue that women doctors have struggled with since they were drawn into medicine. In her groundbreaking study on this topic, Morantz-Sanchez noted that historically most female physicians believed that they had a unique contribution to make to their profession and to society at large. This has been true from the colonial period where their activities, such as nursing and midwifery, were linked to the private sphere; to the antebellum health reform movement where health was viewed as " a female responsibility"; and lastly to their entrance into medicine in ever-growing numbers during the nineteenth century which ushered in a phenomenon that historians have referred to as the "cult of domesticity" or the "cult of true womanhood."[3] During this period, the public arena was the natural place for men, while women's rightful place was the home. Qualities most desirable in a woman were associated with her tenderness, docility, obedience, cheerfulness, and modesty and moral worth. The concept of "separate spheres" reinforced the belief that men and women's natures were opposites and pioneer women who studied medicine were thought to be violating their natural domestic roles in society.[4] While women were presumed to be citizens, they lacked the rights male citizens had such as owning property, voting, working in a profession, and enlisting in the Army. In other words, as historian Kerber maintains: There are hierarchies of citizenship.[5] Since women were at the bottom of the hierarchy, female physicians faced many more obstacles and they needed a special brand of perseverance to overcome them. They also recognized that cooperation was preferred over competition if they were to succeed in mainstream society. If indeed they were different than men, they would bring their tender ministrations to the bedside as only women could.

Yet even as the Victorian era began to wane, the struggles of medical women were repeated over and over again because of the "dictates of a culture still characterized by extreme sex stereotyping."[6] One writer was even more outspoken on the battles of medical women over the years when she stated, "One thing is clear: sexual discrimination is deeply embedded in the fabric of American medicine."[7]

Elizabeth Blackwell, for example, knew first-hand about the stigma associated with her sex. "The first seven years of New York life were years of very difficult, though steady, uphill work," she said. "I had no medical companionship, the profession stood aloof, and society was distrustful of the innovation [of medical women]." Unable to practice in hospitals and dispensaries there, she was sometimes the object of anonymous hate mail. When no one would rent her office space, she solved the problem by buying her own house; and she adopted an orphan girl in 1854 to assuage the feelings of loneliness that accompanied her pursuit to establish a medical practice.[8]

Towards the end of April 1861, Blackwell realized that nurses would be needed in the field, and she started a training program under the auspices of the New York's Woman's Central Relief Association. In her autobiography, however, Blackwell scarcely mentions her wartime experience, other than to note her "special work was the forwarding of nurses to the seat of war." She said simply: "All that could be done in the extreme urgency of the need was to sift out the most promising women from the multitudes that applied to be sent on as nurses, put them for a month in training at the great Bellevue Hospital of New York, which consented to receive relays of volunteers, provide them with a small outfit, and send them on for distribution to Miss Dix, who was appointed superintendent of nurses at Washington."[9] When the government decided to train and supply nurses on a much larger scale, Blackwell was considered a logical candidate, "but because most medical men were suspicious, hypercritical, or jealous of her, Dorothea Dix was appointed Superintendent of Women Nurses."[10]

A few other medical women decided to practice their healing arts on the Civil War battlefields at the same time that Blackwell threw her energy into training nurses. Given societal expectations and the military's negative view of women serving in a man's Army; however, they could not be commissioned as medical officers. In order to treat the wounded and sick, they volunteered instead as nurses, a role which was consistent with the "tender ministrations" of women—even though these women had superior training to the thousands of inexperienced women who rushed to the field. Since they performed the duties of nurses, they were generally perceived as nurses—something that Dr. Mary Edwards Walker, the only woman to be awarded the Medal of Honor so far, could not and would not countenance.[11] In fact, her persistence and determination (which many called obstinacy and stubbornness) in pursuing a commission as an assistant surgeon not only made her a controversial figure, but it made her a highly visible one as well. Like it nor not, she forced the public to concede, however unwillingly, that a woman doctor could take to the field if she chose.

Dr. Mary Edwards Walker.
Courtesy National Archives.

As pioneer women doctors managed to graduate from medical school, they continued to feel the brunt of an unsympathetic public—sometimes in their own families and sometimes as it was reflected in institutional discrimination and even outright ostracism. Such experiences, however, only seemed to make them more determined to succeed. For example, Bertha Van Hoosen, who was born March 26, 1863, in the midst of the Civil War, had to reconcile herself to some of the same kinds of problems Blackwell had. As her parents were not supportive of her plans to be a doctor, she saved money earned from teaching calisthenics and physiology to finance her studies at the University of Michigan Medical School in 1884. Aware of her financial straits, Dr. Mary McLean offered to help the young woman with her studies and housing although it meant finding larger quarters. The search proved difficult, however, as all the rooming house owners were adamant on two points: no woman doctor, and no sign. Van Hoosen recalled, "Dr. McLean opened my eyes to the prejudice, the discrimination, the lack of confidence and paucity of opportunities that had to be reckoned with before success could be secured." Toughened by such experiences, and despite considerable opposition from male faculty, she went on to become the first female faculty member of the University of Illinois College of Medicine despite much opposition from male faculty.[12]

Early women physicians from the South had even more problems when they declared their intentions to study medicine given the views of how a genteel and refined woman was expected to conduct her life. Born into a prominent family in Lynchburg, Virginia, Rosalie Slaughter Morton entered medical school in 1893 at the Woman's Medical College (WMC) in Pennsylvania against her parents' wishes. Her mother "could not bear the thought of my serving all sorts of people in clinics and hospitals," and her father felt she "should not go into competition with those who need to support themselves." Her response was: "I would need less courage to face those dangers, fancied or real, than Joan of Arc had in becoming a soldier!" Undaunted, she became the first woman faculty member in Colombia's prestigious University College of Physicians and Surgeons.[13]

Around the same time that Morton was completing medical school and doing an internship, other women physicians faced the same kind of sexual prejudices at the start of the Spanish-American War in 1898. Nursing was done entirely by men until Congress recognized the necessity of increasing medical services to its soldiers and authorized the employment of contract nurses, regardless of sex, in March 1898. While this was a small victory for female nurses, who were now highly trained having graduated from the hundreds of approved nursing schools that had sprung up after the Civil War, women physicians were still unable to volunteer as physicians. But the window of opportunity was beginning to widen just a bit when on 29 August 1898, Surgeon General George Miller Sternberg appointed Dr. Anita Newcomb McGee Acting Assistant Surgeon in the Army and assigned her to the War Department. She was "placed in charge, directly under him, of all matters concerning" women nurses.[14] With this appointment, McGee was the only woman with that title in the Army, but she was also not perceived as a threat by male military surgeons as her work was purely administrative, and she would not be doing any real medical work.

Dr. Anita Newcomb McGee.
Courtesy Office of the Surgeon General, U.S. Army.

Even as soldiers rallied to the cry, "Remember the Maine" in 1898, women on the home front continued to support their men as they rushed to war. Yet many of them were determined to serve as nurses, albeit on contract with the Government, or else working with private agencies or groups such as the Red Cross. A handful of women doctors were just as eager to volunteer even if they could not do so officially as medical officers. McGee, who was busy in setting up a selection process for nurses, noted: "A few women physicians in good standing were also accepted as nurses" on contract. "Those who opposed the entrance of women into medicine as doctors," it seemed, "welcomed them as nurses...Clearly, women as nurses, engaged as they were in a domesticated version of the doctor's role, posed no threat to the male physician."[15] One of the doctors personally recruited by McGee was Dr. Mary E. Green, a well-known expert in foods—marking the first time a woman physician was recruited for her specialty area in war even though she served as a contract nurse.

It was Green's job to help design and supervise special diets, especially for typhoid victims who were suffering in many of the camps in the southeastern part of the United States. [16]

As World War I escalated, women physicians began to push their agenda for wartime service and military rank. If "action" was the watch word of the day, there was no stopping Van Hoosen and Morton who, along with Esther Pohl Lovejoy and Emily Dunning Barringer, went about promoting the rights of women physicians in war—a battle which would be repeated in WWII. When Van Hoosen served as the first president of the Medical Women's National Association (MWNA) in 1917, she appointed Morton as chairman of the War Service Committee, and the American Women's Hospitals Service (AWH) was put under it. Over a thousand women registered with the American Women's Hospitals the first year it was established. In accordance with the provisions of a special agreement, a large number of these women doctors were certified to the Red Cross for service in France, Italy, Poland and the Balkan States. (The Red Cross had also decided that there was an age limit, with special exceptions, for these physicians between twenty-five an forty years). At the first meeting called by Morton on 9 June 1017, Lovejoy was made chairman of the Executive Committee along with vice-chairman, Emily Dunning Barringer, and Lovejoy was authorized to go to Europe as the official representative of the MWNA. [17]

Van Hoosen had a straightforward platform—"to convince women physicians, first, of the need for cooperative action by women in medicine, and second, that the National could be a positive force for women in the profession." When Morton became chair of War Services Committee of the MWNA, which in 1937 took its current name, the American Medical Women's Association, she lobbied to have women physicians recognized as being equal to men for wartime medical duty. In fact, one of the goals of the MWNA was to change the law governing the Army Medical Reserve Corps. Despite considerable opposition from Congress and the War Department, she proceeded to raise money to organize the American Women's Hospitals which sent hundreds of women doctors overseas for duty during the war and in postwar relief work later on. Towards the end of her life, Morton reflected that having been devoted "to the service of women physicians during the World War" was one of her greatest fulfillments in life.[18]

While giants like Lovejoy, Van Hoosen, Morton, and Barringer continued their activism, the War Department refused to accept women doctors in an official capacity in WWI, as only persons who were "physically, mentally, and morally qualified" could be appointed.[19] To the War Department it seemed clear that women doctors were obviously not physically qualified "persons"[19] At the same time, "many women doctors were eager to cast off the constraints of Victorian gender norms and join their male colleagues in the military medical corps."[20] In the end, the government relented its position and the Surgeon General was authorized to appoint women contract surgeons in the Army.[21] Women physicians were divided over this opportunity as many felt that serving as a civilian on contract without the benefits of rank and salary that male surgeons possessed was beneath them. McGee was also outspoken in supporting this position, as she believed working on contract was an offer that few women doctors could accept. Fifty-six women, however, volunteered, and often they had special skills the Army needed in areas such as anesthesiology and psychiatry.[22]

In World War II, woman physicians engaged in a repeat battle for their wartime rights. The AMWA renewed its efforts in an all-out campaign to help women physicians fight for military commissions. If the organization had learned anything, it was the importance of collective action by women, and it reached out for help to Dr. Emily Dunning Barringer. No better choice could have been made, as she was used to fighting for what she wanted and getting it. Born in 1876, her medical career spanned two world wars during which she played an active part in campaigning for the rights of women doctors.

In 1897 she entered the College of Medicine of the New York Infirmary, which merged with Cornell University School of Medicine. After graduation she applied for a position at Gouvernour Hospital and took a qualifying examination on which she received the second highest grade, but she was refused entrance because she was a woman. Fortunately she had Dr. Anna Putnam Jacobi for a mentor and friend who, being a fighter herself, would not let the younger woman give up.[23] Barringer reapplied later to the same hospital and was accepted although male medical interns in the city were opposed to her appointment.

Barringer became the hospital's first woman resident and ambulance physician. An immediate problem arose, however, when she learned there were no separate bathing or toilet facilities at the hospital unless she shared the men's bathrooms or made a long trip to the nurses' quarters. She solved the dilemma by buying a portable medical tub and hiring "an obliging maid" to help with filling and emptying the tub; but this was nothing compared to the discomfort and misery the other male doctors tried to foster on her as soon as she arrived. On her first night on rounds she was told that she would be expected to perform the routine catheterizations in the male surgical ward. Barringer realized that previously "men alone had dealt with the afflictions and diseases, instrumentation and surgery of the male sexual organs... [As] it is the one of the most intimate of all medical ministrations." It was clear that the male staff had conceived a plan that would ensure her failure on the first night of service, as "a strong well-founded opposition on the part of the male patient to being treated by a woman would be the strongest card the staff could hold." Nevertheless, she had been trained well and she carried out the routines with calmness and efficiency; and after her work that night she soon found "there was a growing demand for the 'Lady doctor' in the clinic."[24]

From 1917 on, Barringer was active with the MWNA; but her crusading put her in center stage when, as president-elect of the

AMWA for 1939-40 and afterwards as president, she was still promoting the wartime rating of women physicians. Fireworks broke out in 1942, however, when the American Medical Association (AMA) turned down a resolution recommending that the Army and Navy offer commissions to women physicians. AMA spokesmen opposed to the Barringer campaign insisted that women doctors "can render their greatest service" by replacing male practitioners who go on active duty.

As the controversy continued, Barringer maintained that, "The Army and Navy are the last strongholds held by men and administered by purely masculine planning. It would upset this man-made scheme to have women enter into it." Her frequent articles "demanding equal rights" appeared in the papers with such effect that half a dozen women's organizations rallied to her cause. By then she had gained the support of organizations like the American Legion and the New York State Medical Society, and she utilized the strategy that had been successful in World War I—securing the help of women leaders across the country. In this case, she solicited the support of Dorothy Kenyon, a well-known judge, lobbyist, and crusader.[25]

In March of 1943 numerous individuals and representatives of various groups throughout the country testified before the Seventy-eighth Congress. They urged the passage of a bill to provide for the appointment of female physicians and surgeons in the Medical Corps of the United States Army and Navy. Dr. Sophia J. Kleegman, of the Women's Medical Association of New York, testified that her sister, Dr. Anna Kleegman Daniels, was a contract surgeon during World War I, and she worked side by side with her men colleagues. Even though she had equal training and did exactly the same work, she was considered "inferior to them" in rank, pay, and denied many privileges, with no possibility of promotion. At that time Surgeon General Gorgas had stated: "Women physicians should be commissioned in the Army, but we are in the midst of a war and cannot take time out to pass the necessary legislation. However, I promise you that in the next war women physicians will be commissioned on a basis equal to the men." What happened to that promise?

A statement prepared by Dr. Margaret D. Craighill, then Dean of the Woman's Medical College of Pennsylvania, was read in her absence by Dr. Emily D. Barringer, who was proud to represent a school where a few years earlier the faculty unanimously expressed a willingness to serve in the Armed Forces: "With nurses now commissioned, women physicians would be in an untenable position without rank if serving with military organizations." The statement contained the names of all the students and faculty of the college who supported the Celler bill, one of two separate bills petitioning that women serve in the medical corps of the Army and Navy. The other bill was sponsored by John Sparkman of Alabama and it was later signed into law on 16 April 1943 as the Sparkman-Johnson Bill. It seemed that women physicians had finally gained the right to be medical officers "thanks to heightened wartime need and their successful, strategic hard work."[26]

Even as women physicians continued to support the AMWA and push for commissioning, however, a few adventurous American women physicians had already volunteered to serve abroad in England under the auspices of the Red Cross in the summer of 1941. As had happened in WWI, the War Department decided to accepted women physicians as contract surgeons towards the end of 1942, and several of the women in England signed contracts with the United States Army hoping this was only a temporary measure. As public pressure continue to mount and the shortage of doctors continued to grow in the military, commissions in the Army Medical Corps were finally awarded to women starting in April of 1943 for the duration of the war and six months thereafter. Although the Army placed no limit on the number of professionally and physically qualified female doctors it would accept, only 1 percent or 76 of the approximately 7,600 women doctors in the United States were ultimately commissioned.[27]

One of the ironies of women's acceptance in medicine has been that although they were well established in the latter part of the nineteenth century, by 1920 the numbers of women doctor plummeted. It is not the intent of this book to discuss these reasons, but it is evident that the decline in the number of medical schools from 162 in 1906 to 69 in 1944 led to increased competition for medical school entrance and internships and residencies, especially for women and minorities. Between the two wars, quotas had also been set for women students which averaged 5 percent and 92 percent of the hospitals did not train women doctors. As late as the 1930s, an average of 250 women who had graduated from medical school competed for 185 internships that were open to them. With the outbreak of WWII, only 105 of 712 approved internship hospitals accepted applications from women. At the same time, 4,844 male medical graduates could choose from among 6,154 internship opportunities. Almost all of the seventy-six women doctors who were commissioned in the Army during 1943 and 1944 attended medical school between World Wars—which means during a period when entry levels for women were low but competition was keen.[28]

Who then were these women who chose to study medicine at a time when competing for entrance was a challenge for the most determined and persistent individuals? Initially the Army's preference was for women doctors who were single and between the ages of thirty-five and forty-five. Once the bill for commissioning passed, however, the requirements changed somewhat as women were to have the same rights and privileges as men, and like men, be assigned where they were the most needed. Applications were preferred from women physicians under age 45. Those under age 38 were to be commissioned as lieutenants; over 38, as captains or majors, depending upon their qualifications and the existence of appropriate position vacancies. For consideration above the rank of lieutenant, special training was required in a recognized specialty as well as further study and experience in the specialty. As it turned out, only two women were over the age of fifty but there were at least seventeen under thirty-five, depending on the date that the count was taken. As expected, most of the women were in their thirties and forties and most were single although a few were divorced or widowed. Only a handful of the married women claimed dependent children, but roughly a dozen claimed a dependent parent, usually a mother.[29]

Dr. Margaret D. Craighill.
Courtesy National Library of Medicine.

Women Army doctors represented 43 medical schools from all over the United States and ten foreign schools. At the top was the WMCP having eight, Johns Hopkins having five, and four from The College of Physicians and Surgeons of Columbia University and the University of Wisconsin. Two other schools were represented by three women each: Long Island College of Medicine and the University of Texas. Several schools sent two women forward from their respective medical schools. Among these were Tufts where in 1955 only 1 percent of the graduates were female, and the University of Michigan, where there were no women graduates in 1956. (See Appendix for a list of other schools that were represented).[30]

Once women became part of the military establishment, they encountered a new set of problems. One issue that plagued the enlisted women was the concern over a woman's morals and conduct as she performs her duty and serves her country. When we consider the Civil War, we know there were definite assumptions about the proper role of the "lady volunteers". Dorothea Dix had stringent standards for government nurses, and applicants needed to produce two letters of reference testifying to their "morality, integrity, seriousness, and capacity for the care of the sick."[31] In considering what made a good nurse in the Spanish-American War, Dr. Anita Newcomb McGee required that they be judged in three areas: professional ability, character, and health.[32] When Irene Toland, a physician working on contract as a nurse, died of typhoid fever while in service during the Spanish-American War, the attending physician wrote: "She died loved by all who knew her, for her zeal and true moral worth as well as her skill."[33] Again, the inclusion of the phrase "true moral worth," emphasizes the qualities to be valued in a refined woman and nurse.

In May 1941, Congresswoman Edith Nourse Rogers from Massachusetts introduced H.R. 4906 which established the Women's Army Auxiliary Corps (WAAC), but it was not until a year later that the bill was established as law with a separate set of rules for women who would serve with the Army. One of the characteristics established by this legislation was that WAACS were required to be of high moral character and technical competence, which was not required of the men who were being inducted into the Armed Forces with the compulsory draft.[34] The changeover from WAAC to full military status as the Women's Army Corps (WAC) took place in the late summer of 1943.

WWII was also the first time that large numbers of women other than nurses were brought into the armed services, which historian

D'Ann Campbell maintains, "constituted a radical—arguably the most radical—break in the history of gender... as women in uniform challenged the centuries-old association of men with warfare, that is, challenged the most deeply anchored preconceptions of gender identity."[35] One of the most important tasks then that Oveta Culp Hobby, the Women's Corps Director, faced was promoting women as soldiers as she needed to create a new category which would proclaim female soldiers as feminine and sexually respectable.[36]

As the Women's Army Auxiliary Corps, later Women's Army Corps (WAAC/WAC) forces began to expand, there were false and exaggerated rumors about the immorality of women. One of the major themes for such rumors was "that Waacs were issued prophylactics or were required to take such items with them when they left the barracks, so that they could fulfill the 'morale purposes' for which the Army had really recruited them." It was this story in a nationally syndicated newspaper column that brought the slander campaign out in the open. Of course, there were concerns over recruiting the best female applicants, but problems were often with the screening process itself, which was often not thorough enough to wean out those women who were not prepared for the physical and mental strain of military life.[37] Clearly there were identified problems that needed attention if the WACs were to survive as a Corps, and it became the job of Dr. Margaret Craighill as the first Consultant for Women's Health and Welfare to make recommendations concerning the health of Army women including the nurses.[38]

When it came to the women medical officers in WWII, they were spared the kind of slander that had been directed at the Army servicewomen. The seventy-six women were all graduates of medical schools, they were considerably older than the WAC recruits, and many had family responsibilities in terms of dependent parents, children, or other family members. When these factors were taken as a whole, it was highly unlikely that such women had left successful practices to find husbands. Of course, it is also true that since there were so few of them, women doctors were generally overlooked as a group by the public and even the Army itself.

The war did little to change prevailing stereotypes regarding the proper social identities of men and women in the Army.[39] And neither the outbreak of WWI or WWII, with their shortage of male doctors, created any serious reconsideration of the role of women doctors in wartime by the end of 1945.[40] It was not until 1952 that permanent legislation to enable women physicians to enter the service with the same rights and privileges afforded their male colleagues was passed. By the late 1980s, one historian observed that, "virtually all liberal women's advocacy organizations were linking military participation to first-class citizenship." There was no doubt that women had formed an increasing proportion of America's military strength "and that they have been placed in positions which erode simple distinctions between *combat* and *noncombat*."[41] By the 1990s, there was also a growing interest in women's war work and a new realization that unless the public acknowledges women's experiences and contributions, the processes involved in war will not be completely understood.

This book is about WWII American women Army doctors with a focus on who they were and what they did. Once they entered the Army (Navy women physicians are not treated here), their experiences were intertwined with the WAAC/WAC. Thus, it was important to discuss the history of the WAAC/WAC as it intersected with the lives of these women throughout their wartime careers. Margaret D. Craighill's accomplishments, in particular, are considered because of her vast influence on WAC medical care and health. Craighill also pointed out that many of the women medical officers were assigned to the care of WAC personnel exclusively or at various times, the very situation that the AMWA was opposed to as this would limit the kinds of experiences women doctors could acquire from being in the Army. Craighill further indicated that there were few specialists among the women doctors in the Army. This research, however, found that while there were few specialty areas, roughly 75% of the women were in them out of the total number of 76. This brings up two questions: What were these specialties and who were assigned to them?

Commissions were given according to age and experience, and by the end of 1945 about one-third of the women Army medical officers had received promotions. In analyzing the professional classifications for each Army doctor, only a very few women were found in fields such as radiology, pathology, tropical medicine, plastic surgery and urology. This reinforces what was clear in civilian practice: gender issues played a key role in determining the choices of women doctors as most specialists were drawn to pediatrics, obstetrics/gynecology, anesthesiology, and psychiatry—fields that were consistent with "feminine" areas of endeavor.

Major Theresa Ting Woo, 1951.
Courtesy private collection.

For some other women doctors, the Army gave them opportunities they might not have had in civilian life. A few of them, for example, got special training once they were in the Army. Theresa T. Woo was a pediatrician who was sent to study tropical medicine. In addition, "her knowledge of Chinese was "of inestimable value to the military intelligence."[42] Jean Dunham, among others, was sent for training in anesthesiology, and Machteld Sano of Belgium passed her Board examinations in pathology after being commissioned. Many women doctors clamored to serve abroad and Margaret Janeway was the first to be sent overseas with the WAAC/WAC. She also worked alongside Craighill as Assistant, Women's Health & Welfare Unit.[43] By the end of the war about one-third of the total women medical officers served overseas. Some of the women were stationed in England while others went to Germany or were on duty in the Pacific area and even in South America.

Dr. Margaret Janeway.
Courtesy private collection.

Women doctors also had to take on a new set of problems never encountered before in civilian life. They had to become accustomed to military protocol and red tape in the form of administrative duties and paperwork. They were frequently given duty assignments that were unrelated to their background and training, there were issues over rank and promotions, there were concerns about overseas duty, treating exclusively or mostly women patients, and pay dependency allowances. Such matters, among others, needed to be considered here as they add to an understanding of the struggles and triumphs of this first group of women medical officers in the Army. And as Mattie Treadwell aptly put it in her classic study of the WAC: They "had passed through the natural evolution of any new cultural phenomenon [with] the mistakes and experiments…"[44]

The work of WWII women doctors has never been treated in depth before, and it is felt that the telling of their stories is long overdue. Since commissioning was not granted until April of 1943, their Army service was relatively short, and for the majority of the women medical officers, it was only an interlude in their professional lives. This brings up several questions. What were their lives like before they volunteered? What did they do when they were in the Army? Did crossing gender lines affect their wartime military experiences? What career paths did they follow in postwar years? I have tried to weave answers to these questions in various chapters throughout the book. In doing so, I have uncovered stories that testified both to the character and the convictions of these women as individuals, as doctors, and as pioneer medical officers. And the stories are as varied and sometimes as incredible as the women themselves: From a Chinese psychiatrist to a Jewish plastic surgeon who fled Nazi Germany; from the author of the first important German textbook in anesthesiology to a pioneer in the research of Sudden Infant Death Syndrome (SIDS); from a medical missionary to an expert in the Manhattan Project, from a pathologist who was married to a member of the French Resistance to a sculptor turned physician, and so forth.

As might be expected, the accounts of some doctors are more detailed than others, depending on how public their lives were and what they accomplished. In cases where there was less information available, readers are referred to the tables and Appendix which summarize important facts about these women and their Army service.

While there are many pictures of these women, it was not always possible to find them wearing their Army uniforms.

Finally, like any good history, it is the author's hope that this is an accurate picture of the experiences and lives of these uncommon women—all Army doctors and all volunteers who proved that combat is not the sum total of war.

~ NOTES ~

1. For the definitive work on women soldiers, see Blanton, DeAnne and Cook, Lauren M. *They Fought Like Demons: Women Soldiers in the Civil War* (New York: Vintage Books, 2002). Also see Hall, Richard. *Patriots in Disguise: Women Warriors of the Civil War* (New York: Paragon House, 1993). For a general treatment of women in war, see DePauw, Linda Grant. *Battle Cries and Lullabies: Women in War from Prehistory to the Present* (Norman: University of Oklahoma Press, 1998). Quote is from Blanton and Cook, 205.

2. See Graf, Mercedes, *On the Field of Mercy* where she identified eight women who served on the battlefield; but only two of them were later recognized for being contract surgeons, Dr. Mary E. Walker and Dr. Sarah Chadwick Clapp.

3. Morantz-Sanchez, Regina, 11-15. She also points out the "subtle and insidious" fear of male physicians that the influx of women would alter the image of the profession by feminizing it in unacceptable ways. For more on the connection between health reform and advances in 19th century medicine, see "Making Women Modern: Middle Class Women and Health Reform in 19th Century America," *Journal of Social History* (10) June 1977.

4. For a discussion of women in medicine from ancient healers to their status in the U.S. up to the 1870s, see Marks, Geoffrey and Beatty, William K. *Women in White* (New York: Charles Scribner's Sons, 1972); also see the monumental work of Hurd-Mead, Kate Campbell. *History of Women in Medicine from the Earliest Times to the Beginning of the Nineteenth Century* (Haddam Conn.: Haddam Press, 1938). Also see Hurd-Mead, Kate Campbell 1867-1941 Papers, Arthur and Elizabeth Schlesinger Library on the History of Women in America, Radcliffe College.

5. See Kerber, Linda K., *No Constitutional Right to be Ladies: Women and the Obligations of Citizenship* (New York: Hill and Wang, 1998). She emphasizes that rights and obligations are reciprocal elements of citizenship.

6. Morantz-Sanchez, *Sympathy and Science*, 88-89. Leigh Marlowe believed that "Sexism cannot be explained on an individual basis. Its roots are cultural, though it works out on a personal and interpersonal level. Consequently, sexism has to be treated institutionally." See "Commentary," *International Journal of Group Tensions* 4, No. 1, March 1974, Special Issue: Who Discriminates Against Women? 136-37.

7. Walsh, *Doctors Wanted: No Women Need Apply*, 272. Gender discrimination was also true in European medical schools where the first ones to open their doors to women were in Switzerland and France. Even the medical school in Paris, which

admitted women from the early 1870s, had strong "opposition from the medical faculty and general public on the grounds that a medical education would affect women's moral purity." See Le-May Sheffield, Suzanne. Women in Science: Social Impact and interaction (Santa Barbara, CA: ABC-CLIUO, 2004), 116.

8. Blackwell, Elizabeth. *Pioneer Work in Opening the Medical Profession to Women* (New York: Humanity Books, 2005), reprinted from London and New York: Longmans, Green and Co., 1895; quote 219. Also see Blackwell Family Papers 1835-1960, Arthur and Elizabeth Schlesinger Library on the History of Women in America, Radcliffe College; and the Blackwell Family Papers, Library of Congress, Washington, D. C. When Dr. Marie Zakrzewska, who established the New England Hospital for Women and Children, could not find office space early in her career, Blackwell let her open an office in her back parlor.

9. Blackwell, *Pioneer Work*, 260-61.

10. Massey, Mary Elizabeth. *Women in the Civil War* (Lincoln: University of Nebraska Press, 1994), 46; reprinted from *Bonnet Brigades* (New York: A. A. Knopf, 1966).

11. Since being referred to as a nurse was such a sore point with Walker, two years after the war she felt compelled to write to the Judge Advocate General's Office for a statement verifying her official Army service. "I am worn out by our great government that has made no appropriation for me," she declared. It was her sincere hope that no one would be allowed "to carry the idea that I had never done any service in the U. S. as surgeon or Physician, but only as nurse, but admitting that I was paid as a contract Surgeon (only) while a prisoner." She ended by asking: "Will you kindly loose no time in stating that Official papers have passed through this office showing that Mary E. Walker, M.D. graduated as Doctor of Medicine in a regularly Chartered Medical College in the state of N. Y. In the year 1855, and was serving as Contract surgeon in the U. S. A. at the time our war closed?" See "Letter of Dr. Mary E. Walker to the Judge Advocate General, April 14, 1867," Entry 6, Letters Received, RG 153, *Records of the Office of the Judge Advocate General*, National Archives and Records Administration (NARA). Also see for "Walker's Relief": Report No. 1671 to accompany H. R. 7153, April 23, 1890, in *Walker's Pension File*, SC 142 715. Whenever she was in the field, she tied the green surgeon's sash around her waist as further proof she was not a nurse. For more on Walker, see Leonard, Elizabeth D. (*Yankee Women: Gender Battles in the Civil War*. New York: W.W. Norton & Co., 1994); Schultz, Jane E. *Women at the Front: Hospital Workers in Civil War America* (Chapel Hill: The University of North Carolina Press, 2004); Graf, Mercedes. *A Woman of Honor: Dr. Mary E. Walker and the Civil War* (Gettysburg, PA: Thomas Publications, 2001).

12. Quote in Van Hoosen, Bertha. *Petticoat Surgeon* (New York: Pellegrini & Gudahy, 1947), 58-59. (This is her autobiography). Also see Schultz, Rima Lunin and Adele Hast, eds. *Women Building Chicago, 1790-1990: A Biographical Dictionary* (Bloomington: Indiana University Press, 2001). In addition, she was the only woman of her time, other than Madame Marie Curie, elected an honorary member of the International Association of Medical Women. For more information, see *Bertha Van Hoosen Papers 1931-1960,* University of Illinois-Chicago. In 1918 Van Hoosen went to Loyola University as professor and head of obstetrics, becoming the first woman to head a medical division at a coeducational university.

13. Autobiography of Morton, Rosalie Slaughter. *A Woman Surgeon: The Life and Work of Rosalie Slaughter Morton* (New York: Grosset & Dunlap, 1937); quotes on 14-15; end of life quote, 396. For more information, see the *Papers of Rosalie Slaughter Morton, M.D.* at the Hoover Presidential Library. More details her struggles in *Restoring the Balance,* 134-140, 146-147. Woman's Medical College went through several name changes from WMC to Woman's Medical College of Pennsylvania (WMCP); and was also known as Allegheny University of the Health Sciences, Hahnemann School of Medicine, and Drexel University College of Medicine. Generally this school is referred to here as WMCP unless reference is made to current archives and materials housed currently at DUCM.

14. "Untitled Manuscript by Anita Newcomb McGee" p. 25, (probably intended as a history of the Army Nurse Corps); in Anita Newcomb McGee Correspondence/ Office Files, RG 112, Entry 230, Box 1, (NARA). For a brief biography, see Dearing, Mary A. "Anita Newcomb McGee," in *Notable American Women, 1607-1950, Vol. 2* (Harvard: Belknap Press, 1971), 465; and Oblensky, Florence E., "Anita Newcomb McGee, MD," *Military Medicine* (May 1968), 398. See also Anita Newcomb McGee Papers at the Library of Congress, Washington, D.C.

15. "Testimony of Dr. Anita Newcomb McGee," *Conduct of the War Department with Spain*, Vol. 1 (Washington: Government Printing Office, 1900), 725; no threat quote in Walsh, 142.

16. For more on Dr. Mary E. Green, see Mary Elizabeth Korstad, *One to Follow: A Tale of Two Women* (New York: Carlton Press Inc., 1990). Mary (Mamie) Green Korstad, M.D. tells about her mother in the SAW; and see, B. L. Selmon, "A Woman of the Century," *Medical Woman's Journal*, Vol. 54, No. 12, December 1947, 42-43. Green's "Thesis on Medical Jurisprudence," submitted for the degree of Doctor of Medicine in the Woman's Medical College, PA., Session 1867-68, housed at (DUCM). The thesis is 17 pages long and it was her hope that "the legal and medical professions will be intelligently brought together, so that medical and surgical practitioners shall thoroughly understand their legal rights and liabilities, and the lawyers be prepared to properly examine medical men as witnesses in courts of

justice…" A Copy of Dr. Green's "Commencement" [Program] on March 14, 1868, is also housed at DUCM.

17. Sometimes there is confusion over Lovejoy's name. She was married twice; and after her first husband, Dr. Emil Pohl died, she remarried Lovejoy in a marriage that lasted seven years. The summary here of AWH is taken from her book about her experiences in France, *Certain Samaritans* (New York: The Macmillan Co., 1927). Space does not permit a discussion of her public health activism and medical relief work: reader is referred to the Oregon Health and Science University (OHSU) Historical Collections and Archives which has correspondence, speeches, and other records related to her work; Archives and Special Collections on Women in Medicine DUCM, Philadelphia. For more on AWH, see American Women's Hospitals Collection, Medical College of Pennsylvania Archives and Special Collections on Women in Medicine, Philadelphia. Also see Kimberly Jensen, *Mobilizing Minerva: American Women in the First World War* (Urbana and Chicago: University of Illinois Press, 2008); Kimberley Jensen has a Blog on-line which contains numerous references to her work.

18. Van Hoosen quote in More, *Restoring the Balance*, 125. Morton end of life quote in her autobiography, *A Woman Surgeon: The Life and Work of Rosalie Slaughter Morton* (New York: Grosset & Dunlap, 1937), 396. More offers a comprehensive account of the MWNA in WWI as well as contrast of the lives of Morton, Lovejoy and Van Hoosen.

19. Treadwell, Mattie E. *United States Army in World War II, Special Studies: The Women's Army Corps* (Washington DC: Center of Military History United States Army), 8.

20. Moore, *Restoring the Balance*, 126. Also see Jensen, Kimberly. *Mobilizing Minerva: American Women in the First World War* (Urbana: University of Illinois Press, 2008). She also discusses nurses and women physicians who she feels embraced military service during World War I as a route to personal, professional, and political advancement.

21. These women contract surgeons served at the Army's pleasure and did not get the military rank, pay, and benefits of commissioned male officers; and the contracts could be abolished at any time.

22. McGee pointed out that there could be consequences for women doctors as the latter step meant "sacrificing their practices, performing the same services as their brothers, but with no rank, no promotions, no standing; when discharged, no bonuses or pensions, and if injured no disability provisions for themselves or their dependents." See Ellen More, "Rochester Over There," Ruth Rosenberg-Narparsteck, Ed., *Rochester History*, Vol. LI, summer 1989, No. 3. 20. List of 55 contract surgeons in "Women Contract Surgeons, U.S. Army, Who Served during the War

with Germany," undated, author unknown, American Medical Women's Association Collection, DUCM. The number is actually 56 if the work of another doctor is considered. Dr. Anne Tjomsland, a 1914 graduate of Cornell Medical School, served as an anesthetist overseas with the Bellevue Base Hospital unit.

23. Dr. Anna Putnam Jacobi was the first woman to be admitted to the New York Academy of Medicine. "She repeatedly prescribed grit and hard work in the face of discrimination," see Morantz-Sanchez, *Sympathy and Science*, 199; so she was an excellent role model for Barringer.

24. See Barringer's autobiography, *Bowery to Bellevue: The Story of New York's First Woman Ambulance Surgeon* (New York: W. W. Norton, 1950), 105-106; 121-123. Also see Noble, Iris. *First Woman Ambulance Surgeon, Emily Barringer* (New York: Julian Messner, Inc.), 1962. Noble notes that she raised money to buy ambulances in WWI by driving up and down the streets of New York in an ambulance herself.

25. All quotes regarding Barringer in "Woman Doctors Seek Officer Status in Medical Corps," *Medical Economics,* September 1943; supplied by Drexel University College Medicine (DUCM). Also see Barringer's editorial, "Women Physicians and the Medical Reserve Corps," *Norfolk Medical News,* January 1943, Volume III, No. 3. Jensen, in *Mobilizing Minerva,* points out that WWI "women physicians who made claims for wartime service in the military medical corps based their campaign on a vision of women's citizenship that included economic and professional equality," p. 97. Women who joined in this effort included those who served as contract surgeons and with voluntary organizations, those who registered for wartime service, members of the Colorado Medial Women's War Service League, the four Oregon women who took direct action to apply for service, the hundreds of women who sent in applications and inquiries, and thousands of others who signed petitions to Washington officials.

26. See Hearings before Subcommittee No. 3 of the Committee on Military Affairs, House of Representatives, 78th Congress, 1st Session on H.R. 824, March 10, 11, 18, 1943; printed for the use of the Committee on Military Affairs (no publisher: Washington, D.C., 1943), 69. "Kleegman's Statement" in Hearings before Subcommittee No. 3, 67; "Craighill's Statement" in Hearings, 71. Medical officers quote in Jensen, *Mobilizing Minerva,* 97.

27. McMinn, John H. and Levin, Max, *Medical Department, United States Army: Personnel in World War II* (Washington, D.C.: Office of the Surgeon General, Department of the Army, 1963), 155. The numbers vary slightly if a count is taken at the end of 1945.

28. Walsh, Mary Roth. *"Doctors Wanted: No Women Need Apply," Sexual Barriers in the Medical Profession, 1835-1975* (New Haven: Yale University Press, 1977); 192, 224-225.

29. See "Requirements for Army Commissions", *Women in Medicine*, October 1943; 9. Statistics were based on the 63 questionnaires that were returned to Dr. Craighill, including hers, in Box 30. The two oldest women doctors (both commissioned captains) were Dr. Catherine Gordon McGregor, assigned to General Duty at a VA facility, and Dr. Mary Jane Walters, a neuropsychiatrist. Seventy-six women medical officers are named in *Medical Department, United States Army: Personnel in World War II* (Washington, DC: Office of the Surgeon General Department of the Army, 1963), 155. This list includes Cornelia Motley who was deferred for residency to 1 July 1945. Only the names of 75 women appear on Craighill's Official Army list, but not Motley's name, which would make it 76. See "Status of Women Commissioned in Army Medical Corps According to Initial Appointment and Present Rank," Histories of the Women's Health and Welfare Unit and Women's Army Corps Activities, Box 29, Margaret D. Craighill Collection, U. S. Army Military History Institute, Carlisle, Pennsylvania; hereafter referred to as Histories, MDC Coll. Differences in statistics are probably due to date when lists were compiled.

30. Craighill's list mistakenly noted that Dr. Agnes Hoeger graduated from medical school at the University of Michigan, but she graduated from the University of Minnesota. Only one woman doctor, Lt. Cornelia Ann Wyckoff, died in service. Obituary for Cornelia Ann Wyckoff in *JAMA*, 23 June 1945, Vol. 128, No. 8, 611. She began active duty as a first lieutenant (there were no 2nd lieutenants) on March 3, 1944; had been stationed at Foster General Hospital in Jackson, Miss.; died in the Touro Infirmary, New Orleans, 27 March, aged 28, of Clostridium welchi infection and heart disease. The only other doctor to die in service, but of disease contracted while in service, was Dr. Irene Toland in the Spanish-American War which is discussed below.

31. Schultz, *Women at the Front*, 15.

32. In choosing applicants, McGee preferred those who had come well endorsed with good hospital records. First preference went to those who had endorsements from the Daughters of the American Revolution (DAR) members who knew them, followed by those recommended by the schools from which they graduated. McGee went so far as to establish a regular method of writing to the superintendents of every school to get all possible information about candidates.

33. See Personal Data Card of Irene Toland in Personal Data Cards of Spanish-American War Contract Nurses, 1898-1939, Record Group (RG) 112, Entry 149, National Archives and Records Administration, Washington D.C.

34. Linda Strite Murnane, "Legal Impediments to Service: Women in the Military and the Rule of Law," *Duke Journal of Gender Law & Policy*, Vol. 14, 2007, 1065.

35. Campbell, "The Regimented Women of World War II," in *Women, Militarism, and War, 107*. Women scientists also had their share of problems in getting entrance into doctoral programs at the turn of the twentieth century and in being accepted in their professions as late as the 1940s. In Women and Science, Le-May Sheffield points out that "many scientists were responsible for the design and construction of the atomic-bomb "although the majority of publications recounting the story of the creation of the bomb do not mention women's scientific participation," 147. Also see Howes, Ruth and Herzenberg, Caroline, *Their day in the Sun: Women of the Manhattan Project* (Philadelphia: Temple University Press), 1999.

36. Noted in Meyer, Leisa D., *Creating G.I. Jane: Sexuality and Power in the Women's Army Corps*. For more on Hobby, see Directors and Division Under the Commanding General, 160.8; Office of the Chief of Staff, 165.5; and Records of the Dir. Of Personnel and Administration (G-1) 165.10, NARA, Washington D.C.

37. Rumors in Treadwell, *The Women's Army Corps*, 201; 604. For more on women in the Army, also see Morden, Betty J., *The Women's Army Corps 1945-1978* (Washington, DC: Center for Military History, 2000); Holm, Jeanne, *Women in the Military an Unfinished Revolution* (Novato, CA.: Presidio Press, 1982). For more on the image of the woman soldier and sexuality and homosexuality, see Meyer in preceding note and Hampf, M. Michaela, *Release a Man for Combat: The Women's Army Corps during World War II* (Koln Weimar Wien: Bohlan Verlag BmbH & Cie, 2012).

38. See Craighill's "Military Record and Report of Separation Certificate of Service," Personal Papers, Box 1, MDC Coll.

39. Campbell, "The Regimented Women of World War II," in *Women, Militarism, and War* 107.

40. When women doctors talked publicly about their role in the military in WWI and WWII, they were referring to the Army Reserve Corps with its limited term of service.

41. Quotes are from Kerber, *No Constitutional Right to Be Ladies*, 299. It would take the Supreme Court until 1980 to make the point that the court regarded gender discrimination as a "badge of inferiority". See *Goldberg v. Rostker*, 509 F. Supp. 586, 594, 596, 603; also noted in *No Constitutional Right to Be Ladies*, 291.

42. "Women Physicians in the Army of the United States," *Women in Medicine*, No. 90, October 1945.

43. Ibid, 9.

44. Treadwell, *The Women's Army Corps*, 763.

MERCEDES GRAF

CHAPTER ONE:

From Pioneer Women Doctors Abroad to "Joining the Home Team"

"The women of the medical profession were not called to the colors, but they decided to go anyway."

— AMWA PRESIDENT ESTHER POHL LOVEJOY

Two important questions must be answered if we are to understand the role of women doctors during war. First, why did they want to volunteer at all? One medical historian maintained that "war service attracted women doctors with a promise of adventure, service, patriotic duty, and professional advancement." There were also many other reasons why they would choose to join in the fight, the reasons being as varied and different as the women themselves. For example, a few were married to a doctor in the Armed Forces and wished to follow in his footsteps, others had a brother or another male relative in the service, or some came from families with a strong military tradition like Dr. Margaret D. Craighill, the first woman doctor to be commissioned. The second question is: Why would they continue their battle for equality into the Second World War? Part of the answer is that the Medical Women's National Association (MWNA) in WWI had already proved that women physicians could do war work overseas as part of American Women's Hospitals (AWH). This group also cooperated with the Red Cross in being a clearinghouse for women doctors who volunteered directly for the Red Cross; and at one point in 1918, "nearly 50 percent of all Red Cross physicians in France were women, many of them affiliated with the AWH." While it was true that women doctors had lost their fight with the War Department over commissions during WWI, they were ready to take on the issue once again in 1941. As Dr. Emily D. Barringer observed: If women physicians did not have "the *right* to go forward with the troops into action", they would be unable to see traumatic surgery and war injuries at first hand, especially the women surgeons who were as well qualified as any male doctor.[1]

Barringer stressed the "right" of qualified women physicians to gain battlefield experiences that would hold them in good stead in postwar years. Since they could not serve during wartime for their own country, she continued, they were "serving in England in British uniforms...with the men physicians of the British Emergency Medical Service of the British Government... where vital accomplishment, not sex, is the measuring rod." In other words, women doctors would not be denied the "right" to serve in wartime, whatever the cost. Around the same time, Dr. Minnie L. Maffett, a distinguished woman surgeon and also president of the National Federation of Business and Professional Women's Clubs, Inc. noted: "Fifty years ago, we did not know that some of our greatest doctors and surgeons could be women. Now we do...After an uphill fight for recognition, women doctors have now proved their worth. It seems almost shocking that they are granted greater recognition in other countries than our own, where equality of opportunity is one of our cherished ideals."[2]

Why would women doctors decide to follow the same course that had been set in WWI and volunteer abroad? One medical historian maintained that the outbreak of WWII and the continued exclusion of women doctors from the military reserves "revitalized the activism and organizational elan of American women physicians." Concerns over the availability of women doctors in wartime led the AMWA to form a War Service Committee to canvas women doctors across the country. The committee sent questionnaires to 8,000 women doctors, with about 2,000 of them responding that they were willing and able to do war service. From this registry, approximately 500 expressed a willingness to accept service overseas.[3] At the request of the American Red Cross, a handful of women was selected from the last group. Great Britain had asked the United States for 1,000 male doctors to help care for the civilian population "because so many of their medical men were needed in the armed services." Unfortunately, the call came after the Selective Service Act had been enacted in the U. S., and "only about 100 male doctors were available."[4] Various accounts indicate that between ten and twelve women doctors were recruited for the British Emergency Medical Service (EMS) the fall and winter 1941, but seven American women were the only ones who decided to stay for one year. (See Table D, Appendix for names).

Barbara B. Stimson, who was one of seven children, hailed from a family with a strong sense of duty and service. Her father was a minister, one grandfather had been president of a college, and her uncle, Dr. Lewis Stimson, helped establish Cornell University Medical College. Her first cousin, Henry L. Stimson, became Secretary of War twice—once in 1911 and again in 1940. Barbara's older sister, Julia (who had wanted to become a physician but her parents and uncle disapproved even though Cornell admitted female students), settled on a nursing career and later enlisted in the Army Nurse Corps and served as head nurse for Base Hospital 21 which was organized by the Red Cross. The hospital drew its medical staff from the Washington University hospitals and it had the distinction of being the first such unit in the country mobilized for overseas service in World War I. Later Julia became the first dean of the Army School of Nursing, and a few months later on 30 December 1919, superintendent of the Army Nurse Corps, a position she held until she retired in 1937. She was drawn back to service in 1942, however, to head the Nursing Council on National Defense, and she became the first woman major in the United States Army.[5]

Mjr. Barbara Stimson (left) & Lt. Achsa Bean,
Royal Army Medical Corps, 1942

When Barbara declared her intention to become a doctor, she had the support of her sister, Julia; and by this time, her parents were more understanding of such a decision. After her graduation from College of Physicians and Surgeons at Columbia in 1923, she applied and got an internship at Presbyterian Hospital in New York City. "I was the second woman to have a surgical internship at the hospital," she explained. "In the 1920s, the housing problem [at the hospitals] made it difficult for women to obtain internships."[6] After her internship, Stimson had a two-year National Research Council fellowship to do experimental work in physiology. She did one year of that work at Western Reserve University and one year at Columbia University, and she received her doctorate in medical science from Columbia in 1934, was a Fellow of the American College of Surgeons, and a member of the American Board of Surgery.

Her specialty in orthopedics was one in which women were scarcely represented because it is a field which had been traditionally dominated by men, even today; and as late as the 1960s there were only four women in Orthopedic Surgery in the United States.[7] Stimson had tried to volunteer abroad once before, but failed. "Because of my sex," she explained, "my application to go to England for the war effort with a volunteer orthopedic group had been turned down." When Dr. Esther Lovejoy, her friend and also the director of the American Women's Hospital Association, called in April 1941 with an offer to serve abroad, Stimson, now age 42 and an established orthopedic surgeon and third in rank on the staff of the newly formed Fracture Service at Columbia Presbyterian Medical Center, decided this was finally her chance. She asked another friend, Dr. Achsa Bean, an assistant physician at Vassar College and two years younger, to join her.[8] Once she agreed, both women applied for a leave of absence from their positions.

Like Stimson, Achsa Bean wanted to volunteer abroad, and while duty and service were long-standing traditions in her friend's family, she could only provide the simplest of explanations for her choice: She wanted to be useful. "I think I can," she admitted, "for there seems to be plenty to do."[9] Although it was a difficult decision to leave an aging mother behind, she was used to doing difficult things. Her family had never been able to help finance her education, so in order to save for college, she taught high school, ran a town library, and for seven summers she was head counselor in private girls' camps in New Hampshire. She received both her undergraduate and graduates degrees from the University of Maine (1922, 1925), and then did graduate study in the department of physiology at Harvard Medical School 1930-31. Bean "always wanted to be a doctor," which was her reason for finally leaving home to enroll at the University of Rochester School of Medicine where she received her MD in 1936.[10] The next year she interned in obstetrics and gynecology, but since years of education had exhausted her savings, she needed to work. She accepted a position at Vassar College as an assistant physician from 1938-1941, and she later became the Dean of Women at the same institution for six years. Bean stated that one of the most important reasons for wanting the security of a university position was because she "had a mother and grandmother to support."[11]

Stimson and Bean, also believed that they had a great deal "to learn from the British... to see... how they organized their women's services, and how they met the unparalleled conditions which reigned since the blitz started." They felt that "when and if the time ever came when it would be necessary to organize the same kind of services in the United States, our country could benefit by the experience of the British and avoid a number of mistakes." This explanation suggests a certain humility on Stimson's part because she was an expert on fractures and one of the outstanding exponents of the "internal fixation" treatment which had revolutionized bone-setting in the United States.[12]

There were many new experiences in store for the two women after their arrival in England the fall of 1941. First, they had to report to the Alien Registration Office for "Certificates" of Registration. Next they signed contracts and applied for temporary licenses to practice at the Ministry of Heath, and finally there were the required interviews to discuss their medical backgrounds. Apparently all the officials had expected senior medical students or interns. "We had caught them completely unprepared for doctors of our experience," Stimson confided.[13] The women were assigned to the Royal Free Hospital in London where they sometimes lectured to the female medical students who were delighted with their accents. Bean wrote home: "This hospital is an old one and is the teaching hospital of a medical school... We are both settling into our work."[14] Stimson described the hospital this way: It "is situated in a district near several railroad stations and on the edge of the City, and hence in an area which had been very badly damaged. The House Staff at the hospital were almost entirely women and the Attending Staff mixed...All of the Staff had gone through harrowing experiences the preceding winter, but were competent and cheerful in spite of obvious weariness. They welcomed us and quickly made us feel at home.'[15]

When Achsa Bean and Barbara Stimson started work, signs of devastation were still everywhere. "We found in London that the big city hospitals were carrying on under great difficulties," Stimson recalled. "Many of them had been badly blitzed, and all of them had had to readjust to the blitzed conditions. Operation rooms, which had been on upper floors, were improvised in basements. Patients had to be moved down from the dangerous zones and temporary wards improvised in lecture rooms, laboratories, and storerooms." As the women walked down the streets, sometimes they saw only a few houses still standing between carefully fenced craters marking the spot where another home had once stood. What impressed them most was the amount of cleaning-up that had been done since the last bombing raid only a few months ago. "Workmen were busy everywhere making much-needed repairs," Stimson said. "The rubble had been carted away, but the crowning touch was the flowers blooming in some of the bomb craters—a delightful gesture of defiance."[16]

The occasional bombings still continued although the Blitz had ended in May and Hitler had turned his attention to Russia. "You should see us in our tin hats and gas masks," Achsa Bean wrote home.[17] She did not, however, expect to be "bombed out" of her house in London, a story she enjoyed relating after her return to Vassar. "Just as she was heading for the luxury of a rarely come by deep bath, the bathroom was blown up" in front of her.[18] Such experiences only strengthened the resolve of Bean and her friend who were eager "for action", and they decided that they wanted to be attached to the Royal Army Medical Corps (RAMC) if it could be arranged. As Stimson noted: "We were already three thousand miles nearer the actual fighting than we would have been had we returned home, and...the need for doctors in the British Armed Forces was very great."[19] Their decision required that they be released from the EMS and transferred to the RAMC; and in order to start the ball rolling, they decided to compose a letter to the American ambassador to seek his help. Then they had to wait and see.

In the meantime, five more doctors were sent to join them. Two American women arrived at the "Royal Free" shortly after Stimson and Bean—Drs. Sarah "Sally" Bowditch, from Massachusetts, and Marion C. Loizeaux, a graduate of Cornell University and a physician at Wellesley College. Stimson recalled: "They were delightful— about our age—and we were glad to be able to help them through the intricacies of reporting their arrival to the Emergency Medical Service and getting the necessary identification cards and coupons... They quickly settled into the hospital routine, helping out when needed."[20] Three more women doctors were sent from America before the winter was out. Dr. Eleanor K. Peck, a pediatrician, came next followed by Dr. Mila Pierce, another pediatrician, and Dr. Josephine Stephens arrived last in January of 1942.

In terms of their backgrounds, all seven women were experienced physicians from recognized medical schools located mostly in the eastern part of the United States, as Pierce was the only one who went to a school in the mid-west. All of them were single (Bowditch was divorced) so they had no dependent children although Bean assumed some of the financial responsibility for her mother and grandmother, Loizeaux claimed her mother as a dependent, and Peck sent her allotment checks home to help various family members although her parents were deceased.[22] The women were also white and from middle-class backgrounds.[21] They were close in age—three of the women were in their thirties, and Stimson, Bean, Pierce and Stephens in their forties. Stimson was also well known in certain social circles because her first cousin, Henry L. Stimson, was the Secretary of War and her elder sister, Julia, had been the Superintendent of the Army Nurse Corps in 1919.

During the first week of January 1942, Barbara Stimson and Achsa Bean received a message to report at the War Office. Stimson recalled: "There we learned that we had been accepted in the RAMC." On 1 February 1942, both doctors entered into the second phase of their transatlantic experience as they transferred to the RAMC and were ordered to duty. On hearing the news, the two women went directly to order their uniforms with the USA flash on the left shoulder. Bean was made a lieutenant since she was not a specialist, but she was promoted to a captain about six weeks later. Stimson was made a major since she did have a specialty in orthopedics.[23]

At this point, the friends were separated and sent to different military hospitals—Bean to one in York, and Simpson to Shenley, which was just outside of London. Stimson said, "It took me quite a while to become accustomed to being saluted by every soldier whom I passed, either on the grounds of the hospital or in the streets of London." But there was more than enough work to occupy her time. "My orthopedic ward was full," she explained "[and] I had a blossoming out-patient session once or twice a week."[24] She was also making frequent trips to the military hospital in Hatfield House to operate on their orthopedic cases because they did not have a specialist in that field.

As the summer of 1942 ended, Bean returned home. Stimson was busy in the outpatient clinic evaluating the fitness of British soldiers for return to duty when she was asked to meet with Dr. Elliott C. Cutler, the commanding officer of the United States Medical Corps in Europe. He was quite frank in sharing the fact that her country preferred not to have her in a British uniform. Stimson was offered the option to transfer to the United States Medical Corp as a contract surgeon which meant being a civilian employee of the Army Medical Department, working for the salary specified in the contract for as long as she might be needed while the Army could abolish the contract at any time. Since the British authorities wished to have her continue at Shenley, she would be "seconded" to them. "In other words," she recalled, "I was to go back to my job at Shenley in an American uniform without rank." She thanked Dr. Cutler politely "and emphatically refused the offer."[25] While Barbara Stimson was deciding to stay with the RAMC, her friend, Achsa Bean was making hard choices of her own. Unlike the Army, the Navy did not hire women contract surgeons. This fact helped steer Bean towards the Navy, and on 27 November, 1942, she applied for a commission in the U.S. Naval Reserve and was appointed Assistant Surgeon 12 January, 1943.[26] She recalled: "My first duty with the Navy was a training course for Naval Medical Officers at the National Naval Medical Center at Bethesda, Md."[27] She reported next for duty as a medical officer at the WAVE Training School at Hunter College in the Bronx where she spent most of her time running the dispensary for the station. As head of Hunter College's dispensary, Bean handled 100-300 WAVES (out of 5,000 at Hunter) who were on sick call, and she conducted physicals and gave vaccinations routinely as 40,000 WAVES moved in and out of the dispensary.[28]

As the New Year 1943 was rung in, Barbara Stimson was still in England with the RAMC. But new opportunities were headed her way. In mid-December she had been asked to report to London where she was told she was being handed a "special assignment", and by the beginning of January, she was on her way to the United States aboard the Queen Elizabeth. Shortly after her arrival in New York, she met with her cousin, Henry who drove her to the Pentagon where he listened to her experiences with the RAMC, and introduced her to one of the Army generals who wanted to hear about the work of women in the British Medical Corps. Then she was invited to a staff meeting of the Army Medical Corps where she answered all the questions that were put to her—but the question of women medical officers did not arise. After the meeting ended, she was flown back to New York and was soon sailing on a return trip to England.[29] Three months later, in April 1943, both houses of Congress passed the bill commissioning women doctors in the Medical Corps of the U.S. Army.

This was the news so many women physicians had been waiting for, particularly Stimson and Bean. The summer of 1943 Colonel Elliott Cutler sent for Barbara Stimson once again. As she walked into his office, he told her he could finally offer her a position with rank in the Army Medical Corps. It was not quite what she was used to doing he told her, since it would be as a gynecologist to the WACs with the rank of major. "Shoemaker, stick to your last," was all she replied when she realized he was not joking about the offer. As the war continued, Stimson was offered administrative positions several times in the United States Medical Corps. "I had no difficulty in refusing the offers," she said since she was doing what she did best.[30]

As fall 1943 approached, Achsa Bean was unhappy over her rank in the Navy—the same issue that caused dissatisfaction later with other medical women in the military during WWII. She had been transferred as an officer in the WAVES to an officer in the Medical Corps of the U.S. Naval Reserve, but with the same rank of Lt. (jg). On 10 November 1943, she wrote to the Chief of the Bureau of Navy Personnel and pointed out that her age and professional qualifications entitled her to a higher rank than Lt. (jg). After all, she had served abroad as a Major (with the classification of Medical Specialist) in the RAMC. "I am forty-three years old," she said, "[and] requirements in the 3rd Naval District lead me to believe that I could enter the Naval Medical Corps Reserve at this time with the rank of Lieut. Comdr." By the following summer of 1944, Bean had finally received promotions to Lt. Comdr. When the war ended and the services of women doctors were no longer needed, she requested a return to inactive to duty and she returned to Vassar in January 1946."[31] She remained there until her retirement in 1963.

Barbara Stimson's career seemed to run a parallel course with that of her friend, Achsa Bean, for November 1943 was also an important time for Stimson. She was sent to North Africa with the RAMC to a base hospital in the hills back of Algiers. "In Africa we were getting the wounded, those too ill or too seriously hurt to be transferred home. It was sort of picking up the pieces and organizing and orthopedic center," Stimson reported. "Britain didn't have enough specialists for every hospital, so it established two orthopedic centers on the east side and two on the west to centralize treatment of specific injuries. There were a lot more hospitals."[32] Soon she was taking care of the remnants of the wounded from the North African campaign and from the Sicilian attack as many of the men continued to be too ill to be evacuated to the United Kingdom. In April of 1944, the center was moved to a base hospital in Italy, which had been set up in an orphan asylum in Pompeii. "In Italy we treated some of the wounded within a very few hours of injury. We couldn't have been more than 75 miles from the fighting," Stimson recalled. "The wounded were brought in by ambulance. The front was much more scattered than it was in Africa."[33] In the summer she was also sent to a hospital in Naples to help out with the mass of fracture cases that were there, and in September she went to an Italian military hospital in Rome.[34]

Since the United States Army had growing concerns over the shortage of medical officers in theatres of war overseas as the war went on, it sent out a memorandum in March 1945 alerting all women medical officers serving with the RAMC that they had " a full liability for service at home or overseas and this is brought to the notice of each individual at the time of inviting her to attend for medical examination and interview prior to appointment."[35] At this juncture, however, Stimson was winding up her work, and she returned to the United States the end of August to resume her civilian work as an orthopedic surgeon. But she had many memories to take with her as well as a military decoration presented by King George VI, and a plaque from the Orthopedic Center of the British Army. She moved to Poughkeepsie, New York, where she was director of the Department of Bone and Joint Surgery at St. Francis Hospital, and still taught once a week at the College of Physicians and Surgeons in New York until her retirement.

By 1963, both women were ready to retire. In a private letter to a close friend, Stimson wrote: "The cottage that Achsa Bean and I have built on the Maine coast near Rockland is a great joy and we hope someday to be able to spend most of our time there." And so they did, until Bean died at the age of 74 in March 1975 at Owls Head, Maine. Stimson stayed on until her death in 1986 at the age of 88.[36] In her lifetime, however, Orthopedics, which had begun to be recognized in World War I, leapt forward in giant steps during World War II and subsequently in other conflicts.

For doctors Stimson and Bean, the military was only an interruption in their career paths since they returned to what they were doing before the war. For another woman, Army service was a life-changing experience. Dr. Sarah (called Sally) Bowditch was a woman who had it all. She came from a family that was well off financially, and her brother was "one of New England's outstanding industrial leaders."[37] One of the few American women to be accepted with the British EMS in 1941, she had been on the teaching staff of the highly respected Johns Hopkins Medical School before volunteering. Not only did she receive her undergraduate and medical degrees (1930, 1935) from Hopkins, but she also completed an internship there. In June 1939, she married Dr. Thomas A. Gonder, who also completed his internship at Hopkins. One of her regrets was that the marriage did not work out, and she separated from him the next year and then got a divorce. This short-lived marriage, however, may have been the driving force that led her to leave Hopkins and go abroad where she could immerse herself in a different kind of medical work.

On arrival in England, Bowditch spent the summer and fall working at the Royal Free Hospital with Achsa Bean and Barbara Stimson. On New Year's Day 1942, she received orders to report to the Northern Hospital in Winchmore Hill in North London, which was about the same time her friends learned they were transferring to the RAMC.[38] Bowditch was sorry to say good-by to these women because they had become close friends, a friendship which lasted throughout her life.[39]

About the same time, the United States government was beginning to recognize that it needed surgeons after it declared war on Japan and as had happened in WWI, women doctors were offered the opportunity to volunteer as general contract surgeons with the United States Army in November of 1942 while the wheels squeaked forward slowly in getting a commissioning bill approved. One of the five remaining women doctors in England, Sally Bowditch was unwilling to accept the status of a contract surgeon, and when the end of the "agreed on" year in England ended, she "returned to the United States at the request of Johns Hopkins" and resumed work as an assistant in medicine. At that point, Johns Hopkins was one of the university-affiliated hospital units being assembled to serve during wartime. Such units had begun in WWI and were called up for the last time in WWII. On 20 April 1942, about 50 of the Hopkins doctors boarded a train in Baltimore and then headed for the South Pacific. These doctors, along with about 60 nurses, formed two medical units, each staffing a 500-bed hospital. The 18th General Hospital Unit, bore the name of Hopkins' famous World War I unit while the other was called the 118th. Part of a unique program that allowed medical personnel to join the military as part of a cohesive team, the units offered women nurses unprecedented opportunities to serve as wartime nurses, as they were given a great deal of autonomy by the Hopkins' doctors who knew and respected them. No women doctors were in either unit. One wonders what would have happened if Hopkins had offered Bowditch an opportunity to serve as a physicians with one of the Hopkins' units instead of calling her home to work.[40] In a strange twist of fate, however, Bowditch applied for a leave of absence when the Sparkman-Johnson Bill passed the following year in April 1943.[41]

Bowditch received her captaincy 22 November 1943 in the Army Medical Corps. She was classified as a dermatologist, was sent for the next three weeks to Lawson General Hospital "for indoctrination", and then ordered to duty on 26 December 1943 at Fort Oglethorpe, Georgia, situated just outside Chattanooga, Tennessee. The Fort had been designated the Third WAAC (later WAC) Training Center with an activation date set for 1 January 1943 with recruits reporting in February. This might have been viewed as a routine assignment, but one of Bowditch's colleagues thought otherwise: "Capt. Bowditch has gone to take charge of all V.D. at Ft. Oglethorpe," she said, "and maybe you think that didn't take some doing to have a woman put in charge of V.D. where male patients were to be taken care of."[42] This assignment was also her first introduction to the field of preventive medicine.

Starting in March 1944, Sally Bowditch served as the Assistant Military Attaché for Medicine at the American Embassy, London. Her duties consisted of liaison work between the RAMC and the Surgeon General's Office in Washington, and it suited her well as she had grown to love England during the time she had been assigned to the EMS. She was the first woman attaché in the embassy's history—a job that gave her "much freedom of action with a minimum of supervision." Bowditch summed up her Army experience this way: "This position has been an experience and an education in itself." From her point of view, however, the work had one drawback: She was "out of touch with active clinical medicine." Nevertheless, she was "able to keep up with current literature, published and unpublished." In a letter to Dr. Margaret Craighill she also confided: "I feel as though I were one of the few people who had really a good time, and I am almost ashamed to admit it!" In 1946, she received the Bronze Star, and she was a lieutenant colonel when she left the service.[43]

Bowditch would have remained in the Army, but that was not possible at the time. Like many other doctors who had served in the Army, however, she had learned some valuable lessons in the service—one of the most important was the advantage of having a medical specialty. She returned to school in 1947 and received a Master of Public Health Degree from Harvard School of Public Health a year later. Almost immediately, she set about putting that degree to work along with the experiences she had acquired in "V.D. at Ft. Oglethorpe". She accepted the position as the assistant director in the Division of Venereal Diseases with the Massachusetts State Department of Health from 1948-1949, but she later resigned along with three other doctors in the agency because of inadequate salary. The Massachusetts Health Commissioner, Dr. Vlado A. Getting, explained: "It is practically impossible to hire competent public health physicians at the entering grade of $4,200, especially since department physicians are not permitted to engage in private practice after working hours."[44]

Despite the problems in Massachusetts, 1949 was the year that helped cement her career choice in preventive medicine. Sally Bowditch became a civilian medical officer at the Army Surgeon General's Office, Preventive Health Division, in Washington, D.C. where she remained until 1953. Following this, she returned once again to Hopkins (1953-1956), this time as dispensary physician and medical coordinator on common chronic diseases. But she was drawn back into government service from 1957 to 1959 when the opportunity arose to serve as Assistant Chief of Health and Welfare for a U.S. Operation Mission in Haiti. Although Bowditch believed this would be a tenuous position unless "the political situation in Haiti clears", she seized the occasion as she recognized the population's extreme poverty and lack of basic health care called for a program of preventive medicine.[45]

Her last position, and probably the most prestigious, was the one she held before her death—Chief of the Department of Health Data, Division of Preventive Medicine at Walter Reed Army Institute of Research (WRAIR) in Washington, D.C. "This work," she wrote to a colleague in 1961, "has nothing to do with statistics, believe it or not. I am concerned with turning out unclassified reports on disease incidence, medical facilities, etc., on a global-wide basis." Furthermore, she indicated, "I am also used to a limited extent in a teaching capacity in some of the courses that are given at WRAIR, such as the three months' course in Military Preventive Medicine... There is also a short intensified course which is given on global medicine to Medical Corps officers who are either internists or preventive medicine specialists."[46]

Sally Bowditch died of cancer at the age of 61 on 21 July 1966 in Washington, D.C. At her death, Bowditch donated the bulk of her family landholding to form a part of Arcadia National Park. Among the many distinctions she held in her life, she was a fellow of the American College of Preventive Medicine, a member of the American Public Health Association, and she belonged to the World Medical Association and the Association of Military Surgeons of the United States.[47]

Marion Loizeaux, like Bowditch, graduated from a prestigious medical school in the East. Born 20 December 1904 in New York, she received her MD from Cornell University Medical College in 1931. After an internship at the Lakeside Hospital in Cleveland, Ohio, Loizeaux became a graduate assistant at Memorial Hospital and Peter Bent Brigham Hospital—the latter being one of the main teaching hospitals at Harvard Medical School. She completed a residency at Grasslands Hospital, Obstetrics/Gynecology Clinic, Woman's Free Hospital in Boston, and she followed-up with a postgraduate course in medicine and surgery at Harvard Medical School.[48]

She was an assistant physician at Wellesley College before she arrived in England around the same time as Sally Bowditch. Because she "had friends in London" she planned to make the most of her leisure time when she was not working at the Royal Free.[49] In November 1942, after her agreed-on year in England with the EMS, Loizeaux accepted a position as contract surgeon with the U.S.

Army. The condition was the same for all volunteers with the EMS: "With the understanding that they remain at the British hospitals where they were working until the Army could use [them] in its ranks." In other words, they had to be willing to take a chance that the bill for commissioning would be passed. At this point, Loizeaux believed, "There was hope, but no promises."[50] She decided to accept the condition and she continued to carry on the same medical duties, only in a "lend lease" capacity.

Towards the end of June 1943, Dr. Margaret D. Craighill, who had been appointed by the War Department as the first Consultant for Women's Health and Welfare with the Surgeon General's Office and was also the first woman doctor to be commissioned in the Army Medical Corps in 1943, was concerned about the insufficient number of potential female medical officers to cover Army women's medical needs in the US and abroad. "They should, therefore," she recommended, "be distributed where they can be used for the largest number, or where conditions demand a specialized type of service."[51] Marion Loizeaux was the first woman to profit from this recommendation as she was already in England in July 1943 when the first battalion of WACs to reach the ETO arrived in London and were assigned to duty with the Eighth Air Force. Just as a second battalion of WACs also earmarked for the Eighth Air Force reached London in the fall, Loizeaux was commissioned 19 September 1943 as a captain, making her the first woman doctor to be commissioned in the ETO. (She was promoted to major 1 November 1944). Next she was ordered for special training to the Medical Field Service School (American School Center) and then ordered for duty to the European Theatre of Operations (ETO). Her assignment was special "Consultant" to the Chief Surgeon on all matters pertaining to the Medical Care of the Women's Army Corps, ETO.

There were several reasons why Loizeaux was a good choice for the special consultant: She had been abroad with Britain's EMS since the fall of 1941, she had done postgraduate work at Harvard, and the Army classified her as an internist. She also knew the Chief Surgical Consultant for the ETO, Dr. Elliott C. Cutler, because he had been the Director of Surgery at the Lakeside Hospital in Cleveland in 1931-1932 when she was an intern there. Since Cutler was also the same man who had offered Barbara Stimson a position as a gynecologist to the WAC, it was clear that he was willing to advance the cause of women doctors. Certainly he was in favor of women volunteering during wartime because he had married Caroline Pollard Parker who had worked with him at Base Hospital Number 5, part of the Harvard Medical Unit in France, during WWI.[52] No doubt, it had been his influence that helped Loizeaux with her new appointment.

In her new position as medical consultant in the ETO, Loizeaux tried to keep in contact with Dr. Margaret D. Craighill. Since it was not until the end of the war that the ETO got around to appointing gynecologists on the staffs of general hospitals that treated WACs and nurses, Loizeaux's role as consultant was even more important, especially as WAC units were scattered in England and France (and later to Germany). Loizeaux also confided to Craighill that she felt she was "running a sort of one-man show." There were also great concerns that conditions overseas placed a greater strain on accepted standards of conduct. Loizeaux reported to Craighill that she was giving social hygiene lectures in London to small groups of WAC "at their request" and that these talks "include not only sex, but also other problems that we meet over here." These lectures were intended to provide the women with necessary information about pregnancy and venereal disease "although the subject is an extremely touchy one with women who have been poorly educated concerning sex hygiene."[53] While Colonel Oveta Culp Hobby, Director of the WAC, had incorporated some information in hygiene manuals that were passed out to Army women, both Colonel Anna W. Wilson (later Lt. Col.), WAC Staff Director of the ETO, and Loizeaux believed it "had been a mistake" not to include more frank advice on sex. They felt that the manual contained a moralizing tone that was "too Victorian" for the times.[54] There is "lots of unofficial business," Loizeaux wrote, knowing that Craighill would be able to read between the lines. "It is a slow process, but interesting. I have discovered that when the WAC see a problem in its practical light they get to work and help wholeheartedly."[55]

About fifteen months later in July 1944, Loizeaux wrote a much more detailed eight-page letter outlining some of the specific medical concerns that existed in the ETO with the WAC. In general, she noted that they followed the instructions and procedures in "the Circular Letter" put out by Craighill's Office. She had only one criticism to make, and that was in regard to the monthly physical inspections, which were frequently conducted in a careless manner. "In some instances," she explained, "the doctor looks at the throat, opens a button or two on the shirt and says 'okay'". As a result, she felt it was important to remind "the WAC officers that they are the ones responsible for the health of their women and they should be interested in the physical inspections." Loizeaux added that pregnancies were not really a big problem with the WAC in the ETO and there were very few cases of venereal disease although it was impossible to give a current rate on the latter because the WAC strength had increased so rapidly. In other words, overseas conditions did not worsen either the WAC pregnancy rate or the venereal disease rate as had been feared. If pressed to give numbers related to these two problems, Loizeaux remarked that there had been thirty-seven pregnancies (including both married and extra-marital pregnancies) and between 7-9 cases of venereal disease.[56]

One unforeseen problem for WAC in the ETO was "the unsatisfactory model of military shoes for women, and the shortage of proper sizes" with many persons complaining of metatarsal bursitis and fallen arches.[57] The field shoes were made of good leather in golden tobacco brown shade that matched the WAC utility purse and leather dress gloves. They were generally comfortable, but Loizeauz felt the shoes did not have much support in the instep for those people "whose feet are not rugged…and the WAC shoes over here are of one last, and the orthopedic people insist that all feet are not the same shape."[58] In fact, the "non-effective rate", or absence rate, surged for WACs "during the period when they were being admitted to the hospital for adjustment of shoes."[59] According to Loizeaux, when it came to dealing with these orthopedic problems, "everybody passed the buck until it got to the point where everybody who need-ed a pair of shoes was sent to the 2nd General Hospital." One WAC even wrote a poem on how she spent fifteen days in the hospital try-ing to get a pair of shoes after hers were stolen. Following a survey made by Preventive Medicine, the situation quickly changed and the Senior Consultant in Orthopedics got involved with the problem. Loizeaux concluded that, "WAC officers will do a better job now in demanding that they get shoes that fit, and I believe too that the local doctors will take more responsibility in the matter of correct fit of shoes."[60]

As far as the overall "non-effective rate" for WACs was concerned in the ETO, Loizeaux admitted that it had been twice as high as the men. But she believed this was an unfair comparison as there were considerably fewer women than men and "the errors in statistics are very great." The rates began to drop as more women were sent to the ETO and their increased numbers allowed for better comparisons. Newly arrived troops tended to get over the usual respiratory infec-tions as time went on, but the seasons of the year were another factor that contributed to illness.[61] Army historian Treadwell, for example, noted that the "regulation WAC uniform was completely inadequate for work in unheated buildings during the approaching winter and for the projected movement to the Continent, but time permitted remedial action."[62]

In considering psychiatric problems among the WACs, the num-ber of cases was not that high, but the cases remained fairly constant. Loizeaux was convinced that better and more careful screening at home prior to being sent to the ETO would have been preferred. It was also the case that "women were found to develop psychological disorders somewhat less frequently than men, but "Female complaints" were the cause of almost one-fourth of WAC hospitalizations. The medical consensus was that women having menstrual disorders should have been dealt with prior to their dispatch to a Theater of Operations.[63]

When Marion Loizeaux was asked to comment on her experience in the Army Medical Corps, she was most concerned about the obstacles women medical consultants faced in the line of duty. Prewar plans had made no provision for them in regard to position vacancies and job descriptions. Worse, no effective official channels of communication had been set up between the consultants in the Office of The Surgeon General and those in the various Commands in the United States and the overseas Theaters of Operations. "[I]n every instance except the North African Theater of Operations, the surgeons had been made subordinate to other staff sections, and in many cases, their offices had been fragmented and medical functions assigned to other staff sections."[64] Like Sally Bowditch, she was awarded the Bronze Star for meritorious service.

The year 1946 was also a banner year for Marion Loizeaux. She became one of ten women doctors named to administrative posts with the Veterans Administration (VA), and she and Dr. Margaret D. Craighill were the only two women nominated for membership in "The Society of Medical Consultants in World War II" after the organization was established in 1946.[65] But working with the VA influenced the rest of her career, and in keeping with her new-found commitment to veterans' interests, she later accepted the appointment of Chief, Long-Term and Geriatric Service, with the VA Hospital in Albany, New York. She also managed to fit in being a clinical instructor in medicine at the Albany Medical College.

After her retirement, Marion Loizeaux spent her summers enjoying the outdoors in Maine. Residents, who knew she had been a physician in WWII, recalled, "she kept a little camp next to the Mill Creek Bridge and spent as much of each summer there as she could. That the little cottage had no conveniences and was served by an outhouse didn't trouble this formidable lady a bit, even as she advanced into old age. For years Dr. Loizeaux was an institution on Vinalhaven. She never ceased to express her gratitude for the island and for her little place on it."[66] She died at the age of 88 on 12 March 1993.

Dr. Eleanor K. Peck, like Barbara Stimson, was a graduate of the College of Physicians and Surgeons at Columbia, but she was ten years younger as she was born 4 July 1908. (She was also the youngest of the original group of seven women who arrived in England). She landed on 31 October 1941 and was quickly assigned to the Hospital for Sick Children in London on Ormand Street. "[It] is one of the most famous Children's Hospitals in London," she wrote home. "The hospital itself is taking care only of a minimum of patients, but is prepared to take care of air raid casualties in fair numbers. Part of my job is to be in connection with the blood transfusions to start with." On a more personal note she was happy to have a visit right away from Achsa Bean, who she had known in New York, and from Sally Bowditch who she grew to be friends with over the coming year. "They were a cheery sight and quite full of enthusiasm and gave me the dope on all the things that have to be done about registration and the like," Peck noted, and "they are situated only four or five blocks away which makes it very nice so I am not to be too lonely." Within weeks, however, Eleanor Peck had more news to report: "I have been officially appointed blood transfusion officer here now and that means a bit of organization before we can get going."[67]

But many changes happened the following year and there was little time to think about being lonely. In December of 1942, Eleanor Peck accepted a position as contract surgeon with the US Army. Immediately afterwards, she was lent-leased" to the Ministry of Health, and she continued working at the Hospital for Sick Children in

London in her new capacity. Peck's letters home continued to update her family as news came her way. In March, she stated: "My status at this moment is that of contract surgeon to the U.S. Army Lend-Lease to the Ministry of Health… You may also have heard by now the good news that the Bill to have women physicians commissioned in the Army has probably gone thru [sic] the House Committee… This may then mean that we will be fully commissioned sometime in the near future. We are not WAACs. However, the uniform we wear, when we do, will be that one which has been designed for all women in the Army. Loizeaux is getting hers made now as she is already called up". [68]

Fortunately there were other tasks that helped relieve the tension she was feeling over the commissioning bill. "For the last couple of months I have been working hard on a bit of research," she wrote in May, "and the climax is to be this next week when I am scheduled to attend the annual meeting of the British Paediatric Association and give a paper! Can you imagine it?" In her study, she investigated the records of the Children's Hospital for the three and a third years' period from September 1939 to January 1943. She concluded that "it would appear that early and efficient treatment might shorten the course of this prolonged illness, and save much in the cost of hospitalization and nursing care."[69]

By 16 June of 1943, Eleanor Peck was beginning to feel more hopeful. "I have no orders to move from here but they many come before too long though I am still in the dark. We still have not been able to apply for commissions as they say there has been no official notification of the fact here." Ten days later she wrote again. "The time is approaching, I have been told, when my departure into the service is imminent. I had a conversation with Loizeaux today and she told me that there is a job that is waiting if I want to take it. Its nature I am not able to disclose, nor is the matter finally decided, but I suspect that it will not be any more hazardous than my present job and will not take me away from this part of the world."[70]

Finally, in August of 1943, Eleanor Peck was assigned to the Office of the Surgeon, Eighth Air Force, where two WAC battalions were situated. Another detachment of 300 WACs served with the Supreme Headquarters, Allied Expeditionary Force (SHAEF) and were stationed in Bushey Park, London before they accompanied SHAEF to France and eventually to Germany. Peck's job was to advise on WAC problems and help set up medical care for women in the Eighth Air Force. She also "visited all installations with WACs and carried out monthly physical inspections." She was still a contract surgeon, however.

The fact that Dr. Peck was not commissioned immediately after the passage of the Sparkman-Johnson Bill in April of 1943 caused some concern for friends and family who wanted her to have the recognition she deserved. One newspaper editor wrote: "Her brother-in-law wants to know why she is still a contract surgeon. He says she is a person who would not push herself...He, of course, would feel less concern about her if he knew she was part of the Army and so entitled to certain of the benefits and protections."[71] At long last, on 10 February 1944 she was finally commissioned, but only as a lieutenant. Eleanor Peck had her own thoughts on this overly long process. "Witness the fact that the four of us (not Sally Bowditch) who were commissioned over here had a long delay in getting a commission despite the fact that we were virtually sitting on the doorstep begging to be let in when the bill was passed in Congress, and despite the fact that there was complaints at home that women were not volunteering. My appointment was the longest delayed until February of 1944. This was of course a bit dampening to one's enthusiasm."[72] It was not until the following September that she was promoted to captain.

Like Loizeaux, however, she had concerns about the responsibilities of medical officers because there was no uniform policy as to how women doctors in the Medical Corps should be utilized. "In this theater [ETO] we have fought for the right to be doctors and therefore to take care of both men and women. There has however been a strong force to assign us primarily for the care of women." Peck concluded: "On the whole if one were to ask me whether I felt that I would have been more useful at home or in the Armed Forces, I should probably say at home."[73]

While Eleanor Peck did not go into any detail in regard to the frustration she felt with certain aspects of her assignment at the Eighth Air Force, it had been a difficult situation from the beginning. The Surgeon of the Air Force had asked for a woman medical doctor "in order to do physical inspections and conduct lectures on hygiene...The real object...was to have a woman advisor for an area where there were no women officers, neither medical nor nurses." It was felt that if any problems came up, she would be the one to offer solutions. It didn't work out that way, however, because "the WAC didn't like it." She was transferred to the Second Medical General Dispensary, and the Air Force "did not wish a replacement for Dr. Peck." For a time she was a General Medical Officer mostly responsible for female personnel which included about 1000 allied women, but she was moved back to a complete unit where she took care of "both male and female personnel."[74]

When she considered her overall Army career, however, Peck concluded: "I would not have traded the experience that I have had. There has been the chance to show a variety of individuals that good medicine can be practiced in the Army and that it can be done even by women. From the patient standpoint there has been very little expected opposition though at times sight consternation at the sight of a woman."[75]

Little is known about Peck's postwar years, but she returned to Poughkeepsie, New York, to practice pediatrics and she was certified by the American Board of Pediatrics in May of 1947.[76]. She was honored as the "Woman of the Year" by the Poughkeepsie Branch of the American Association for University Women in 1979, and she died 30 May 1996 at the age of 87.[77]

At the turn of the twentieth century, when Mila Pierce was growing up on the Southside of Chicago, she often went on Sunday outings with her parents (both doctors) in the family carriage. She had only one dream: "[T]o go to college—to that mysterious University of Chicago with its gray stone towers in the distance across the Midway." Everyone agreed she should go there one day, and she received her undergraduate degree in 1922; and in 1925, was one of ten women who finished at Rush Medical College at the University of Chicago. She completed her internship at Evanston General Hospital where it was expected she would do outstanding work "as she had been chosen by the committee" and was not "to let them down." The internship provided only board, room, and uniforms, but she needed money to pursue a residency. Pierce accepted a job at the University of Iowa health service for women and saved enough during the school year to begin a residency in June 1927 at Children's Memorial Hospital in Chicago.[78]

On completing a residency, it was customary for a doctor interested in a subspecialty to volunteer to work with a senior staff member who had expertise in that field. But she was interested in blood disorders, and there was no one there with such an interest. The chief of staff suggested that she develop a special clinic just for such patients, but Pierce did not feel she knew enough to undertake such a task. He replied, "The best way to learn a subject was to study it." She was reminded, however, that there were no funds for extra laboratory tests, so she would have to conduct them herself. She immersed herself in the study of hematology, and in 1930 enrolled in a postgraduate course in the histology of the blood-forming organs at the University of Chicago with one of the leaders in the field, Dr. William Bloom. For the next several years, Pierce continued her work in this area until she was drawn to the study of childhood leukemia. Next she seized the opportunity in 1939 to visit the Children's Hospital in Birmingham, England, as a visiting fellow with Dr. Leonard Parsons, also well known for his work on blood disorders and anemias of childhood.[79] Her visit was cut short as she became aware of impending war, and she vowed to return if and when war broke out.

After returning to the States and Children's Memorial Hospital in Chicago, Illinois, where she headed up the pediatric hematology clinic she had also established there, she decided to act on her promise—so it might be conjectured, that loyalty was another motivation for joining the war effort. In June of 1940, the Director in charge of enrollment of medical technologists for the Red Cross sent out a letter to Rush Medical where Pierce had received her MD in 1925. "We have received an application for enrollment as Physician from Mila I. Pierce...It is necessary that we have...as much information as possible concerning the applicant's training, experience, qualifications, and degrees received."[80] No one seemed to be in a hurry to expedite the transition, however, and it was not until December 1941 that she was able leave.

For the next year, Mila Pierce served as a pediatrician with the British EMS at children's hospitals, which were short of staff, in Liverpool and Birmingham. Then the Army offered her the appointment of contract surgeon in November 1942. "I accepted the appointment," she said, "but was allowed to continue with my hospital appointment (Children's Hospital, Birmingham)." She went to the Hospital for Sick Children in London next and on 20 November 1943 she was commissioned as a captain but remained working at the same hospital until after "D" Day 1944. "During this entire period, "she explained, "my training as a pediatrician was well utilized as the British hospitals were particularly short of trained pediatricians." After "D" Day she was transferred to the 81st General Hospital in Wales "where the commanding officer and chief of medical service accepted a woman medical officer with complete fairness." She was assigned as ward officer in the cardiovascular service, which covered two wards.[81]

While on duty one snowy night in January of 1945, Mila Pierce was running between wards. She slipped on an icy ramp and fractured a bone (a femur), which was cause for automatically sending her back to the United States to recover. Dr. Marion Loizeaux, then special consultant to the ETO, wrote: "Captain Pierce's accident was most unfortunate. I had a talk with her CO the day after she was evacuated... He spoke very highly of her, and said she was one of the most superior medical officers he had. She would have gotten a promotion I am sure if this had not happened... She hated very much to return."[82] Back again in the States, Pierce was on "patient status" until July of 1945.[83]

"When able to return to limited duty," Mila Pierce said, "I was assigned to the University of Chicago's high-security Manhattan Project." She recalled that the campus was strangely quiet that summer.

> The various projects undertaken by the Atomic Energy Commission were housed in several different buildings, each strictly guarded and with little communication among them. I was to work on the top floor of the anatomy building under Bloom, who had undertaken the staggering task of evaluating the effects of plutonium and its fission products. Using experimental animals, he compared the histologic effect on blood-forming organs with standard irradiation given in different doses. The task was necessary but tedious. It was not until the first test bomb was exploded at Los Alamos that all the personnel involved in the Manhattan Project were invited to a meeting in the physics building and the full magnitude of the project was made known. I shall never forget the awed silence of that audience and the mixed emotions flooding my mind as I realized that such destructive energy could be directed against a great population of human beings.[84]

Over the next four decades, Mila Pierce accepted academic appointments at major institutions in Chicago, Illinois. At the end of the war, she accepted a full-time academic appointment as assistant professor in the Department of Pediatrics at the University of Chicago. She was later Professor of Pediatrics at Northwestern University and at Rush Medical College, and when she retired from Rush she was named Professor Emeritus.[85] For more than fifty years she did research and published scientific articles on leukemia "having witnessed a drastic turnaround in the mortality rate of childhood victims of the disease—from 60 percent dying of leukemia...to 75 percent being cured today."[86] Among her many honors, she was a pioneer in the field of exchange transfusion for the Rh factor", one of the few women to have received the highest award given by the national pediatric society, and recipient of the Distinguished Alumnus Award from Rush Medical College in 1983.

In June of 1983, A *Sun Times* columnist was interested in writing an article on Dr. Pierce, and she wrote to Rush-Presbyterian-St. Luke's Medical Center asking for information on the well-known professor of Pediatrics. In response, the Medical Center supplied this information: "Dr. Pierce is 82 years old...Despite her age, she maintains a busy practice in pediatric hematology/oncology with a special interest in treating childhood leukemia...Dr. Pierce never married and has lived in Hyde Park since the 1950s. She is a charming woman, well liked by her colleagues and patients. She is a bit shy, but has agreed to being interviewed..."[87]

Before the year was out, however, Dr. Pierce was no longer single. On 10 December 1983 at the age of 82, she married her 1920s classmate from Rush Medical College, Dr. Paul S. Rhoads. After their marriage, she used his name professionally and on all her publications after that date. He preceded her in death 24 January 1987 at the age of 88. She died 31 March 1997 at the age of ninety-five.[88]

Dr. Josephine M. Stephens was born 15 March 1902 in Monongahela, Pennsylvania.[89] She attended the local high school there and received her degree in 1923 from Smith College. Like many aspiring women medical students, she taught school for one year in order to save money before she went off to the University of Pittsburgh School of Medicine where she graduated in 1928.

Those who knew Stephens described her as "brilliant, energetic, keen, and with excellent ideals…She is a talented musician and has been gifted with literary ability." She was also remembered as the "mystery girl" of the freshman class until she began to "unfold" over the next three years. The 1928 Yearbook concluded with this comment: "We have often admired her reticence, as well as her timely remarks. It's our opinion that medicine will profit by her type of woman.[90]

Josephine Stephens devoted the next dozen years to the practice of medicine. She went on to finish an internship at West Pennsylvania Hospital in 1929, and "she hung out her shingle in Monongahela five years later." By December of 1941, the local newspaper, the *Charleroi Mail*, printed a headline, which read: "Woman Doctor to Serve Abroad in British Service." And go abroad she did, arriving in England the beginning of January 1942 to join the other American women doctors there. On her arrival she was sent to the Nottingham City Hospital as part of the British EMS, and by the end of the year, she accepted a position as contract surgeon 16 December 1942.

She continued working for the EMS until she was commissioned a captain 27 November 1943, and she was swiftly assigned in December to the General Dispensary in the London area. The Supreme Headquarters there asked for a woman medical officer because there were a large number of women in the area, and "it was thought it would be a good place to put a woman medical officer who liked general practice." The medical consultant describe her duties this way: "She runs the women's sick call and this includes not only WAC, but Red Cross and civilian workers. She is treated like any other officer of the unit."[91] Several other assignments followed in rapid order—all classified as general duty. Thus, between April 1944 and July 1945, she went to two General Dispensaries in London and Paris, the 152nd Station Hospital, and then lastly to the 119th General Hospital. For the most part, all her patients were WAC enlisted women.

When Josephine Stephens was asked to give her impressions of her Army experiences, however, she was straight forward in her assessment, pointing out two common problems with rank and work load: "Insufficient rank was the cause of any difficulties or unpleasantness that I met in the Army. It was very evident that in this respect I was at a disadvantage with women officers in the WAC and ANC [Army Nurse Corps] with whom I worked and lived. I'm sure," she went on, "that our associations would have been more pleasant for all concerned had there been comparable rank in our respective services. ... Within my own service I found that my responsibilities exceeded the authority that my rank conferred—in charge of all women patients at the dispensaries where I worked. I found I received a disproportionate load of the work." She concluded: "It gave me no satisfaction although I appreciated the implied accomplishment that the post I left in London to move to Paris was filled by two officers, one of superior rank and at a time when work there had slackened."[92]

After she left the service, Stephens returned to her home in Monongahela, Pennsylvania. She resumed her medical practice as a pediatrician and became a member of the board of directors of the Southwestern Pennsylvania Heart Association. Eventually she became president of the Association (later retiring from that office in 1960), and she was a clinical instructor in pediatrics at the medical school she had attended. She died 6 April 1994 at the age of ninety-three.[93]

Yet even as these women doctors ventured abroad and finally became contract surgeons and later commissioned medical officers, some of their colleagues were set on the same course in the United States. Eventually seventy-six women doctors would be awarded the commissions they coveted. And as other civilian women were finally permitted to volunteer in capacities other than as nurses, the War Department relented in its strong stand against enlisted women although it had been even more unfavorable to an attempt by the Surgeon General to commission women doctors in the Army Medical Corps (AMC). With the establishment of the WAAC in 1942, it was evident that a director was needed and Mrs. Overta Culp Hobby was tagged for the job. Her first step was to make it clear that "Waacs will be neither Amazons rushing to battle, nor butterflies fluttering about."[94] At the same time, another leader would be needed who could oversee the health of the large numbers of women personnel joining the ranks. As shall be seen in the next chapter, Dr. Margaret D. Craighill was appointed Consultant to The Surgeon's General's Office (SGO) and she became the first woman to achieve Major in the AMC. A practicing physician, a dean of a woman's medical school, and a member in a family with a long military tradition, she was a superb choice for the job.

~ NOTES ~

1. Moore, *Restoring the Balance*, 126 and 137. Barringer quotes in Barringer, Emily D., "War and the Woman Physician," *New York State Journal of Medicine*, Vol. 42, No. 2, 15 January, 1942; right, *italics*, mine.

2. See Hearings before Subcommittee No. 3 of the Committee on Military Affairs, House of Representatives, 78th Congress, lst Session on H.R. 824, March 10, 11, 18, 1943; printed for the use of the Committee on Military Affairs (no publisher: Washington, D.C., 1943). "Maffett's Statement" (read in her absence) in Hearings before Subcommittee No. 3, 6770.

3. Quote in More, *Restoring the Balance*, 182; and questionnaires to 8,000 in Walsh, *Doctors Wanted: No Women Need Apply*, 226. Also see "Women Physicians Win Medical Corps Status", *MWJ* May 1942, 115; and "American Women Physicians Serve in English Hospitals", *New York Times* 12 October 1941.

4. *MWJ*, "News of the Month", January 1942. Quotes in Stimson, "Memoir", 1. Stimson and others agree that 10 women arrived in England early on, but two others came later who did not get commissions: Dr. Grace Haskin who worked with the EMS in the Midlands at Sheffield, which was the center for head injuries; and Dr. Jane Kilham who went on the inactive medical list because she had an infant. See "Loizeaux to Craighill, 17 April 1944", letter, Box 5, MDC Coll.

5. For information on Julia Stimson, see Sarnecky, Mary T., "Julia Catherine Stimson: Nurse and Feminist," *Journal of Nursing Scholarship*, Volume 25, No. 7, June 1993, 113-120 and Sarnecky, *A History of the U.S. Army Nurse Corps*. Philadelphia: University of Pennsylvania Press, 1999. Also see Hunt, Marion, "Julia Stimson and the Mobilization of Womanpower," *Gateway Heritage*, Vol. 20, No. 3, 1999; James, Edward T., et al. *Notable American Women: A Biographical Dictionary, Vol. 3*. Harvard: Belknap Press, 1971; 379.

6. "'She's a Doctor'" Say Colleagues Lauding Head of Medical Society", *Poughkeepsie Sunday New Yorker*, 28 February 1960. Stimson's birth date was 14 February 1898.

7. In this book, orthopedic is used rather than orthopaedic. Even today women make up only 3% of board-certified orthopedic surgeons. See Barbara Boughton, "Female Orthopaedic Surgeons Rare", *M. D. News* (Bay Area Edition,) April 2008.

8. "Joining British Army Enabled U. S. Women Doctors to Learn," *Austin Minnesota Herald*, 5 March 1942; no page indicated. The FBI and Scotland Yard conducted intensive investigations on both women.

9. From "Dr. Achsa Bean Writes of War Conditions", unidentified newspaper clipping supplied by Vassar Library.

10. Quotes are from "Sketch of Achsa M. Bean," supplied by the Alumni Office University of Maine at Orono. Her original application for Commission in U.S. Naval Reserve dated 27 November 1942 gives school information and dates; supplied by supplied by the Bureau of Medicine and Surgery History Offices, U.S. Navy; hereafter referred to as BUMED. Bean's birth date was 6 March 1900.

11. "Mother to support": Quoted from unidentified newspaper clipping dated 2 February 1965, in Bean's file; supplied by Vassar Library, Vassar College.

12. "Internal fixation" is a treatment, which discards plaster casts so that the patient can be more active a few days after the fracture had been set.

13. Stimson "Memoir", 18.

14. Bean's quotes in "Bean Writes of War Conditions". The Royal Free Hospital was the first teaching hospital in London to admit women for training.

15. Barbara B. Stimson, "Three-and-a-Half Years in the Royal Army Medical Corps," *JAMWA*, May 1946, 48-49. The doctors also learned that during the Blitz, the London hospitals had been so crowded with injured people each night that places had to be found nearby to which the patients could be moved to make room for the next night's arrivals. The Royal Free solved the problem by building large Nissen (prefabricated steel structure) huts on the grounds of the mental hospital in Arlesey.

16. Devastation quotes in "Three-and-a-Half Years in the RAMC" preceding note; and Stimson Memoir", 23.

17. Ibid, "Bean Writes of War Conditions".

18. Bath quote from "Memorial Minute: Achsa Mabel Bean 1900-1975", Bean Biographical File, provided by Vassar Library.

19. "Their Hunch Proves Good," *The Montreal Daily Star*, (undated) supplied by the Vassar Library, Bean's Alumna File.

20. Quotes from Stimson "Memoir," 28.

21. The AMWA had just discontinued its policy of rejecting membership applications from "colored" women physicians in 1939.

22. It was not until 7 September 1944 that an amendment was passed so that female physicians could receive increased rental and subsistence allowances as for officers with dependents. It was not, however, retroactive, and it worked a real hardship on the women whose parents were dependent on them.

23. Quote from Stimson "Memoir," 40; also see *JAMWA*, Vol. 45, No. 5, 172. Information on ranks from "Bean to Dr. Ava H. Chadbourne, 18 November 1955, letter, supplied from Alumni file, Vassar College Library.

24. Quotes from Stimson's Memoir, 46, 48.

25. Quotes from Stimson's Memoir, 51.

26. Bean's "Application for Commission in U.S. Naval Reserve," and copy of her "Appointment in Naval Reserve", BUMED.

27. "Excerpt from Bean's Letter to Dr. Ava H. Chadbourne Dated 18 November 1955," from Bean's File, Vassar Library.

28. Information provided by WIMSA; see her individual record there.

29. Summarized from Stimson's Memoir, 50-55.

30. Quotes from Stimson's Memoir, 55.

31. Bean to the Chief of the Bureau of Navy Personnel, 10 November 1943, letter, provided by BUMED, U.S. Navy. She finally resigned from the U.S. Naval Reserve under honorable conditions 8 December 1953.

32. "'She's a Doctor'", *Poughkeepsie Sunday New Yorker*, 28 February 1960.

33. Ibid, *Poughkeepsie Sunday New Yorker*, 28 February 1960.

34. See Stimson, "Three-and-a-Half Years in the Royal Army Medical Corps," *JAMWA*, May 1946, 48-49.

35. See "Memorandum for Deputy Directors of Medical Services Eastern, Northern, Southern, Scottish, Western and AA Commands, London District and Northern Ireland, Dated 5 March 1945," Box 5, MDC Coll..

36. "To Ruth from Barbara Stimson, letter, Undated, but received 11 December 1958 and placed in Alumnae File, Vassar Library. See her Obituary, "Owl's Head Orthopedist Dr. Barbara Stimson Dies," Portland, Maine, *Press Herald*, 31 October 1986. Bean's obituary in "Memorial Minute, Achsa Mabel Bean 1900-1975, Vassar.

37. See "Bowditch is Dead, Industrialist, 58," unidentified newspaper clipping supplied by Alan Mason Chesney Medical Archives, Johns Hopkins University; hereafter referred to as AMC Archives.

38. After WWII the Northern hospital was renamed Highlands and merged with South Lodge in 1966 to form a district hospital for Oakwood, Southgate and surrounding areas. They remained friends until Bowditch's death at the age of 61 in 1966 which preceded that of Stimson and Bean. See her obituary, "Dr. Sarah Bowditch, 61, of Milton, Dies in Maine," The *Boston Globe*, 24 July 1966.

39. "Women Doctors Seek War Tasks," MWJ, January 1942, 28.

40. Request to return to Hopkins in "Medicine and the War," JAMA, 26 May 1945, Vol. 128, No. 4. Also see the Institutional Records of the Johns Hopkins Hospital: "Hopkins Units in World War I and World War II", Record Group 7, Alan Mason Chesney Medical Archives, Johns Hopkins. Also see "When Hopkins Went to War," *Annals of Hopkins*, fall 2006.

41. Sparkman Bill: Public Law No. 38, 78th Congress enacted 16 April 1943.

42. Since Ft. Oglethorpe was centrally situated, it was a convenient location for drawing trainees from all parts of the country. Quotes about "VD" in Dr. Jessie D. Read to Dr. Craighill, 11 January 1944, letter, Box 5, MDC Coll.

43. Quotes in Bowditch's Army Questionnaire, Box 30, MDC Coll.; Bowditch to Lt. Colonel Margaret Craighill 25 September 1945, letter, Box 5, MDC Coll.

44. "Inadequate Pay," unidentified newspaper clipping supplied by AMC Archives, Johns Hopkins University.

45. 1957 was the start of the Duvalier family dictatorship in Haiti. As one of the poorest countries in the western hemisphere, its children suffer from a variety of problems and illnesses including water-borne diseases, intestinal parasites, etc. Haiti quote in a note appended to her address label as part of her alumni records, AMC Archives.

46. Quotes in "Bowditch to Dr. T. B. Turner, Dean, Johns Hopkins Medical School, Received 8 February 1961, letter, Registrar's Office," AMC Archives.

47. "Dr. Sarah Bowditch, 61, of Milton, Dies in Maine," The *Boston Globe*, 24 July 1966. She also made a substantial gift in the form of a trust to Johns Hopkins upon her death. Her date of birth was 3 February 1905 in Milton, Massachusetts.

48. Biographical information for Loizeaux supplied by Cornell Archives. Sometime after WWII she became Board certified in internal medicine.

49. Stimson Memoir, 28.

50. "No promises" quote in Loizeaux to Major Craighill, 17 April 1944, letter, Box 5, MDC Coll.

51. Craighill to Chief, Personnel Service, 24 June 1943, letter, Personal Papers, Box 2, MDC Coll.

52. For information on Dr. Elliott C. Cutler, see Francis A. Countway Library of Medicine, Harvard University that holds a collection of his files from WWII. For biographical information, see Frederick P. Ross, "Master Surgeon, Teacher, Soldier

and Friend: Elliott Carr Cutler, MD (1888-1947)," *American Journal of Surgery* 137 (1979): 428-32.

53. Quotes in Loizeaux to Craighill, 17 April 1944," letter, Box 5, MDC Coll.

54. Manual and sex, in Treadwell, *The Women's Army Corps*, 397-398.

55. Loizeaux to Major Craighill, 17 April 1944," letter, Box 5, MDC Coll.

56. Loizeaux to Major Craighill, 15 July 1944," letter, Box 5, MDC Coll.

57. Problem with feet, Treadwell, *The Women's Army Corp*, 397.

58. All quotes on shoes, in Loizeaux to Major Craighill, 17 April 1944, letter, Box 5, MDC Coll.

59. Treadwell, 397.

60. Quotes in Loizeaux to Major Craighill, 17 April 1944, letter, Box 5, MDC Coll.

61. Overall "non-effective rate" in Loizeaux's Letter preceding note.

62. Uniforms in Treadwell, 382.

63. Ibid, 398.

64. Quotes in Loizeaux's Questionnaire, Box 30, MDC Coll. Also see, "Capt. Loizeaux, First Woman Physician Commissioned in European Area," MWJ, March 1944, 32.

65. "Ten Women Doctors Named to VA Posts," *The New York Times*, 28 November 1946, 47.

66. "Island Circumambulation, A Walking Tour of the Perimeter of Vinalhaven", a blog on-line, posted by Phil Crossman.

67. Eleanor Peck to Family, Sunday 2 November 1941, letter, in the Eleanor K. Peck Letters, Women Veterans Historical Collection, University of North Carolina Archives, Greensboro, North Carolina; hereafter referred to Peck Letters, WVHC, Greensboro. Also Peck's Letter of 8 December 1941", Ibid. The hospital was also referred to as the Great Ormond Street Hospital for Sick Children.

68. Eleanor Peck to Family, 23 March 1943, letter, WVHC, Greensboro.

69. Eleanor Peck, 8 May 1943, letter, ibid. Also see, "Proceedings of the Royal Society of Medicine: Section for the Study of Disease in Children, 26 February 1943, Vol. XXXVI, 21-22.

70. Eleanor Peck's Letters, 16 June 1943, and 26 June 1943." WVHC, Greensboro.

71. Job description in Peck's Questionnaire, Box 30; To Major Craighill from Eleanor Choate Darnton, Women's Editor *The New York Times*, February 23, 1944, letter, Histories, Box 29, MDC Coll.

72. Peck to Major Craighill, 4 September 1945," letter, Box 5, MDC Coll., Ibid, p.2.

73. All quotes from Loizeaux to Major Craighill, 17 April 1944," Correspondence, MDC Coll.

74. Peck to Craighill 4 September 1945, Box 5, MDC Coll.

75. Peck's Questionnaire, Box 30.

76. *American Journal of Diseases of Children*, 1947;73(6):744-745.

77. Online site for American Association of University Women: w.aauwpoughkeepsie. org/woman.html See Social Security Death for Peck. Her birth date was give as "about" 1909.

78. Quotes from Mila I. Pierce Rhoads "Beginning a Career in Pediatric Hematology: 1926," *JAMA*, 16 September 1988, Vol. 260, No. 11, 1806, 1807. Those were the days when children's hospitals were supported only by volunteer contributions and were dedicated to the care of indigent children. On the wards, visiting hours were permitted only twice a week for parents unless emergencies arose. As she started her work, a new building was under construction, which was adding a wing for private patients and allowing attending physicians to admit some of the patients.

79. Summarized from "Beginning a Career in Pediatric Hematology," *JAMA*.

80. American Red Cross to Rush Medical College, 29 June 1940, letter, in Pierce's Alumni File, provided by Rush University Medical Center, Medical Center Archives, Chicago, Illinois; hereafter referred to as Rush Archives.

81. All quotes are from Pierce's Questionnaire, Box 30, MDC Coll.

82. Loizeaux to Major Margaret Janeway, 2 April 1945, letter, Correspondence, Box 5, MDC Coll.

83. "Resident patient" quote from her Questionnaire, Box 30, MDC Coll.

84. All quotes from "Beginning a Career in Pediatric Hematology," *JAMA*.

85. Summarized from "Mila I. Pierce," The American Journal of Pediatric Hematology/Oncology 8 (4): 342-345, 1986.

86. To *Chicago Sun-Times* from Francie Murphy, Assistant Manager Media Relations, Rush-Presbyterian-St. Luke's Medical Center, Chicago, 7 June 1983, letter, provided by Rush Archives.

87. Quote is from "Letter of *Chicago Sun-Times*," preceding note.

88. Rhoads had graduated in 1924 one year ahead of her. He was a deeply religious man and humanitarian well-known for combining his interest in medicine with religion. Many of his 150 bibliographic entries deal with how to enhance the physician-clerical relationship. Paul S. Rhoads obituary in *JAMA*, 18 March 1988, Vol. 259, No. 11. See article on Pierce's marriage to Rhoads: "Looping Chicagoland" in Sneed & Lavin column, *Chicago Tribune*, 15 December 1983. Her birth and death dates are from the Social Security Death Index.

89. Birth date from Social Security Death Index; quotes are from sketch of "Stephens, Josephine M., A.B. Monongahela" in the Class of 1928 Yearbook, provided by University of Pittsburgh, Medical Alumni Association.

90. See "Dr. Stephens Feted Before Leaving for Service with British Red Cross," *Charleroi Mail*, Charleroi Pennsylvania, 30 December 1941; quote from "Woman Doctor to Serve Abroad in British Service, 30 December 1941, Ibid.

91. Stephens's duties: "Loizeaux's Letter", Ibid.

92. Quotes from Stephens Questionnaire, Box 30, MDC Coll.

93. Obit. in *JAMA*, 16 August 1996, Vol. 274, No. 7, 590; she was later honored as a distinguished "Pitt" Faculty member.

94. Culp quote in Treadwell, The Women's Army Corps, 48.

CHAPTER TWO:

From Contract Surgeon to Army Medical Officer

Before WWII, mobilization planners assumed, as they had prior to WWI, that any American involvement in war would be mostly defensive. With the German occupation of Denmark, Norway, Belgian, and the Netherlands in the spring of 1940 and the fall of France in June, the United States sensed an imminent danger. Congress responded by approving the federalization of the National Guard and calling up the Organized Reserves in 1940 and the following September, the nation's first peacetime draft law was authorized for an army of 1.4 million men. The Surgeon General's Office (SGO) initiated the first important modifications in its structure since 1935 which included setting up or enlarging subdivisions within the Professional Service Division, while the creation of a preventive medicine division in 1940 signaled the importance of preventive medicine as large numbers of recruits were being gathered in camps. It did not consider women doctors part of that initiative. Nevertheless, while American women doctors in England accepted the offer to be contract surgeons towards the end of 1942, other women doctors in the States were started on the same path, despite its second-class status.

In June 1942, the Services of Supply took steps to procure female doctors, not for service with the Army Medical Corps, but with the WAAC. This handful of women served as civilian contract surgeons for a short time when first placed on duty; and if they were found acceptable, they were made members of the corps, in the status of "second officer", which was not a commissioned status. As Esther Pohl Lovejoy had once observed about WWI women contract surgeons a little more than two decades earlier: "They were without commissions," but "they were on the job."

Of course women had a variety of reasons for volunteering on contract although the AMWA rejected the idea of medical duty in the WACCS as given its lack of rank and status, contract service continued to represent an inferior kind of status, just as it had in WWI. Jensen pointed out, however, that some women physicians in the First World War "held notions of patriotism and professionalism that allowed them to view contract service with the military in a more positive light." The same was true in WWII, although another historian offered an alternative explanation. She believed that while a few women accepted positions as contract surgeons, they filed protests with the War Department at the same time. The women doctors stated that "they hoped this would lead to a regular commission."[1]

Between December of 1942 and July of 1944, 16 women physicians signed on as contract surgeons according to Craighill's records, but if you add the names of the three other female doctors who served abroad in England—Pierce, Stephens, Loizeaux—the total rises to nineteen that can be identified. (See Table 1) Of these, eleven women were immediately sent to the First WAAC (later WAC) Training Center at Fort Des Moines, Iowa. Dr. Elizabeth Garber of Dunkirk, Indiana, and Dr. Mary Moore of Colorado were the first two to sign on in July 1942. They were followed in September by Dr. Eleanor Gutman and Dr. Margaret Janeway of New York; in November by Dr. I. E. Fatheree and Dr. Poe-Eng Yu, and in December by Dr. Eleanor Hayden (later d'Orbessan) and Dr. Nita Arnold. In 1943, six more women were appointed, and in 1944 the last two volunteered. Unfortunately, only scanty information was located for some of the women, and in the case of two doctors who had initials but no first names, little or nothing could be found at all, i.e. Fatheree and Loving. In Fatheree's, case, for example, it is known that she listed Columbus, Mississippi, as her address; and she was sent in November of 1942 to serve as a troop train physician with a WAAC troop movement en route to a training center at Daytona Beach, Florida, where some 20,000 women recruits had started to arrive in October.[2] It can be conjectured that she was also assigned to the hospital there as the Army anticipated that it would need 'special' wards reserved for the hospitalization of its service women.

(Clockwise, from the left): Elizabeth Garber, Mary L. Moore, Eleanor Gutman, Eleanor Hayden and Poe-Eng Yu.

When the eleven women contract surgeons were sent to the First WAAC Training Center, they were assigned first as assistant ward officers in the Station Hospital, and then, as they became more familiar with Army procedure, they went to the WAAC Dispensaries or the out-patient department of the hospital or became ward officers. Training, however, did not follow any formal pattern although the women were carefully supervised by the Commanding Officer of the hospital, Colonel T. E. Harwood Jr. "They were treated on an equal basis with the men and were assigned where their qualifications best suited them." The other five women found that different opportunities awaited them—in the ETO, the Army Medical Museum, the WAAC Dispensary in New York City, the San Antonio Ordnance Department at Camp Stanley, Texas, and Bradley Field, Connecticut. In December1942, they were authorized to wear uniforms similar to those worn by men.[3] After commissions were available to women physicians on 16 April 1943, those already in the WAAC were offered the opportunity to transfer to the Medical Department for the duration of the war plus six months.

Of the sixteen contract surgeons that first served in the United States (excluding Dr. Eleanor Peck who was abroad), five went on to become commissioned in the WAAC early in 1943: Drs. Garber, Gutman, Hayden, Janeway, and Yu. For various reasons, not all of the contract surgeons went on to be commissioned; but sources available for some of them reveal that they were just as highly qualified.

One fact that emerged in identifying these women was that several of them either had a relative who was physician or else they married one. In the case of Dolly (also Dollie) Morgans, both her parents were physicians as well as her paternal grandmother, and so it seemed natural that she would choose a medical career. She received her degree in medicine from the University of Vienna where she specialized in dermatology and before the Second World War started, she had spent a little more than ten years in Europe in study and travel abroad. It was said that she was in Berlin when the Reischstag was burned in 1933, and in Vienna at the time of the early rioting of students at the universities. As soon as she learned that the WAAC needed doctors, Dr. Morgans volunteered her services and she was ordered to the first WAAC Training Center at Fort Des Moines.[4]

Dr. Dollie Morgans. Courtesy private collection.

While Dr. Morgans had been inspired by her parents and grand-mother to study medicine, it was a pathologist uncle who turned out to be a role model for Sophie Spitz. Born 4 February 1910 in Nashville, Tennessee, of Jewish parents who had emigrated from Germany, Spitz supported herself during high school and college working as a technician in her uncle's clinical laboratory. Following her graduation from Vanderbilt University in 1929, she continued at the medical school associated with the university until she received her medical degree in 1932. After she accepted an internship, she moved to New York to work at the New York Infirmary for Women and Children, and it was while she was here that she was inspired by another pathologist, Dr. Elise Strang L'Esperance.[5] Under her tutelage Spitz advanced to resident pathologist and director of Laboratories. At the same time, she combined this work with service at the Memorial Hospital for Cancer and Allied Disease—beginning as assistant bacteriologist from 1939 to 1941 and then as assistant attending pathologist from 1941to 1956. During this same period of time she held the title of Assistant Medical Examiner for the City of New York and assistant professor of pathology at the Sloan-Kettering Division of the Cornell University School of Medicine. As medical examiner she sharpened her skills as an autopsy pathologist, but she also suffered from the hazards of the job when she received a wound during an autopsy, an injury that left her with ankylosis, or a stiffening of a finger joint.[6]

In September of 1942 she married Dr. Arthur Allen, a pathologist who had joined the Army a few months earlier. Because of the war, Spitz asked for a leave of absence from Memorial to serve as a contract surgeon. At the initiation of Colonel James Earle Ash, then director, she was assigned to the Armed Forces Institute of Pathology from 1944 to 1945 where she was part of a group of outstanding pathologists gathered together to meet the Army's expanding needs, most importantly in tropical diseases, an area that had been foreign to most pathologists—but changed because of the war.

As part of her assignment, Dr. Spitz prepared "study sets'" for medical personnel of the Armed Forces, using materials at the Army Institute of Pathology that had been sent from various installations situated in tropical climates, as well as material that she personally collected from Puerto Rico, Panama, Colombia, and Venezuela. She also prepared collections of study sets about tropical diseases that were supplied to practically all of the medical schools in the United States as a means of alerting students to the possibilities in this special field.[7] She was also on the faculty of the Army Medical School and she lectured to many groups of medical officers who were enrolled for the course in tropical diseases.[8] It was during the same period that she completed several important projects including coauthoring with Colonel James E. Ash, who was then Director of the Army Institute of Pathology, an atlas and text on the pathology of tropical diseases.[9] She also wrote important articles on malaria as well as a paper with her husband on the comparative pathology of the rickettsia diseases. For the last effort, she was awarded a commendation ribbon by the Surgeon General.[10]

Following the war, Sophie Spitz returned to work at the New York Infirmary and also at the Sloan-Kettering Cancer Center and she continued her research efforts, especially with what was then known as Juvenile Melanoma. She recognized that these lesions have benign behavior despite their microscopic resemblance to melanoma, and the lesion now bears her name today. Today she is recognized as a prominent pathologist of her time because of her contributions to pathology and for her foresight in advocating the use of the Pap smear when it was first devised.

At her memorial service, Colonel Ash recalled that she had a "courageous, forceful, yet generous and warm personality, a brilliant intellect and an indefatigable and purposeful worker, who was uncompromising in defense of her ideas and ideals." She was also a painstaking teacher "as the number of pathologists in training at the Armed Forces Institute of Pathology and at the Memorial Cancer Center, to which she returned after the war, would spiritedly agree."[11] One biographer noted that "despite her brilliant intellect and hard work, she did not receive full credit during her life for her manifold accomplishments. Spitz died at the age of forty-six from colon cancer on 11 August 1956, and she left no children. She also never heard the term "Spitz nervus," which was named in her honor.[12]

Like Dr. Sophie Spitz, Effie Matilda Ecklund also married a physician and volunteered as a contract surgeon because she wanted to follow her new husband into military service during WWII. She was born 6 March 1901 in Charlevoix, Michigan, moved with her family to Chesterton, Indiana, when she was growing up; but spent most of her adult life in Chicago, Illinois. Her parents were Swedish immigrants and her father, who had worked in the steel mills and also been a farmer, later became a chiropractor.[13] She decided to follow in her father's footsteps and became a chiropractor in Hyde Park and the Englewood district of Chicago, eventually setting up a private practice there. During this period she married her first husband, who she subsequently divorced.[14]

The thought of a medical career seemed to be the only thing on her mind for the next few years. Ecklund began to take some classes at the University of Chicago, not far from where she lived, and she obtained her B.S. degree, premedical and first two years of medicine at the University of Chicago, which she followed up with a MD from Rush Medical College in 1937.She interned at Walther Memorial Hospital, and it was here she was introduced to Dr. Harry A. Lerner whom she married 8 January 1941.[15] "I went into general practice as soon as I had finished my internship," she said, and then from August 1941 to October 1942 she was the resident in otolaryngology at the Presbyterian Hospital.[16]

But this was wartime and the couple were both eager to do something for their country. Lerner volunteered for the Army and received orders to Camp McCoy, Wisconsin.[17] "My residency was to cover a year, so in August 1942 I left the hospital", Ecklund explained. She moved near the camp so she could spend time with her husband when he was free. "I was very restless and tried to find something to do that would help the war effort. I did go to the Red Cross to roll bandages, but this seemed like child's play after having a medical practice. Finally, in desperation, I wrote to the Surgeon General in Washington, D.C... Within a very few days I received a letter and a contract from the general." He informed the young wife that he could not promise that she would be sent to Camp McCoy, but she was needed at Fort Des Moines, Iowa, if she were willing. This was a serious decision and Ecklund waited for about two months before she signed on as a contract surgeon in the spring of 1943 and she went to Fort Des Moines. "I reported to the colonel," she explained, "and was assigned to work in the infirmary at first, but when the commanding officer learned that I had some training in otolaryngology and also knew how to do refractions, I was sent to work with the doctor in charge of this work." In the end, she wound up at one of the three infirmaries connected with the complete hospital unit there.[18]

When her contract ended, Ecklund began a whole new set of experiences. She accepted a residency in ophthalmology at Cook County Hospital in Chicago, Illinois, and at the end of the year she decided to go into private practice in LaGrange, Illinois. Out of the Army now, Lerner began a search for a residency in radiology and finally accepted a two-year residency at Boston University. Ecklund flew back and forth over that period and in the summer of 1978 they both moved to Oak Park, Illinois, where she continued her private practice and Lerner went to the radiology department of West Suburban Hospital. They remained together until his death in 1986. She lived on until 17 December 1995.[19]

Dr. Ednah Swasey Hatt was no different than doctors Sophie Spitz and Effie Ecklund as she also married a doctor and followed him off to war. She was, however, the oldest of the three women having been born 12 September 1895; but like them she attended a prestigious medical school. While she was at Tufts Medical School, she also studied alongside Rafe Nelson Hatt whom she married 9 March 1918. This must have been an exciting year for them both as she graduated cum laude from the medical school and Rafe started his internship in orthopaedics at the Massachusetts General Hospital in Boston. He soon made rapid strides in his field and he was offered a post in charge of an orthopaedic unit at Honolulu which was followed up two years later with an appointment at the Springfield Shriners' Hospital where he worked with crippled children. While the young wife also continued to practice, she managed to have three children who were born between 1918 and 1932.

In August 1942, Nelson entered the AMC and he went overseas immediately following the invasion of Sicily in 1943 to serve as a front-line surgeon. In April of the same year, Ednah signed on as a contract surgeon and was sent to Bradley Field, Connecticut, which was an Army air base. It is not known what duties she performed or how long she stayed there, but most likely she was assigned to the Bradley Field Station Hospital although WAC personnel and nurses were also on base who might need medical screenings and care. After her husband left the AMC in 1946 with the rank of Lt. Colonel, however, the couple decided to return to Honolulu so he could accept the post of chief surgeon of the Shriner's Hospital where he had been previously. Rafe died 27 May 1949 at the age of fifty-nine but Ednah lived on until her passing 24 October 1969 in Massachusetts.[20]

We know little about the background of Mary L. Moore other than that she lived in Rifle, Colorado, and was a graduate of the Colorado School of Medicine. Her contract started 16 July 1942 and was annulled less than a year later on 30 April 1943. She did, however, write to a colleague describing her experiences at Fort Des Moines where she was in charge of one of the infirmaries which serviced some 2,500 young women. Sick call started at 7 a.m. and usually ended at 9 o'clock "when we begin to examine all of the newcoming WAACS. We do between 250-422 a day, a team of seven doctors," she wrote. "By the end of the week the greater mass of them are finished, and so on Saturday we give shots—they're typhoid tetanus and smallpox. We give some 3,000 or so every Saturday. And then Saturday night and Sunday night the doctor working as the officer of the day is up all night with shot reactions." She explained that there were also a number of interesting cases in the hospital "and a considerable number of mental cases, odd as it may seem."[21] But while this may have seemed strange to her, such cases were a reflection of some of the early problems with recruitment and screening that had concerned Oveta Culp Hobby, the first Director of the WAACS/WAC in February of 1943 when the decision was made to recruit 150,000 women by June of that year.

Another contract surgeon in WWII, Dr. Ellen Cover, had also volunteered in WWI. When the American Women's Hospitals Service (AWH) could not persuade the War Department to commission women physicians in WWI, it launched a successful campaign to deliver voluntary medical relief in various places throughout the world. By war's end it had won Red Cross backing to send women's hospital units overseas and had raised a large sum of money for the purpose. Ultimately AWH sent about 130 women physicians, dentists, nurses, ambulance drivers, and general purpose assistants abroad, and they worked either for the Red Cross or directly for AWH units. Cover was the only woman doctor that we know of who served in two world wars—in WWI as a relief worker and as a contract surgeon in WWII, and she was also an acquaintance of Esther Pohl Lovejoy, who had been authorized to go to Europe as the official representative of the MWNA in 1917.[22] Her passport from 1920 indicates that she was a physician and surgeon for the AWH and that she had been approved by the Serbian Commission for relief work there and in Greece following her efforts in France two years' earlier.[23]

Cover was born 11 October 1888 in San Antonio, Texas, and she was a graduate of Texas Woman's University and the University of Texas Medical School at Galveston. Following internship at the New England Hospital for Women and Children at Boston and Worchester Memorial Hospital at Worchester, Massachusetts, she served abroad and while in Europe she took postgraduate work in Paris, Dublin, and London. After returning to the States she spent more than thirty years as a psychiatrist at San Antonio and Austin State Hospitals.[24] This work was put on hold for a short time when she volunteered as a contract surgeon for the Army during WWII. She served in the dispensary at the Ordnance Depot, Camp Stanley, Texas, starting 1 April 1944. When her contract was over she returned to civilian medicine and was active in both the Texas State Medical Association and the AMA until her death 27 October 1965.[25]

The Army Medical Corps commissioned two Chinese woman physicians during WWII Theresa T. Woo and Poe-Eng Yu, but only Yu started out as a contract surgeon. (Her work is discussed in the

Chapter Three, psychiatrists). No Japanese or African American women doctors served in WWII. In May 1942, in fact, The Surgeon General recommended against commissioning Japanese-American citizens in the Medical Department. Even if they might meet all the requirements for commissions, he maintained, "They would be placed at a personal disadvantage and in many embarrassing positions. They would inspire a lack of confidence and distrust throughout the Army...rendering no military value and being under suspicion at all times."[26] At the height of the war, however, the WMCP risked taking an unpopular stance and admitted students from Japanese internment camps to its medical school. Dr. Toshiko Toyota began her studies with the class of 1943, but the resulting chaos surrounding the acceptance of Japanese-American students delayed her studies and forced her into the class of 1944. After she and the other students graduated, they had very successful practices and they continued to face some discrimination in postwar years—but it is not clear whether this was due to racism, sexism or a combination of both. Some other Asian-Pacific-American women did enter military service in an important capacity during World War II, however. The WAC recruited 50 Japanese-American and Chinese-American women and sent them to the Military Intelligence Service Language School at Fort Snelling, Minnesota, for training as military translators. In August of 1944, the Secretary of War announced that qualified Nisei (American citizens of Japanese ancestry) would be appointed as nurses in the Army if their loyalty was vouched for by the Provost Marshal General's Department, and that The Surgeon General would direct their assignment to duty. By February 1945, only four were appointed, and this did not change during the war. There were no African American women doctors in the Army until 1955 when Clotilde Bowen became the first one to have this distinction.[27]

Although the Army needed and wanted medical officers, women were sometimes discouraged from seeking a commission. Dr. Priscilla White, an expert in diabetes, was someone Craighill personally wanted to see in the Army as she was "anxious to get some of the better type women into the service. We need them," she stated emphatically, "and there is distinct criticism because they have not volunteered in any large numbers." It was believed, however, that since she was doing such an important job in civilian life that she should not be removed from it. "The theory back of it is that the Army does not deal in diabetes and whereas she could replace a man in a general hospital, in a medical service, there are too few persons with her specialized medical skill to allow her to be sidetracked."[28]

Dr. Bella S. Van Bark, a psychiatrist at Brooklyn State Hospital was interested in exploring a commission but she did not want her assignment to be exclusively with the WAC. "Women medical officers are not being used exclusively for the WACs," Craighill informed her, "I cannot, however, give you any assurance of a definite assignment or that it will not be with the WAC." She explained that every attempt was made to assign medical officers according to their qualifications and the needs of the service, rather than according to their sex. While women medical officers were not being used exclusively for the WACs "they must take their chances along with the men medical officers in such assignments."[29] Apparently Van Bark decided against such a risk as her name did not appear on the list of the first women medical officers to be commissioned, but she went on to have a long and distinguished career in psychoanalysis.

The Army also rejected some promising women candidates for commissions, such as Dr. Alice McNeal, the first female anesthesiologist in Alabama and the first female chair of an academic anesthesiology department in the United States. Born in Hinsdale, Illinois, in 1897, McNeal graduated from Rush Medical College in Chicago in 1921, and finished internships at Women's Hospital in Philadelphia and Durand Hospital in Chicago. In 1943, the operating team to which she belonged was called up as part of U.S. Base Hospital. Forty Chicago doctors went, but Dr. McNeal was left behind because she was a woman and the Army refused to commission her.[30]

Another physician also experienced rejection by the Army even though she had served faithfully as a contract surgeon. Dr. Nita Arnold had been practicing as a psychiatrist for almost a decade in Chicago before signing on as a contract surgeon 25 December 1942. She very much wanted to become a medical officer in the Army Medical Corps, and she felt that she had earned her chance since from late December 1942 to May 1943 she served with the WAAC as a psychiatrist and was stationed at Ft. Des Moines. When the bill to grant commissions to women was passed, her contract, as well as some others, was cancelled and she was told to apply for a Commission—which is what she did. After several months of waiting, she was informed that she could not be commissioned, but no reason was given.

The cancellation of the contract was upsetting to Arnold since she had never received any negative evaluations. Her Commanding Officer at the Station Hospital admitted later, however, that he had asked for a cancellation of her contract because he felt she was "disloyal to him." Had her contract been cancelled for misconduct or neglect of duty she could have asked for a hearing, but since she was honorably discharged, she was deprived of the opportunity which would have allowed her to present her side of the case. Arnold maintained that "the refusal to commission me has far reaching effects on my life." She was at a loss to answer her colleagues' questions as to why she was no longer in the Army. This was also particularly distressing since the Army needed and wanted psychiatrists in the service.

Although the case was investigated, Craighill informed Arnold "that an appointment as a contract surgeon does not necessarily mean that one would also be commissioned." Furthermore, she was advised that she was "not the only one who failed to get a commission under similar conditions." Craighill also assured Arnold that there was "much essential work to be done by civilian women doctors", especially those with her training, and she could see no reason for her "to feel apologetic or embarrassed about being out of the service."[31] In the end, the Ranks had closed against Arnold and there was no further appeal.

As women started to volunteer in large numbers and commissions were granted to women medical officers, one thing was still needed—a medical consultant who could be responsible for recommendations concerning the health of women personnel of the Army. Four days after the commissioning bill was passed, Dr. Margaret D. Craighill became the first woman to achieve Major in the AMC, and she was appointed Consultant to The Surgeon's General's Office (SGO). With a huge sigh of relief, Director Oveta Hobby said, "This is our first ray of hope. Now we have real cooperation from The Surgeon General. Major Craighill has been given the whole problem."[32]

One of six daughters, Margaret Craighill was born in Southport, North Carolina 16 October, 1898, and she grew up in Mobile, Alabama, where she was privately educated. but she attended a public high school in Portland, Maine. She received both her undergraduate and graduate degrees (1920, 1921) from the University of Wisconsin, enrolled in medical school at Johns Hopkins, but "dropped out of school for year while working in the Chemical Warfare Service at Edgewood Arsenal" in Maryland, where she studied the toxicology of war gases in animals. In 1922 she married Dr. James Leonard Vickers, but the marriage was unsatisfactory and the couple subsequently divorced. Years later she married Rear Admiral Alexander S. Wotherspoon who had a distinguished career and had seen service in both world wars.[33]

Craighill received a medical degree from Johns Hopkins University in 1924, and then interned the following year in gynecology and surgery at the hospital associated with the university. In 1925-26, she became assistant in pathology at the Yale Medical School, but then returned to Hopkins Hospital for the next eighteen months as assistant resident in Gynecology. She decided to spend the next six months training in radium therapy with Dr. Howard A. Kelly, and then entered private practice from 1928-40 in gynecology and obstetrics in Greenwich, Connecticut. She was still engaged in her own practice when she was invited to be Dean of Woman's Medical College of Pennsylvania in 1940. She accepted this on a part-time basis the first year while continuing in practice in Greenwich, but it seemed clear to her that she could not continue to devote her time to two major interests at once. In April of 1941 she retired from her practice and began the job of "reorganizing the medical school, hospital and school of nursing of the Woman's Medical College of Pennsylvania."

Margaret Craighill came from a military family as her father and grandfather, Colonel William E. Craighill and General William P. Craighill, respectively, were West Point graduates. Her father, who entered the Corps of Engineers, saw service during the Spanish-American War and in the Philippines, and in China during the Boxer Rebellion. Her grandfather became Chief of Engineers, U.S.A, and president of the American Society of Civil Engineers. With the advent of the Second World War, she, too, wanted to volunteer for the Army. She asked for a leave from the WMCP, becoming the first woman physician to be commissioned directly in the Army with the rank of major, and she was assigned 28 May 1943 to the Division of Preventive Medicine in The Surgeon General's Office (SGO) in an advisory capacity in relation to medical problems of women personnel of the Army.[34] While she was Dean at the WMCP, Craighill must have inspired many female students there with her patriotism and zeal to serve during wartime as records indicate that the college had thirteen medical graduates in both the Army and Navy, more than any other institution.[35]

As soon as she was commissioned, Craighill was classified in obstetrics/gynecology and her responsibilities began to expand since policies of all kinds had to be made in relation to medical conditions of the WAAC/WAC. In June of 1943, she indicated that there were an insufficient number of potential women medical officers adequate to cover WAAC medical needs both in the country and abroad. She

recommended that there should be a woman medical officer assigned
to the WAAC service in at least every major field of operation and in
such other areas in which there was a concentration of approximately
500 WAAC personnel. The next month she was appointed Liaison
Officer between The SGO and the WAAC for the purpose of maintaining more intimate contact with Headquarters and expediting the
action on routine medical matters for which The Surgeon General
was responsible. In January of 1944, however, a Women's Medical
Unit was established in the SGO and she was placed in charge to
develop policies and coordinate all activities within the SGO relating to the medical care and welfare of women in or connected with
the Army.[36]

After Craighill volunteered for duty, her military occupational specialty was listed as obstetrician and gynecologist. While Craighill's
duties were not only numerous but varied, it was soon evident that
her training in gynecology was going to be a much needed requirement for the job. While recruiting had begun in 1942 and proceeded
at a rapid pace, efforts were doubled in 1943 because the recruiting prospects had dropped earlier in the year. WAAC Headquarters
directed the Army Recruiting Service to make certain that recruits
were thoroughly screened by mental and physical tests. And as there
were concerns about their morals and background, inquiries were
to be made to their references, police courts, and schools. Women
were also required to prove any occupational claims and they were
to be interviewed finally by a WAAC officer who had the power of
administrative rejection.[37]

As WAAC recruiting efforts plummeted, the Adjutant General
took a step which was to remain a controversial issue—he lowered
acceptance standards and simplified recruiting procedure in order to
meet increased quotas. One outcome was that a preliminary health
certificate from a civilian doctor was no longer required, since this
put the applicant to some expense and was supposedly duplicated
by the Army examination. As soon as the requirement for a civil-

ian doctor's examination was dropped, physical and psychiatric standards fell at an alarming rate. Returns from the field indicated that one of the main problems was "not willful negligence", but either the absence of an adequate authorized induction examination for women or medical examiners' ignorance of proper standards of such an examination.[38] A worse problem was the fact that the public had the impression that the Army was scraping the bottom of the barrel for WAACs since they were reduced to recruiting its own previous rejects and the rejects of the other services. One incident was cited in which the parents of one recruit had their daughter removed from an insane asylum to enlist her and when the officer called in the family to present them with a discharge, the parents cried and the girl "leaped over and bit her mother."[39]

Director Oveta Hobby believed that quality was being sacrificed for quantity and that serious damage was being done to "the positive image that highly skilled women had created within the Army." She asked that recruiting be transferred to her control so that she could restore the quality standards.[40] Furthermore, she urged The SGO to set up a specialist team to develop and publish detailed guides for the medical examinations required for women and their later medical care. Sometime later The Surgeon General stated that "there are problems of health peculiar to women", and it was at this point that he appointed Maj. Margaret D. Craighill as the person responsible for recommendations concerning the health of 60,000 WAACS and 30,000 nurses, and for visits to them at stations both in the United States and overseas.[41]

As one of her first official acts, Craighill set about publishing standards for proper gynecological and psychiatric screening of applicants. At the same time, conversion from an auxiliary corps (WAAC) to full military status as the Women's Army Corp was achieved late in the summer of 1943 and WAAC "relative ranks" were converted to Army ranks. This conversion eliminated one of the major impediments to recruiting and morale. It also resolved much of the internal confusion as the WAC was integrated into the normal Army command channels. Coming as it did in the middle of the slander campaign against women in the Army, "the conversion gave them the official message that they were needed and wanted by the Army. Nevertheless, "there was a constant, all-pervasive awareness that women had invaded a male preserve."[42]

Even as Hobby struggled to restore quality standards and then later retain them, Craighill was forging ahead with her own agenda in regard to recommendations for the proper examination for women in the examining stations and she sent out memoranda to that effect as well as directives fixing the new standards. This was followed up with visits to Service Command Headquarters and to various stations which conducted such examinations; and she made visits to WAVE and Women's Marine Reserve Training Schools to compare the programs of the three services. She directed that there be a reduction of the number of authorized stations for WAC enlistment examination in order to standardize procedures and to make qualified medical officers available, where needed. Coinciding with this she consulted with psychologists in WAC Headquarters and with representative of the Neuropsychiatry Division to set up and maintain a screening program for WAC applicants related to social, educational, and psychiatric backgrounds.[43]

Craighill also began an investigation of special problems related to women such as pregnancy, venereal diseases, gynecological conditions, foot problems, and psychiatric issues. Prior to Hobby's appointment, the early WAAC Regulations contained a provision that only married women would get an honorable discharge for pregnancy, with others receiving a summary discharge. This was unacceptable to Hobby and in December 1942 she secured a change in the regulation to permit an honorable discharge by reason of "unsuitability for the service." Thus, the new WAC and Army Regulations required an honorable discharge for all pregnant women. Since delays in discharge overseas, however, were inevitable Director Hobby finally is-

sued a directive stating that if discharge had been delayed until pregnancy was so advanced that the mother's or unborn child's life would
be endangered by travel, the mother might be retained in service
overseas until the infant was both and both returned to the States.[44]

While the incidence of unmarried pregnancy was not regarded
as great enough to merit any special studies, as the incidence rate
in the WAAC was about one fifth that among women in civilian
life, a particular problem for medical officers was that of quick and
accurate certification of pregnancy in order to expedite discharge.
Craighill started to gather monthly statistics on discharges for such
cause in the Continental United States as well as for those women
going overseas; and on her field visits, she and her staff made inci-
dental notes of the factors that seemed to lead unmarried women in
to "misconduct" and resulting pregnancy. They found several factors
which appeared to have some relationship: Women a long distance
from home were more susceptible, detachments with the least recre-
ation facilities had the most pregnancies, most pregnancies occurred
where women were subject to the most restrictions, bed check, etc.,
and length of service or assignment to one station could lead to resulting fatigue and boredom. On the other hand, detachments with
a good company commander had low pregnancy rates, and oddly
enough, none of the cases occurred in women who were accustomed
to drinking.[45]

Venereal disease (VD) during WWI had traditionally been a cause
of rejection for potential recruits, although the Medical Department
later in 1917 informed medical officers that men with VD could be
accepted as long as they were not incapacitated or actively infectious.
Once accepted during the war, however, they were excluded from the
peacetime Army.[46] During the early administration of the venereal
disease control program in WWII, the treatment of venereal disease
was a responsibility of the Medical Consultants Division. Because
of the need for centralizing the responsibility for all phases of venereal disease control, however, Brig. Gen. Charles C. Hillman, Chief,

Professional Services, recommended to The Surgeon General on 3 November 1942 that the treatment phase of venereal disease control be transferred to the Venereal Disease Control Branch of the Preventive Medicine Division. This change was intended to bring about a desirable unification of the venereal disease control program.[47] In the early mobilization phase, individuals known to have venereal disease were rejected for military service primarily because the available facilities and personnel were inadequate to cope with such resulting problems. Early in 1942, the Army training program was now sufficiently advanced and the administrative and professional procedures well enough organized so that diagnostic and treatment facilities necessary for the induction of men currently infected with VD (as well as those men previously deferred for VD) could be established. As soon as The SGO initiated and developed the necessary plans, two orders were immediately sent to all service commands. On 7 December 1942, the induction of registrants with uncomplicated venereal disease was authorized; and on 10 December 1942, the types of venereal disease with which men could be inducted were outlined and regulations were provided for the rate of induction of these individuals so that existing facilities for their management would not be overtaxed.[48]

At the same time, the National Research Council made a strong recommendation regarding VD control among female components of the Army, and approval was granted in early May 1943 for the establishment of a WAAC Liaison Section in the Venereal Disease Control Branch. On 28 May 1943, Maj. (later Lt. Col.) Margaret D. Craighill, was assigned to the branch as chief of the WAAC Liaison Section. Since her responsibilities with respect to medical problems of the WAAC soon came to extend beyond the field of venereal disease (which never constituted a serious problem among this group), she was transferred on 15 July 1943 to the Operations Service, Office of the Surgeon General, and the WAAC Liaison Section was discontinued.[49]

During WWII, the WAAC rate of venereal disease was almost zero. In fact, many WAAC units never had a single case, and in training centers the occasional case was due to faulty enlistment examinations.[50] Still vicious rumors persisted, with one rumor among military personnel in New England at the Fort Devens area being that the WAAC venereal disease rate was skyrocketing. After 6,000 women were examined, only eleven cases were discovered, eight of them having existed before enlistment and having gone undetected by entrance examinations—a rate less than any civilian community.[51] Nevertheless, as was the case with pregnancies, Craighill also gathered data on venereal diseases. In addition, diagnostic facilities were provided, standards of diagnosis and treatment were established, and an educational program with conferences, pamphlets, and moving pictures was developed.[52] Even with her inspection trips overseas, and in the North African and Mediterranean Theaters, Craighill pronounced that the cases among WACs were "very infrequent"— less than one per month, with only fourteen cases being reported by the end of 1944. When it came to the men in the same areas, however, the rates were frequently "alarming: and the disease endemic.[53]

As another one of her immediate actions, Craighill made a tour of Army induction stations to seek the cause of medical examiners' errors, which had seriously affected the early recruiting program. She discovered that most stations were not giving any pelvic or gynecological examination at all nor were they giving a psychiatric examination. Her immediate remedy was to secure a directive that gynecological and psychiatric examinations would be given every WAC applicant and she was instrumental in the appointment of a board of Army doctor to set standards of acceptability which were quickly circulated.[54] One complicating factor for women was the higher WAC rate of morbidity (the frequency of reporting to sick call). The rate of admission to the hospital was about the same for women and men but the length of stay was considerably less for the women. Craighill maintained that the smaller loss of time by hospitalization for women could not be attributed to especially efficient gynecological care as such was almost nonexistent in Army hospitals as they were not set up with a view to caring for females.[55]

In late 1943 The SGO made a survey of the locations of Army doctors who had been civilian specialists in gynecology, but it was not until after the victory over Japan that an organized effort was made to place specialists in hospitals servicing large numbers of women.[56] Thus, in November 1943 considerably less than half the 650 male Army doctors classified as gynecologists and obstetricians were employed in their specialty; and of those who were, they attended female members of the Medical Department and the dependents of Army personnel. The use of a larger percentage in this specialty had to await the entrance of large members of WACs.[57] There were few such specialists among the female doctors as only three other women medical officers besides Dr. Craighill were classified as an obstetrician and gynecologist.

The last two crucial areas than demanded Craighill's attention were foot problems among the WAC and their psychiatric needs. Fortunately she had the help of Capt. Marion Loizeauz (later Major), who had uncovered that the problems with service shoes were related to being too stiff, too wide, or lacking enough arch support. In the end, what really helped was that in 1945 the Army ceased to use the men's foot-measuring outfit, and replaced it with a new women's foot-measuring outfit so that a better fit was assured, and this further eliminated the problem of ordering shoes in the wrong sizes. By the 1960s, however, with the emphasis on appearance for all women in the Armed Forces, women wore their low quarter-lace oxfords only for marching or when necessary on the job. In all other instances, pumps were generally mandatory because they were considered more feminine.[58] As soon as she was appointed, Craighill found that no action had been taken in regard to women's psychiatric disorders. As she began to visit visiting training centers, she noted that they were filled with "inadequate persons" who presented major problems with "disposition".[59] As one of her many important accomplishments while consultant, she launched an historical survey of the psychiatric problems incident upon the service of women volunteers in nonprofessional occupations who were recruited for the Army in WWII. This survey covered a three-and-one half year period beginning in June 1942. In this work, she focused particularly upon the administrative policies and professional medical problems of these females as well as the emotional impact of a new and unusual environment of war upon women military personnel.[60]

Motivations for military service were important in predicting success in the Corps and they were almost as divergent as the women themselves. While many women enlisted in the WAC for altruistic reasons such as patriotism or a need to substitute for a husband or male family member who might be dead or disabled, others were immature women who had volunteered in the hope of meeting men or for glamour and excitement. In the latter group, the women's enthusiasm often could not stand up to the reality of military life with all its monotony. There were also the escapists who were trying to get away from either internal conflicts or external problems in their environment and those who had been maladjusted and were constantly looking for greener pastures that they could never find. Craighill concluded that many of the so-called neurotics were in the escapist group, and it was mostly women from this group who were responsible for numerous company problems and who were given disability discharges. WAC volunteers were also more prone, than male draftees, to conceal symptoms of emotional disorder and past history of mental disease.[61]

Two factors quickly surfaced that affected psychiatric suitability for the WACs, age and misassignment. WACs were accepted who were between the ages of twenty and fifty, but neuropsychiatric rejection rates were nearly twice as high in the over 40 age group when compared to the twenty to twenty-four age group. Discharges within the first six months of service showed a similar trend. Because of this, the SGO recommended an upper age limit of thirty-eight but this did not occur until after VE day. Craighill stated, "It was the opinion of many medical officers that, with few exceptions, women over 35 should not be sent overseas."[62]

A major cause of psychiatric breakdowns among the enlisted WAC proved to be due to misassignment. Craighill found that the women were willing to put up with almost anything as long as their jobs were satisfying. She said, "If their work was in accordance with their training and if there was enough to keep them busy, sick call was at a minimum."[63] An extensive study on fatigue among 5,000 WACs further demonstrated that the incidence of fatigue was influenced more by psychological factors than physical ones. Interest in the job seemed to outweigh any other factor.

Until after the change to WAC in 1943, recruiting centers did not emphasize the importance of physical standards, and few attempted psychiatric evaluations. Oftentimes psychiatric examinations were not encouraged in many areas until experience later demonstrated the need for better recruiting procedures. With pressure from the SGO, however, the quality of examinations improved which was related partly to the appointment of Col., later Brig. Gen. William C. Menninger to head The Surgeon General's Neuropsychiatric division in the spring of 1944. By the end of 1994 Menninger had arranged that explicit directions be sent to medical examiners and he also set up a pioneer mental hygiene unit at Fort Des Moines under the direction of Maj. Albert Preston, Jr., a Menninger-trained psychiatrist.[64]

Army psychiatrists agreed that the Corps as a whole faced one common problem—its volunteer nature which was responsible for many difficulties that affected both the selection of women recruits and the proper utilization of them as individuals.[65] Women, for instance, experienced unusual hardships from a loss of individuality, unaccustomed group living, regimentation, and the discipline associated with Army rules and regulations. A particular hardship was the lack of privacy in the Army. Craighill stated that, "The crowded dormitory and the community shower room and latrine were really traumatic for many Overseas this situation was a definite factor in increasing tension and precipitating psychoneuroses, especially after a year or more under such conditions."[66] Overall, psychiatric conditions in the WAC were of more than usual importance, because they occurred in a conspicuous minority group although the number involved was small, probably about one-tenth of the Corps.[67] Craighill concluded that with proper leadership, satisfaction in job assignments, and a feeling of being needed, they performed "with skill and enthusiasm." The use of women as staff directors, however, continued to be needed as it was a help in bringing better understanding to higher commands concerning the special problems of the Corps.[68]

Craighill was promoted to Lt. Colonel 23 August 1945, and she was separated from service April 1946. After the war ended, she became a consultant on women veterans' medical care, the first position of its kind within the Veterans Administration on 2 January 1946.[69] In this new position, she surveyed Veterans Hospitals and Homes and other government hospitals where women veterans were receiving care and treatment. General Omar N. Bradley noted that she had made an outstanding contribution to the problem of caring for disabled veterans. "From the standpoint of morale," he noted, "Colonel Craighill is to be commended for the inspiration and encouragement she gave to medical and other professional employees at the stations she visited, many of whom have served throughout the entire period of the war under difficult and trying conditions."[70] She was awarded the Distinguished Service Medal for her wartime efforts.

During her Army service, Craighill developed a keen interest in psychiatry. Early on she had admitted: "The psychiatrists have been, perhaps, the most fortunate in receiving assignments suited to their training" in the Army Medical Corps.[71] Of course, she was speaking of the women as this was not true for the males. As a matter of fact, spokesmen for the Army neuropsychiatrists late in 1942 asserted that despite their best efforts to keep these men in jobs devoted to their specialty, the younger graduates were often assigned as general practitioners to ground force units or organizations alerted for oversea movement. The problem was not only related to fact that The SGO lacked authority for some time, but that within the service commands themselves the assignment system seemed to have been hampered by lack of personnel with training adequate to perform the task most efficiently.[72] Nevertheless, one positive outcome of WWII for the medical profession was that neuropsychiatry emerged as a physician specialty and because of the success in the treatment of psychiatric patients by the military's psychiatric services during the war, Congress was persuaded to pass the National Mental Health Act 3 July 1946 which called for the establishment of a National Institute of Mental Health.

With her Army experiences behind her, Craighill had the foresight, the desire, and the courage to shift gears, and in September of 1946, she reentered into training at the Menninger School of Psychiatry, Topeka, Kansas, as part of its first class. She served as Chief of the Psychosomatic Section at the Winter VA Hospital from 1948-51 and she was on the staff of the Menninger Clinic before 1951 ended. But Craighill had been greatly influenced by her encounters with Menninger as well as her exposure to military psychiatry when she served as Consultant, and she was still not fully satisfied with her training. In fact, "one of the unforeseen results of the psychoanalytic teaching with its emphasis upon psychotherapy was that there an unprecedented demand for psychoanalytic training by the young medical officers upon their discharge from the Army."[73] Like so many of the male psychiatrists in postwar years, she too decided to pursue further studies in psychiatry; and she graduated next from the New York Institute of Psychoanalysis in 1952. After this she entered private practice in medicine and psychoanalysis from 1951 through July 1960 in New Haven, Connecticut. She also served at the Connecticut College for Women in New London as its chief psychiatrist.[74] Craighill died in her home in Connecticut 20 July 1977 at the age of seventy-eight, just a little over a year after the death of her husband, Rear Admiral Wotherspoon.[75]

~ NOTES ~

1. For SGO modifications, see Gillett, *The Army Medical Department* 1917-1941, 535-37. Lovejoy quote and Jensen quote in *Mobilizing Minerva*, 86; historian Walsh quote, *Doctors Wanted, No Women Need Apply*, 229.

2. *Personnel in World War II*, 1963, 154; Statistics in "Women Contract Surgeons in World War II", Histories, Box 29, MDC Coll. Eleanor Hayden's last name was misspelled as D'Orbison in Craighill's records—it is corrected here.

3. Quote in "Women Contract Surgeons in World War II," Box 29, Histories, MDC Coll. See "Commissions for Women Physicians," *Women in Medicine*, July 1943, 15.

4. Morgans in "Section on War Service", *MWJ* August 1943. There was no other information available about this woman.

5. Spitz biography provided by her husband, Arthur C. Allen, MD., "Introduction to 'Melanomas of Childhood' by Spitz", Classics in Oncology, Vol. 4, No. 1, January/February 1991, 37.

6. Finger injury: Philip E. Shapiro, MD., "Who Was Sophie Spitz? The Woman Behind the Eponym, *The American Journal of Dermatopathology*, October 1992, Vol. 14, No. 5, 442.

7. Shapiro, 444.

8. Lectures: See, Col. J. E. Ash, MD., "In Memoriam: Sophie Spitz; An Appreciation 1910-1956", *American Journal of Clinical Pathology*, 1958 Dec. 30(6), 553.

9. This text was revised subsequently by Drs. Binford and Connor at the Armed Forces Institute of Pathology and published in 1976 at the same Institute.

10. Ribbon: Allen, 38.

11. Ash quote, Allen, 38. She also encouraged several women to attend medical school and assisted them financially by either providing work for them or contributing from her own pocket.

12. Term "Spitz nevus", Shapiro, 445. Her younger twin brothers, followed in her footsteps by becoming physicians, both specializing in internal medicine.

13. Ecklund family history in "Memoirs of Effie Lerner: A Saga of Swedish Immigrants", draft of a manuscript, unnumbered pages, written by Effie Ecklund but never unpublished; on line, Family Tree of Raymond G. Ziemer, ancestry.com. Hereafter referred to as Ecklund memoir.

14. First husband's name was Kilbrid "who beat her and caused her to lose her baby," Ecklund Memoir. Because she had a hysterectomy when she was married to Dr. Lerner sometime later, she never had any children.

15. Training noted in Section on War Service", *MWJ*, October 1943.

16. Quote in Ecklund Memoir as are all other quotes hereafter.

17. While in service, Dr. Lerner served in active duty in North Africa and Italy through 1945. He was chairman of the Department of Radiology at West Suburban Hospital in Chicago (1971 until he retired in 1978) where he worked thirty years. He also held an academic position of assistant professor of Radiology at Rush Medical School, Chicago. He died in 1986. See Radiology, Vol. 163, No. 1, 1987, 287.

18. Ecklund Memoir.

19. See Ecklund Social Security Death Index.

20. See Ednah Hatt Social Security Death Index; she is listed in the *Boston Medical & Surgical Journal*, vol. 186, January-June 1922, 19. See Tribute to R. Nelson Hatt (1889-1949) "In Memoriam, Doctors of Hawaii" in *Hawaii Medical Journal* 1969, Nov-Dec; 29(2):144. Information on Ednah was provided by Tufts Archives and digit Coll.

21. Moore's story in "Letters to the Editor", MWJ April 1943. Other information provided from biographical notes, WIMSA. See Holm, *Woman in the Military* for more on recruitment.

22. Cover's name and station appear on the list of "Contract Surgeons", Histories, Box 29, MDC Coll. The date her contract was annulled was not in the record. Also see Ellen S. Moore, "The American Medical Women's Association and the Role of the Woman Physician, 1915-1990", *JAMWA*, September/October 1990, Vol. 45, No. 5, 167; Moore, "A Certain Restless ambition": Women Physicians and World War I, *American Quarterly*, Vol. 41, No.4, Dec., 1989, 636-660. She is also mentioned in Esther Pohl Lovejoy's, *Certain Samaritans*, 46.

23. A copy of Cover's passport can be found in "Emergency Passport Applications, Argentina thru Venezuela, 1906-1925", ARC Identifier 1244183/MLR Number A1 544; Box #4555; Vol. #171, NARA, Washington, DC.

24. Cover's work: *Texas State Journal of Medicine*, Vol. 9, May 1913-April 1914, 113.

25. See Cover "Obituary" in *San Antonio Express*, 29 October 1965. Death is also noted in "The Alcalde", the *University of Texas Alumni Magazine*, April 1966, 39.

26. Surgeon General quote: See *Personnel in World War II*, 153.

27. Helpful information on the WMCP women doctors provided by Alex Miller, archivist, DUCM Legacy Center. Other information on minority women provided by Women in the Military Service of America (WIMSA). For information on African-American women who served in the WAC during WWII, see Brenda L. Moore, *To Serve My Country, To Serve My Race* (New York: New York University Press, 1996). For an extensive bibliography, see: "We Served America, Too! Blacks in the Women's Army Corps During world War II"; A Selected Bibliography; compiled by Dr. Janet Sims-Wood, Assistant Chief Librarian, Moorland-Spingarn Research Center, Howard University, Washington, D.C.

28. Craighill to Dr. Reginald Fitz, Chairman, Massachusetts State Committee, 8 September 1943, White letter, Official Correspondence, Box 5, MDC Coll. Born in Boston, White attended Radcliffe College and graduated third in her class from Tufts University Medical School in 1923. Her research greatly increased the survival rate of babies born to diabetic women. Dr. White taught at Harvard Medical School and was an assistant professor of medicine at Tufts. She received numerous honors and was the first woman to receive the Banting Medal, the American Diabetes Association's highest scientific award.

29. Craighill to Dr. Bella S. Van Bark, Brooklyn State Hospital, 29 October 1943, Letter, Box 5, MDC Coll. A Trustee of the American Institute for Psychoanalysis and a member of its Faculty Council, she received her medical degree from the Woman's Medical College. She died on Dec 19, 1992, from a brain tumor.

30. Refusal of McNeal's commission noted in "Medicine: Equality for Women Doctors", *Time Magazine*, 26 April 1943. Also see More, *Restoring the Balance*, 184. See short biography by Wright, A. J., "Dr. Alice McNeal: Alabama's First Female Anesthesiologist," paper, Southern Association for the History of Medicine and Science, 2009. The author would also like to give thanks to Wright for providing notes and correspondence in regard to McNeal.

31. "Dr. Nita M. Arnold Accepts Position of Psychiatrist with the WAAC Training Center," MWJ, April 1942, 105; mentioned also in *JAMA*, 27 February 1943; 121 (9):682. She had been a citizen for eight years and her husband was in the Army Air Corps. Arnold's case is outlined in two letters: "Dr. Nita Arnold to Craighill," letter Dated 17 April 1944; "Major Craighill to Arnold," Dated 19 April 1944," both letters in Official Correspondence, Box 5, MDC Collection.

32. Hobby quote in Treadwell, 178.

33. "Army to Assign Woman Doctor: Major M.D. Craighill to Be Stationed in Preventive Medicine Division," from brief biography and unidentified newspaper clipping, Official Papers, Box 2, MDC Coll. Also see *Who's Who of American*

Women, 5*th* ed.; Marquis Who's Who (1968). Rear Adm. Wotherspoon obituary in *Newport Mercury*, Newport, RI, 19 March 1976.

34. See Craighill's Military Record and Report of Separation Certificate of Service, Personal papers, Box 1, MDC Coll. Also see "First Woman Commissioned Officer in the Medical Corps, U.S. Army," *MWJ* June 1943. Her quotes are from her own "Personal Biography" in the Army Surgeon General Biographical Files, RG 112, 390/18/33/6-390/18/34/7, National Archives, College Park, MD.

35. Eight WMCP Army Medical officers: Drs. Delores Amar, Angie Connor, Martha E. Howe, Adele Kempker, Jane Marshall Leibfried, Anna Patton, and Margaret Elva Shirlock; 7 in the Navy: Drs. Harriet Josephine Davis, Sylvia Ruby, Gioconda Rita Saraniero, Louise Wetherill Slack, Elizabeth Alice Stone, Bernice Gertrude Rosenthal, and Pauline Kathryn Wenner. Johns Hopkins produced the next largest group of women doctors with five in the Army (including Craighill) and three in the Navy Five from Johns Hopkins: Drs. Margaret Craighill, Sarah Bowditch, Elizabeth Bryan, Marjorie Hayes, and Isabel Harrison: 3 in the Navy: Drs. Edith Michael Buyer, Agnes Conrad, and Orra Almira Phelps.

36. Memorandum for Chief, Personnel Service, Use of Women Medical Officers in Foreign Fields, 24 June 1943, Personal Papers, Box 2; and Memorandum to the Director, WAAC, 29 July 1943, Personal Papers, Box 2, MDC Col. Also see file 333 in the 1943-44 and 1945 segments of the General Correspondence of the SGO, 112.18, NARA, Washington, D.C.

37. See Treadwell, 169; 177.

38. Lower standards, Treadwell 173; willful negligence, Treadwell, 177.

39. "Bit", Treadwell 177.

40. WAC image, Holm 49.

41. "Peculiar to women", Treadwell, 178. Craighill's Army papers noted that at the time of enlistment she was five feet eight inches tall, weighed 140 pounds, and had grey hair and blue eyes.

42. Positive aspects of conversion, Holm 54; "Male preserve", 50.

43. Memorandum for Chief, Operations Service Regarding Annual Report for Fiscal Year 1944, from Craighill 20 June 1944, Personal Papers, Box 3, MDC Col.

44. Pregnancy in Treadwell, 264, 501. Holm points out that during this period there was never any question that pregnant women, married or not should be automatically discharged. At that time, the idea of having pregnant women in the military in uniform was abhorrent to many men and women alike. Moreover, without child

care facilities, it would be impossible to care for an infant and remain in the service. See Women in the Military, 125.

45. Treadwell, incidence, 193; factors, 621.

46. Gillett, The Army Medical Department 1917-1941, policy, 135; peacetime, 499.

47. Preventive Medicine in World War II, Vol. V, 146.

48. Preventive Medicine, 148.

49. Preventive Medicine, 151.

50. Zero rate: Treadwell, 193.

51. VD rumors, Treadwell, 207. For more on rumors in general see, Office of the Chief of Staff, 165.9 which contains the WAC Director's formerly security classified general correspondence, 1942-46 and 1949-50. Within that file is file 330.14 documenting Craighill's investigation of such alleged instances among WAAC and WAC personnel, NARA, Washington, D.C.

52. Memorandum for Chief, Operations Service Regarding Annual Report for Fiscal Year 1944, from Craighill 20 June 1944, Personal Papers, Box 3, MDC Col. Also see Records of the SGO, 112.18, file 024.10-11 which contains reports and correspondence of Craighill for the Women's Health and Welfare Unit, which replaced the Women's Medical Unit in August 1944, NARA, Washington, D.C.

53. Male rate: Treadwell, 372.

54. Standards: Treadwell, 603-604.

55. WAC morbidity rate, Treadwell, 610-611.

56. Survey of Army doctors, Treadwell, 612.

57. Personnel in WWII, 296.

58. Pumps, Holm, 182. She notes that during peacetime in the early sixties there was such an emphasis on appearance that "all training programs were heavily sprinkled with courses to enhance feminine appearance and bearing. Service women were taught how to apply makeup correctly and appropriately."

59. Inadequate persons, Treadwell, 622.

60. Craighill, Margaret D., "The Women's Army Corps," Chapter XV in Leonard D. Heaton and Robert Anderson, eds, *Neuropsychiatry in World War II*, Volume I: Zone of Interior, Washington, DC: Medical Department United States Army, Office of the Surgeon General, 1966, p. 421. Hereafter referred to as WAC chapter.

61. Craighill points out that for a time the supply of men was considered to be inexhaustible and thus any doubtful male inductee could be readily rejected. This policy was reversed with women volunteers in order to build up a desired strength of the WAC.

62. Craighill, M.D.: "Psychiatric Aspects of Women Serving in the Army: The Motivation of Women Volunteers", *Am. J. Psychiat,* October 1947, 227.

63. "Psychiatric Aspects of Women Serving in the Army", 228.

64. Major Preston: Treadwell, 622.

65. Treadwell, 623. There were also gains related to being in the WAC such as emotional maturity, etc.

66. Privacy issues, Craighill, "Psychiatric Aspects of Women Serving in the Army," 229.

67. Craighill, WAC chapter, 473.

68. Craighill, WAC chapter, 474.

69. "Woman Is Named Veterans' Consultant," *Oakland Tribune,* 2 January 1946.

70. General Omar N. Bradley to the Surgeon General, War Department, Washington, DC, 28 December 1945, letter, Personal Papers, Box 2, MDC Coll.

71. "Women Medical Officers, AUS," Histories, Box 29, MDC Coll.

72. *Personnel in WWII,* 291.

73. Psychoanalytic quote, *Neuropsychiatry in World War II,* Vol. I, Zone of Interior (Washington, D.C.: Office of The Surgeon General, Department of the Army, 1966), 85. Two factors that might account for this trend were the leadership of Brig. Gen. William C. Menninger as Chief Neuropsychiatric Consultant in The SGO and the daily experience of psychiatrists "who saw the value of psychodynamics in understanding the characteristic defenses and physical symptoms of people under pressure."

74. From clippings and biographical material provided by Special Coll., DUCM.

75. "Dr. Margaret D. Craighill, at 78, Former Dean of Medical College", *New York Times,* 26 July 1977. Also see Connecticut Death Index for 1949-2001.

Table 1.
Sixteen Contract Surgeons Listed
in Craighill's Records

Name:	Station:	Signed On:	
Arnold, Nita	Ft. Des Moines, Iowa	12-25-42	
Ecklund, Effie	"	3-23-43	
Fatheree, I. E.	"	11-09-42	
Garber (Tate), A. Elizabeth*	"	7-15-42	Yes
Gutman, Eleanor*	"	9-10-42	Yes
Hayden, Eleanor*	"	12-04-42	Yes
Janeway, Margaret*	"	9-10-42	Yes
Loving, M.	"	1-07-43	
Moore, Mary	"	7-16-42	
Morgans, Dolly	"	1-25-43	
Yu, Poe-Eng*	"	11-04-42	Yes
Cover, Ellen	San Antonio Ord. Dep., Camp Stanley, TX	4-01-42	
Hatt, Ednah	Bradley Field, Conn.	4-30-43	
Lichtenstein, J.V.	WAAC Disp., NY City	3-15-43	
Peck, Eleanor K.**	Overseas	12-42	Yes
Spitz, Sophia	Army Medical Museum	4-21-43	

"Yes" indicates the woman doctor went on to be commissioned in the Army Medical Corps

**Peck was not one of the original contract surgeons who volunteered in the States.*

CHAPTER THREE:
Enter the Women Neuropsychiatrists/ Psychiatrists

Gender issues impacted on medical women's choices as they strove to advance in certain fields, psychiatry being one of them.[1] While they might be attracted to a particular specialty for personal reasons, it was also true that it was easier to specialize in a field where there was less difficulty coping with "male-female" competition such as in pediatrics vs. surgery, for instance. By the time of WWII, many female doctors continued to choose fields in keeping with their special talents as women—an expectation that still carried over to the twentieth century because of Victorian influences. One historian believed that it was "through a combination of choice and prejudice against them" that women were scarcely represented in certain specialties like ophthalmology and plastic surgery.[2]

There is little dispute that social expectation and prejudices stood in the way of most women hoping to attend medical school up into the 1960s. Yet being accepted into medical school was only the first of many hurdles for women desiring to become doctors. After graduation from medical school, they faced new challenges with internships and residencies. By the end of the nineteenth century many women doctors increasingly accepted specialization as a mark of expertise, thus aligning them with their male colleagues. As the years passed, however, fewer choices were available to women doctors because most of the national specialty societies denied admission to women until a long time after the creation of the specialty boards in the 1930s. Moreover, when the system for residency training for specialists was formalized during the 1920s and 1930s, the competition was exceptionally keen as there were fewer residencies than internships available. By 1940, the number of residencies had doubled, but "only 6.5 percent of hospitals with residency programs enrolled women residents, and 97.3 percent of board-certified specialists were men."[3]

Trends regarding women's specialty choices stabilized by the 1960s and have remained fairly constant. In her book, *Women in Medicine*, Lopate indicated that in a survey taken in 1966 summarizing the percentage of women and men receiving certification by specialty boards, the top seven choices among the women were pediatrics, psychiatry and neurology, internal medicine, anesthesiology, pathology, obstetrics and gynecology, and radiology.[4] As late as 2000, the American Medical Association (AMA) indicated that although the number of women physicians had increased at an astonishing high rate, six of the top seven choices remained constant, only in different proportions. The survey further noted: "Though female physicians continue to make significant gains, they are still vastly under-represented in all surgical specialties as well as other specialties such as gastroenterology, cardiovascular diseases, and otolaryngology."[5]

In a commencement speech Dr. Margaret Craighill gave to the Woman's Medical College of Pennsylvania in 1944, she also talked about specialties and women doctors. "The position of women doctors in the Medical Corps of the Army is not good... practically all of these are serving With the WAC." She explained that the difficulty with assignments was due to a number of factors. "Many of the women have no specialty, and it is hard to fit them in. They are too old, or their ranks too high to use them in ordinary ward duties, and they have not the specialty training for chiefs of service, except in a few cases." In conclusion, she warned her audience: "If you have an established practice and are serving a community, I advise you not to leave it."[6]

While it is unlikely that any male physicians ever heard Craighill's speech, they were inclined to agree with her views about established medical practices. On the whole, male neuropsychiatrists were not willing to leave their specialty in civilian practice despite the Government's efforts to recruit them which included sending out personal letters through the newly established Neuropsychiatry (NP) Branch of the Army. As a matter of fact, no psychiatrists were obtained by this effort; and of those who were willing to consider a military career during WWII, many preferred the Navy, Army Air Forces, or other Government agencies like the U.S. Public Health Service or even the U.S. Coast Guard.

At the start of war there were fewer than twenty Regular Army medical officers with some training and experience in psychiatry, and it was not until August 1942, seven months after Pearl Harbor, that a psychiatrist was assigned to serve as the chief consultant in neuropsychiatry to The Surgeon General's office (SGO) to plan for the various aspects of such a wartime program. Thus, the proper distribution and utilization of neuropsychiatrists was one of the first problems facing the newly formed NP Branch in 1942. By July 1944, however, a total of 1,490 medical officers were listed as psychiatrists, although the majority of these men were merely psychiatrists "by command." Of this group, only 136 were certified in psychiatry, 121 in neurology and psychiatry, and 14 in neurology.[7]

At peck strength, the medical corps consisted of 48,837 doctors, including the women who numbered 76, by November of 1944.[8] When Army women in WWII are considered who were in specialty areas, the neuropsychiatrists were in the most demand, and they constituted the largest specialty group.[9] (See Table 2) Twelve other women were classified as "Medical Officers, General Duty" although the internists also had general duties at one time or another, despite their specialization. Women gynecologists were also needed, but there were simply not enough to fill the bill when it came to meeting WAC needs. Since only four women served in this capacity, it turned out that the greatest number of physicians meeting women's medical needs were male doctors. The Army noted that three women doctors had a pediatrics specialty before the war—Elizabeth Garber Tate, Mila Pierce Rhoads, and Theresa Ting Woo—but all were assigned to other duties once they were commissioned officers. This was also true for the numerous male pediatricians, who, like the females, also had to perform duties outside their area of expertise and training.[10] When comparisons are made between female and male Army doctors, therefore, it is evident that both groups shared similar problems in terms of being assigned outside their specialty, as well as being assigned to meet WAC medical needs.

In regard to other specialty areas, only four women doctors were classified as pathologists, and while the Army needed anesthesiologists, only six of them could be found in this specialty as contrasted with WWI when women contract surgeons were recruited specifically in this area and were the only ones sent overseas. In terms of implications for medicine, however, one outcome of WWII was not just an expanding interest in psychiatry, but also in anesthesiology. All medical corps officers were classified by a letter code system, later changed to a number code system, and this was used to fit them into a series of job categories. For example, an orthopedic surgeon, instead of having the previous symbol "S", was assigned the code number 3153.[11] Such methods were used so that officers could be given assignments in keeping with their abilities and qualifications, but unfortunately they did not always tend to promote the kind of uniformity that was desired by the SGO for medical specialists. For male psychiatrists, for instance, many of the younger men were lost to neuropsychiatry when they were assigned to combat units and The Surgeon General had no assignment jurisdiction over medical officers so that he could assert proper use of these specialists.[12]

Although women medical officers never saw combat, there were other problems with their proper use. The professional classification of psychiatrists was helpful in the early stages of the war, but it soon became "antiquated" as the original ratings did not reflect the professional development of the psychiatrists. Capt. Fern Thomas, for example, who was a highly experienced neuropsychiatrist, found herself at a VA Hospital where the male doctor over her had less experience. Lt. Elizabeth C. Bremner maintained that she should have been a captain given her civilian experiences; and Margaret E. Shirlock, who was commissioned a captain, reflected that "after two years, in grade, I think a promotion is warranted."[13]

Severe shortages with physicians compelled the Army to train medical officers in neuropsychiatry; so the School of Military Neuropsychiatry was established and its primary purpose in the beginning stages was to offer an opportunity for review and military orientation to newly joined or already trained or experienced psychiatrists and neurologists. Not long afterwards, it became an intensive training center in psychiatry and neurology for general medical officers to function as neuropsychiatrists. The first class was enrolled 20 December 1942 and by September 1945 total of 1,000 had been graduated. While the School started under Colonel Porter at Walter Reed, it was moved to Lawson General Hospital, Atlanta, Georgia, December 1942. In October 1943 it was relocated to Mason General Hospital, Brentwood, Long Island, New York, as that hospital had been designated as a specialized treatment hospital for neuropsychiatric casualties, and it was felt that the neuropsychiatry (NP) program could benefit from the increased clinical facilities there.[14]

Also in October 1943, the basic training program for women medical officers began at Lawson General Hospital (GH) in Atlanta. This course, which lasted four weeks, was similar to that provided for the men with the exception of combat training. Lectures were provided on military courtesy and customs of the service related to Army regulations. When they weren't attending classes, the women worked on the hospital wards, but at the completion of the course, they remained in the medical replacement pool until assigned to a permanent post. Craighill questioned the need for having a course for women officers which was separate from the men, as both "subsequently worked together on identical jobs."[15] Her advice was not heeded, and after women medical officers were commissioned they went for basic training and were either sent to their assignment next or went on for specialized training, i.e. in neuropsychiatry or tropical medicine. After her arrival at Lawson for basic indoctrination, for example, Capt. Elizabeth L. Bryan wrote home: "We have conferences, Retirement Boards, Court Martials, etc., in the a.m. and classes each afternoon…There is so much we must learn so that in a jam we will act quickly and correctly." In a separate letter, she elaborated: "MCRP means Medical Corps Replacement Pool. After a while they get too many of something around and someone gets replaced or sent off somewhere else. I am being trained to be an assistant of some sort, but so far my training has been mostly general."[16]

Of the women medical officers who were classified as neuropsychiatrists in the Army, almost all were single when they were commissioned as only Zdenka Hurianek was married although she did not use her married name of Moore. (Elizabeth Bremner was divorced and Grace Fern Thomas was a widow). Seven of the women were sent for further training to Mason General Hospital after they volunteered—Drs. Alcinda Pereira de Aguiar, Bernice Joan Harte, Zdenka Hurianek, Adele C. Kempker, Hilde G. Koppel, Teresa McNeel, and Margaret Shirlock who had dual classifications in General Duty and Neuropsychiatry. In terms of the backgrounds of the women medical officers, Craighill commented on the "apparent frequent occurrences of women of foreign birth among those being commissioned." This was certainly true for those classified in NP as five of them came from abroad, which constituted a third of the group.[17] (See Table 2).

Dr. Teresa McNeel, AMC.
Courtesy of McNeel family collection.

Despite the fact that Army medical officers, both women and men, were frequently assigned outside their specialty, this did not make it any easier to get a transfer. Such was the case for Capt. Catherine Gordon McGregor, classified as a Medical Officer, General Duty, who asked to be reassigned to neuropsychiatry because she maintained that she was engaging in too many administrative tasks to suit her. Unfortunately she never got the psychiatric training she wanted. Even if she had, however, she might not have liked what she got because with the rapid expansion of the Army, practically all Regular male Army neuropsychiatrists had to assume administrative and command assignments, which meant that they were performing a variety of medical duties other than psychiatric ones.[18]

While the women physicians did not assume command assignments like the men, they also found their time consumed with duties other than medical—Board meetings, teaching, paperwork, and supervisory duties among others. Capt. Adele Kempker, for instance, reported: "We are under peak load of work." While in the AMC, she worked entirely in the Neuropsychiatric (NP) service where she said, "I have thruout [sic] given lectures and talks to various civilians and military and community groups as assigned." The military groups consisted of "occupational therapy, physiotherapy and dietetic students at Lawson General Hospital." Born 16 July 1903 in Vermillion, South Dakota, Kempker graduated from the WMCP in 1933 and received neuropsychiatry training at Mason General Hospital." In later years, she used her Army training to her advantage because by 1968 she was practicing at the VA Hospital in Jefferson Barracks, Missouri. She died 5 January 1992 in Midwest City, Oklahoma.[19]

Two other women shared similar concerns when it came to dealing with nonmedical tasks. Lt. Bernice Joan Harte from the medical school at Middlesex in Waltham, Massachusetts, indicated that after her transfer to Ft. Des Moines, "most of my time was taken up by boards, sick call, physical exams, etc. with only a minimum of psychiatric work."[20] And Elizabeth L. Bryan was disgruntled when she was assigned as an instructor to a WAC school where she had to teach elementary courses that did not require the credentials and experience of a psychiatrist.[21]

In considering the women psychiatrists as a group, certain patterns emerged. They were generally older than most Army doctors (ten out of sixteen were age forty and over); they were very experienced with psychiatric issues (many had worked in state institutions before volunteering), almost one-third were foreign born, and half of them went to work in VA facilities in postwar years. It was no surprise then that the majority of them received their captaincy when they were commissioned, as rank was determined on the basis of age, training, and experience.

Capt. Alice Ellen Rost is a good example of a woman psychiatrist who was older, highly experienced, born abroad, and worked in a

VA hospital after discharge. At age 46, she was also one of the most senior of the women psychiatrists. Born 9 June 1898 in Breslau, Germany, she acquired her medical degree at Friedrich Wilhelms University in 1923, interned at the Wenzel Hancke Hospital in Breslau the next year, and remained to do a psychiatric residency in neurology from 1924-1929. She did postgraduate work at the Psychiatric Institute at the University of Frankfurt 1929-1933, but by 1939 she was in the United States employed as a psychiatrist at the Albany Medical Center Hospital in New York, and assistant clinical professor of psychiatry there in 1940. She also worked as a neurologist at the Benedictine Hospital (formerly referred to as Sahler's Sanitarium) in Kingston, New York, which was known for the treatment of mental and nervous disorders and drug additions.

After she was appointed [22] December 1943, the local newspaper in Kingston printed an article which also contained a picture of her in uniform. It boasted: "Dr. Alice E. Rost...has been commissioned a captain in the Army Medical Corps. She has left for duty at Lawson General Hospital, Atlanta, Ga." But Lawson was only one of four stations in which she later served in the NP service as a ward officer and then as Chief. Her patient contact was not limited to servicewomen, as she predominantly treated male patients and, at one point, she was an Assistant Chief of a section which had twelve male and two female wards of 60 beds each. Like the other psychiatrists, however, she was involved in a variety of duties such as neurological and psychiatric consultations from other services, and serving on various Boards for Nurses' Retirement, Officers' Retirement, and POW Repatriation.[22]

Rost was also called on as a medical witness and asked to give testimony in the case of several WACs accused of lesbian activity at Ft. Oglethorpe. The situation arose because of a letter a mother, Mrs. Josephine Churchill, had written to the Judge Advocate General regarding her daughter. "It is no wonder women are afraid to enlist," she wrote. "It is full of homosexuals and sex maniacs." It appeared that when her daughter came home on furlough she started receiving letters from one WAC that revealed what was going on at Ft. Oglethorpe in regard to practicing this "terrible vice." Naturally an investigation was ordered, and Dr. Rost was asked to conduct several observations and interviews of the servicewomen involved or thought to be involved. On 26 June 1944, Rost reported: "I am a diplomat of the American Board in Neurology and Psychiatry, of both divisions... I am a qualified psychiatrist with the State Department of Mental Hygiene in New York State. I am a qualified examiner in lunacy in New York State... I am an instructor in neurology and psychiatry, the Albany Medical School, which is part of Union University, Albany, New York. I am Associate Neurologist and Psychiatrist with the Dispensary of the Albany Hospital. From all these appointments, I am now on leave of absence; and also visiting psychiatrist at the Kingston Hospital, Kingston, New York, where I have my residence."

In regard to homosexuality, Rost maintained that it was "a certain bent of character and is part of the personality, but not an illness" and could not be cured. When it came to the WAC situation, she felt that such women were "not detrimental" to the Corp: "[W]hat two groups do to their mutual satisfaction in the privacy of their bedroom, is their own business. That is putting it a little crudely." Since the women in question had also "conducted themselves inconspicuously and that they handled their love with discretion", they need not be discharged. At the same time, she admitted that there might be specific instances in other cases where a "confirmed" lesbian might have to be discharged under Section Eight. Like many psychiatrists of her time, however, she challenged prevailing generalizations and stereotypes in regard to the homosexual personality.[23]

In Rost's case, a handful of war years seemed to have left an indelible mark on her, and had it been possible to remain in the Army, she would have done so as she once maintained she was "not eager for an early discharge." After she left the Army, she returned to Kingston for a short time, and then committed herself to veterans' problems by becoming the Chief Psychiatrist at the new VA Clinic at Albany, New York, from 1946-1949. By 1957 she was the attending psychiatrist at the Albany Medical Center Hospital where she had worked before the war, and continued to engage in private practice. Rost passed away at the age of ninety-two 4 May 1991.[24]

Another medical officer also claimed Germany as her homeland. This was Hilde Gertrude Koppel who was born in Kobern, Germany, 26 September 1910 and completed her medical training at the University of Bern in Switzerland. As soon as she had her medical degree in hand, she immediately accepted a position as intern for 1937-38 at the Frankfurt Jewish Hospital in Frankfurt, Germany.[25] Staying on was a bold decision as the Nazi Party was in power and many Jewish doctors, among other groups, were being rounded up or marked for deportation to various camps. Although Koppel was young, single, and idealistic, it was impossible to escape the dangerous anti-Semitic attitude that was everywhere. One woman who worked at the hospital in 1938 recalled: "Daily there were reminders of the worsening situation...the morgue drawers were full of the bodies of Jews who had thrust their heads in ovens rather than face the Nazis."

At some point, Koppel was finally persuaded that her best option was to get out of the country while she could. In April of 1938 Koppel emigrated to the United States. It is not known how she managed to flee, but one of the AMWA's priorities was to help women physicians escape from Europe, so she may have had contact with colleagues who helped or advised her. Nevertheless, by July 1939, she was at Community General Hospital in Syracuse, New York, where she trained in infectious diseases for one year. She followed-up the next year with a psychiatric residency at Stony Lodge Hospital, a child and adolescent inpatient facility overlooking the Hudson River in Ossining, New York. From 1941-43 she worked at Bellevue Hospital Center in New York, and in 1943 she became a naturalized citizen.[26]

Citizenship was an important step for Koppel, because it meant she could now volunteer with the AMC, and on16 November 1943, she received her commission as a captain. As soon as her basic indoctrination ended at Lawson General Hospital, she was sent to the School of Neuropsychiatry, Mason General Hospital, for further training and then posted to Bushnell General Hospital. At that time, Bushnell was a large military medical setting with three specialized centers in tropical disease, amputation, and maxillofacial reconstruction. The Hospital also contained two other specialties in neurology and psychiatry, and Koppel, who was one of "two women doctors" assigned to Bushnell, found that she was also the only woman doctor who served in the neuropsychiatric ward although a detachment of WAC medical and surgical technicians also worked in the complex. With her prewar training in infectious diseases, however, she could just as easily have been assigned to the tropical disease center instead. After Bushnell, she was sent to the 318*th* General Hospital at Camp Grant, Illinois, and then she shipped overseas to the Southwest Pacific Area (SWPA), making her only one of two psychiatrists to be sent abroad. It was probably no coincidence that she was sent to the SWPA, as in May 1944, large WAC units had started to serve in Australia, New Guinea, the Philippines, Hawaii, Guam, and other U.S. Possessions in the Pacific. Koppel was posted for seven months on Oahu and Okinawa and then was assigned to the 307*th* Hospital as the chief psychiatrist in Osaka, Japan, sometime towards the end of 1945.

On the Army Questionnaire that she returned to Major Craighill, Koppel merely checked responses that indicated all her Army experiences had been satisfactory and in accord with her special training in neuropsychiatry. She wrote only one comment: "Will the adjusted service rating score be lower for female medical officers?" This appeared to be a subtle acknowledgment that differences existed in the Army's treatment of female and male doctors—or as Campbell maintained: Army life could be satisfying for individuals, "but a disaster for women as a gender."[27]

In post war years, Koppel continued to direct her energies to her specialty and she maintained a private practice in psychiatry where she did consulting work and engaged in therapy with individuals, couples, and families. In 1946-47 she also engaged in further training in child psychiatry with the Jewish Board of Guardians in New York, an agency that had its start in the New York's Jewish community in the 1890s and was committed to counseling and mental health issues with those most in need. The Board also helped to train mental health workers and was involved in research to help the professions of psychiatry, psychology, and social work. The next year she went for more training at the New York Psychoanalytic Institute and took courses in 1948-49, but she did not graduate until 1959. Koppel married at some point and had at least two children although she continued to use her own name professionally. She died 5 March 1984 in White Plains, New York, at the age of 73.[28]

Before the women were commissioned during 1939-1942, "an officer's assignment was not always, or entirely, based on his classification, nor was he always kept fully occupied in the position for which he was best fitted. This gave rise to complaints of misassignment." When female medical officers were sent to the various medical sties later on, they also had to deal with the problem of misassignment for varying periods as that was just part of Army life. Capt. Mary J. Walters, for instance, was put in charge of the Eyes, Ears, Nose, and Throat (EENT) office at one station while Capt. Elizabeth L. Bryan was detailed to teach WACs.[29] When such problems were considered, Bryan held: "Probably it is psychiatry that needs reform even more than the Army."[30]

Dr. Mary Jane Walters.
Courtesy University of Pennsylvania Archives.

Generally speaking, many male Army psychiatrists had been employed in state institutions before the Army.[31] As was mentioned earlier, this also applied to the women. Resident positions in institutional work at many state reformatories and asylums had also been available to them starting towards the end of the nineteenth century. One medical historian observed that, "Women physician pressed enthusiastically for the chance to do asylum work, both for the clinical experience it provided and because of their increasing interest in psychiatry."[32] This pattern was reflected in the female psychiatrists as a group: Drs. Adams, Bryan, De Aguilar, Hurianek, McNeel, Nersessian, Shirlock, and Thomas—had all been involved in institutional work before the war.[33] It is also more than likely that a few of the other women psychiatrists had asylum experience before they volunteered as complete records were not located for all the women.

One advantage of working at a state institution was that the specialist was frequently concerned with the care of psychotic patients. This was an experience that was useful in the military because the Army always has some psychotic patients which amounted to about 10 percent of the total psychiatric load, although the main thrust in the military was on the patient suffering from neurotic and other personality difficulties. Hence, most psychiatrists commissioned directly from civilian life had much to adjust to when they went into uniform, and this included the women physicians as well.[34] Lt. Elizabeth C. Bremner, a child psychiatrist before the war, indicated that she couldn't wait to get back to working with young patients; and Lt. Bernice Joan Harte (who had six different assignments as a neuropsychiatrist in two years), said: "I am sick and tired of hospitals and the Army both."[35] Finally, Capt. Clyde Adams admitted that her assignment did not match her training and skills and on 29 September 1945, she reported: "I requested relief from active duty."[36] Meanwhile, Capt. Hilde G. Koppel asked: "[W]hat are the chances of discharge?"[37]

Capt. Zdenka Hurianek from the WMCP, was the only married psychiatrist and the only woman medical officer from Arizona. Born 6 September 1902, she was a psychiatrist in civilian practice, but she was still sent for specialized training to the School of Military Neuropsychiatry in March 1944. Later she was assigned as a ward officer for both women and men patients at Darnall General Hospital in Danville, Kentucky, a facility which had been converted over from the Kentucky State Hospital for Army use.[38] Described as having a "sunny" disposition, she was a good choice for an officer in charge as she did not complain when she was also put in charge of occupational therapy at the hospital.[39] As a matter of fact, she relished being "treated the same as any medical officer" and even pointed out that she had assumed "Officer of the Day" (O.D.) duties—a task that a few other women medical officers resented.[40]

The hardships of her early years probably prepared Hurianek for the discipline of Army life. Born in 1903, she grew up with parents who were ranchers in southern Colorado and the nearest school was a seven-mile trip by horse and buggy. Because of this, she did not start school until she was ten and when she was thirteen she began high school lessons in a country school with one teacher and seven students. She eventually passed the state teachers' examination and taught elementary school for a year until she entered Denver University. "I always wanted to be a doctor," she confided. But she never told this to her parents as she felt, "They'd feel bad because they couldn't afford to help."[41] She continued to work while she was in school, but she still earned a Bachelor's degree with a major in chemistry in three years. For the next few years she accepted jobs as a laboratory technician until she saved enough money to enter medical school at the WMCP, which she followed-up with an internship at the Woman's Hospital of Philadelphia, which was associated with the medial school.

Early on in her career, Hurianek related that she "wanted to be in internal medicine." She did not indicate why she shifted her interest later on, but it is well known that psychiatry has its benefits for women, especially those with children. "It's a good profession for a woman because she's not on call at all times and can lead a private life," she explained. On a personal note she also believed: "Married women are better adjusted emotionally and more free to study. 'The man hunt is over.'"[42] Apparently she took her own words to heart as she began to work next as a resident psychiatrist at St. Lawrence State Hospital in Ogdensburg, New York, which was considered a progressive hospital as it opened the first coed nursing school associated with a mental facility in the state.[43] While she was working there in 1938, she married a pharmacist, Thomas J. Moore.

The couple had one son who was born in March of 1942, and was not quite two years old when she volunteered with the Army. Hurianek indicated that she never received a dependency allowance for her son while in service.[44] This was a concern shared by other women medical officers as the war dragged on because they received no entitlements for their dependents—nor would they for several years. It was not until Senate Bill 1641 became P. L. 625 on 12 June 1948 that women won an important battle on their way to securing equal rights with men in the Army. The Integration Act, however, had "certain inherent barriers. While officers and enlisted women could claim husbands and/or children as dependents, it had to be proven that they were in fact dependent upon the women for "their chief support." The wives and children of male members of the Army were automatically considered dependents.[45]

After she was separated from service, she entered private practice in Phoenix, Arizona, but she continued to be affiliated with three different hospitals in the city, and she was also a psychiatrist for the Juvenile Court in Maricopa County. As of 1 July 1969 she accepted a full-time position as a psychiatrist with the Veterans Administration Hospital in Phoenix, but she retired from the VA in July of 1971.[46] Hurianek was a member of various organizations including the American Psychiatric Association, the American Medical Association, and the Maricopa County Medical Association, among others. She passed away 13 July 1975 at the age of seventy-two and was survived by her son.[47]

Lt. Alcinda Pereira de Aguiar (later capt.) also worked as a psychiatrist in two state institutions before she volunteered for the Medical Corps 15 May 1944 at the age of forty-five.[48] Not much is known about her early life and career, other than that she was born in Viana do Castelo, Portugal 15 November 1899, graduated from the medical school at Oponto University, Portgual, in 1925 and interned at Porto Hospital 1924-25. She emigrated to the United States in December of 1925 at the age of twenty-six and then embarked on a psychiatric residency at St. Francis Hospital, Pittsburgh, Pennsylvania, 1929-30.[49] She accepted a position as assistant physician 1930-32 at the Rome State School in Rome, New York, where she treated patients who were classified as insane, mentally retarded, and had behavioral problems. In 1932 de Aguiar resigned her position to enter private practice, and On 2 May 1935 she became a naturalized citizen. Before she volunteered in the AMC, she was on the staff at the Wrentham State School in Wrentham, Massachusetts, as a ward psychiatrist from 1939-44.[50]

Her Army career was off to a good start when, for three months from June to September 1944, she received special training in neuropsychiatry at Mason General Hospital. Following this she became a ward officer in the NP Service at Lawson General Hospital where military transport planes landed wounded soldiers; at Oliver General Hospital which was formerly the Forrest Ricker Hotel and was purchased in 1942 by the Army and transferred to the Veterans Administration in 1950; and at Camp Butner General Hospital in North Carolina where the Army trained combat troops for deployment and redeployment to the European and Pacific Theaters.[51] In all the wards, de Aguiar worked almost "exclusively" with men patients as she took care of only "a few" women patients at any point. In regard to her duties, she reported she worked "mostly in open ward with severe psychoneuroses (men coming from overseas)…gave psychotherapy and in most instances narcosynthesis," which is a method of treating an acute traumatic neurosis by working with a patient while under the influence of a hypnotic drug. When asked about her willingness to stay in the Army, she replied: "I wish to be separated as soon as the emergency in NP Service will permit."[52] She gave no reason for this statement, so it is surprising that she changed her mind later.

When the Korean War started, there was the same pressing need for doctors, and lawmakers passed the legislation allowing the services to commission women physicians into the reserves of the Army,

Navy, and Air Force. As soon as this enabling legislation took effect, the Army recalled three reserve women doctors to active duty, and de Aguiar was one of them along with Clara Raven, pathologist, and Theresa T. Woo, now a public health specialist. She left her civilian practice in Boston where she was a prominent psychotherapist and was immediately assigned as a Major to a psychiatric hospital in To-kyo, Japan, because psychiatrists were needed to treat soldiers with battle fatigue. While she was there she also participated in research for the treatment of soldiers with sodium amytal. One woman medi-cal officer noted that, "[S]he was so successful in restoring back to duty to Korea some of the psychotic soldiers, that she was accused by some unbelieving colleagues of performing 'hocus pocus' with her patients." In the end, she gained recognition and approval for her work, but she was unsuccessful in her request to be assigned close to the fighting front.[53]

Following the Korean War de Aguiar returned to Massachusetts where she established a private practice and held various positions starting as a ward psychiatrist at the VA Hospital, Bedford, Mas-sachusetts (1947-62). Afterwards (1967-71) she was the director of psychiatry at the Westborough State Hospital, formerly known as Westborough Insane Hospital, which had taken in its first patients in 1886 and had been the second hospital in the world under ho-meopathic management.[54] She also did consulting work before end-ing up in Westerly, Rhode Island in the 1970s. She was a member of several medical groups including Pan American Medical Asso-ciation, World Federation for Mental Health, AMA, and the Royal College of Psychiatrists. She died in Bedford, Massachusetts, 15 July 1987 at the age of eighty-eight.[55]

Grace Fern Thomas also worked in a state institution system, only she went to the Mid-west, the South and the West coast to do it. Al-though she was born 23 September 1897 in Gothenburg, Nebraska, Thomas spent the last years of her adult life in California.She re-ceived her BS degree from the University of Nebraska in 1924, her

MA from Creighton University in Omaha, Nebraska, in 1926 and her MD from the University of Southern California (USC) in Los Angeles in 1934. She interned at the Los Angeles County Hospital and completed a residency at the Riverside County Hospital in Arlington California 1935-36. Her strong thirst for knowledge over the next three decades drove her to do postgraduate work at the University of Colorado in 1942 and at the Institute of Living in Hartford, Connecticut in 1943. Only her war service in 1944-45 interrupted her studies as she did further postgraduate work at the USC in 1946, at UCLA 1947-1950, Columbia University 1953, and received another MA in Religion which was awarded in 1968 from the USC. Her thesis topic combined her interests in both psychiatry and religion as it was entitled: "Collaborative psychotherapy by psychiatrists and clergy in problems of guilt and suffering."

Her primary identification was as a psychiatrist as she was a Diplomate of the American Board of Psychiatry and Neurology, Fellow of the American Psychiatric Association, and a member of various organizations which included the AMA, the AMWA, the Association of American University Women, the Institute of Religion and Health, and the Central California Psychiatric Association. Thomas believed in the strong connection between psychiatry and religion, or between the body and the mind, and she was ordained to the ministry of the United Methodist Church in 1968. She appears to be the only WWII woman doctor who became a minister.[56]

At the age of forty-seven Thomas was appointed a captain on 6 July 1944, classified as a neuropsychiatrist, and posted to the VA hospital in Palo Alto, California, with twelve years' experience in her specialty not counting her internship and residency.[57] On her arrival, she immediately encountered one of the problems associated with the classification system for psychiatrists. "At my first station," she said, "work to which I was assigned was not primarily neuro-psychiatric and not in keeping with my specialization (insulin and electro-shock therapy)." And if that were not bad enough, she observed: "At the same time, a male medical officer who under-ranked me, was assigned to shock therapy in a charge capacity without any adequate previous experience." In keeping with her own request, she was transferred to a second VA hospital in Los Angeles where she expected they would be utilizing her services full-time as a "shock specialist"—which is what she had been promised when she interviewed there. By the time she arrived about two months later, administration had changed. "I was not assigned to shock therapy," she reported, "but was placed in charge of the Acute Male Service with a multitude of other routine duties." Eventually, however, about half of the electro-shock therapy work was finally added to her schedule.[58] Overall, when her VA experiences were considered, Thomas felt that it was unfortunate that "male medical officers with comparable training and experience have [the] rank of Major" when compared to the women. (Indeed, only five women medical officers achieved the rank of Major in the Army Medical Corps—Craighill, Janeway, Carter, Loizeaux and Bowditch, with Craighill being promoted to Lt. Colonel).[59] By the end of her service in the VA in 1945, Thomas wrote: "I am presently on sick Leave and also confined to Pasadena Regional Hospital for the treatment of 'acute physical exhaustion.'"[60]

All of her life, Thomas coped with a certain restlessness, and this was evident not just in her quest for knowledge, but in her frequent job changes. She was always on the go from 1924 when she was an instructor in chemistry and biology at Duchesne College to 1927-1932 when she worked as a lab technician at various hospitals. Even after acquiring her medical degree, she held two posts as staff psychiatrist until she entered the Army in 1944.[61] After the service, Thomas entered private practice (1946-51) but she could not stay put and she held at least nine different positions in mental health over the next two decades as director or chief from 1951 to 1971. One of these positions was as chief of the mental hygiene clinic of the VA hospital in Albuquerque, New Mexico (1951-54) and the other was as chief psychiatrist at the Porterville State Hospital in California in 1965.

By 1970 she was back in private practice in California although she also worked as a consulting psychiatrist at a Catholic social service agency from 1974-78.[62] Thomas passed away 28 December 1991 in Stanislaus County, California.[63]

Capt. Agnes Aznive Nersessian referred to herself as Agnes A. in her professional career.[64] Like some of the other women, she also had institutional experience before being commissioned. Little is known about her early life, other than that she was born 15 December 1902 and emigrated to the United States from Armenia when she was nineteen years old and proceeded to graduate from Temple University School of Medicine in Philadelphia in 1932. She interned at the New England Hospital for Women and Children the following year and then accepted a residency in 1933 at the State Hospital in Northampton, Massachusetts.[65] From 1933-39 she was an assistant physician at Foxborough (Foxboro) State Hospital in Massachusetts, which opened in 1889 for inebriates (alcoholics) but later started to treat individuals with psychiatric disorders.[66] By the end of 1939 she was on the staff of Norwood Hospital in Massachusetts and she also had her own private practice in Norwood right before the war.[67]

Nersessian's case illustrates the discrepancies that existed in the Army classification system. Her medical code was missing on one list, but on two other lists her Army classifications referred to her either as a neuropsychiatrist or a surgeon; nevertheless, her prewar training indicated that her specialty was, indeed, psychiatry. (Since she did not submit a questionnaire to Major Craighill, we do not know with certainty what her exact duties were which would have clarified her specialty). She made captain at the age of forty-one and was assigned to work at various places which included the two large WAC training centers at Ft. Des Moines, Iowa, and Ft. Oglethorpe in Georgia. A member of the American Medical Association, Nersessian was certified by the American Board of Psychiatry and Neurology and the National Board of Medical Examiners.[68] A soon as she was discharged in 1946, she starting working as a psychiatrist and neurologist at the VA hospital in Boston where she remained for more than a decade. She succumbed to cancer November 1974 at the age of seventy-two.[69]

Elizabeth C. Bremner was only thirty-four years of age when she volunteered with nearly ten years' of experience in medicine. She indicated she was from Columbus Station, Ohio, was divorced, and claimed both her mother and father as dependents.[70] Although she specialized in child psychiatry, her early interest in neuropsychiatry was fostered by her internship at Toledo State Hospital (also known as the Toledo Asylum) in 1935 following her graduation from medical school at Ohio State University.[71] She was appointed a lieutenant 21 July 1944 and posted to the station hospital at Ft. Oglethorpe, Georgia, where she was made Chief of the NP Section. When she looked back on the value of her efforts to the war towards the end of 1945, Bremner observed: "[I] was in child psychiatry and feel that my real contribution is in that field and sooner I'm back to it the better. Should be Captain—have had 9 years' psychiatric experience, certified by the Amer. Bd. in Psychiatry and Neurology in 1943."[72]

While Bremner's military service had been only with adult patients, she did not lose her zeal for the developing child—as she proceeded to become well known for her work in child and adolescent psychoanalysis in the following years.[73] Sometime in the 1950s she married Dr. Albert J. Kaplan, another psychiatrist, and she proceeded to use her married name, now signing herself professionally as Elizabeth Bremner Kaplan.[74] In the 1960s she was a clinical professor of child psychiatry at Hahnemann Medical College and Hospital in Philadelphia, Pennsylvania, and she was on the faculty of the Division for the Psychoanalysis of Children and Adolescents of the Institute of the Philadelphia Association for Psychoanalysis. She and Albert were married twenty-five years and "their house was always filled with music, and many noted musicians played chamber music" at the gatherings there. She lost a long bout with cancer in November 1981 and Albert followed her 22 July 1982.[75]

One of three medical officers who graduated from Ohio Wesleyan University and the WMCP (see Table), Margaret E. Shirlock was born 31 December 1899, and commissioned as a captain at the age of forty-four with dual classifications in General Medicine (or General Duty) and neuropsychiatry.[76] She also had institutional experience before WWII since she worked for twelve years as a senior resident physician at the Vineland State School in New Jersey, formerly known as the New Jersey Home for the Education and Care of Feebleminded Children. The school also housed a psychological laboratory which was known nationwide for studying mental deficiency; and Shirlock was active in several projects and research studies on the "feeble-minded child" and clinical aspects of mental deficiency while she was there. Prior to her entry, she was the resident physician at Skillman Village for Epileptics at Skillman, New Jersey.[77]

Her military experiences spanned a two-year period. After being sent for training at the School of Military Neuropsychiatry in the winter of 1943, Capt. Shirlock was posted to four stations consecutively: Tilton GH, Ft. Dix, New Jersey; Lawson GH, Atlanta, Georgia: Mason GH, Long Island, New York; Station Hospital at Ft. Oglethorpe, Georgia. Not one to complain, she pointed out that her quarters were generally adequate and comfortable although she was housed in the nurses' barracks. Like Army doctors everywhere at the time, however, Shirlock believed that even though she put forth her "very best effort in the various assignments", the results were unsatisfactory "due to the maze of channels" she had to deal with constantly. Furthermore, there was often "more work than could be handled properly." She maintained that "to a certain degree in several cases, chiefs made work unpleasant and hindered the carrying out of a constructive program," and while she had not learned much in the way of "new medicine and new procedures", she learned more about "dealing with and working with people, as patients, co-workers, and superiors in a military organization."[78]

Following the war she returned to her home in New Jersey, got married, and started using her new name. From that point on, she was known professionally as Margaret S. Foery. She passed away 21 May 1994, and her death was noted by the Medical Women's International Association. She is buried in Monmouth Memorial Park, Tinton Falls, New Jersey.[79]

Clyde Adams was just a few years younger than Margaret Shirlock. Born in Martinsville, Texas, 21 September 1902, she spent her girlhood in nearby Nacogdoches, Texas. She received her medical degree at the Galveston Medical Branch of the University of Texas sometime in the 1920s following her graduation from what is now the Texas Women's University in Denton. She spent a year in the Texas state hospital system as a young doctor, decided on a career in psychiatry, completed her Board work in 1941, and two years later was listed with the American Psychiatric Association.[80]

At age forty-two Adams accepted a commission as a captain in the AMC 26 January 1944, and by May she was making a trip to Ft. Oglethorpe to buy cotton uniforms that the women medical officers could not find in Atlanta where they were stationed. Apparently she was well-liked as another doctor recalled that the "Texas LADY doctor... is a fine girl."[81] Adams served as a ward officer at all three locations to which she was assigned: Lawson General Hospital, Atlanta, Georgia, Winter General Hospital in Topeka, Kansas, and the Army Service Forces (ASF) Regional Station Hospital at Ft. Riley, Kansas. While she dealt with some women patients, her work load was "predominantly" with men patients. She maintained that her Army experiences were generally acceptable with the exception of the last one at Ft. Riley. "I do not feel that my present assignment is satisfactory because it consists mostly of consultation work with psychoneurotic patients and I am best fitted by personal preference, training and experience to deal with psychotic patients." On 29 September 1945, about twenty months after she volunteered, she requested relief from active duty.[82]

Following the war, Adams started to practice in San Antonio, as of 1948 had moved to Rusk, Texas, and by 1953 she was listed as a psychiatrist on the staff of Rusk State Hospital in Rusk, Texas.[83] That same year Rusk was also preparing to transfer out some male mental patients to Terrell State Hospital to make room to accept those who were considered criminally insane. One wonders why Adams accepted the position there in the first place as Rusk had been investigated by the state over the years for various reasons such as getting the needed additional appropriation for maintenance of the old buildings which were originally constructed as a penitentiary in 1878, closed in 1917, converted to a mental hospital in 1919, and named Rusk State Hospital in 1925. It had been pointed out, for example, that "The ward buildings are old and need repairing, and the blocked marble floor in one building needs replacing. Considering the condition of the old buildings, they were clean." One report also noted: "The hospital unit is very clean. The average death rate is between 10 and 15 per month." The peak patient population was also 2,426 in 1946.[84]

On 26 November 1953, one newspaper reported that as a result of an ongoing investigation at Rusk State Hospital, three employees were suspended pending a state probe. Three more individuals were asked to resign, namely: "Dr. Clyde Adams, female psychiatrist", and two female supervisors. Resignations were demanded "for the good of the service."[85] No further information was given regarding the firings, but The Texas State Board of Medical Examiners did not seem to have taken disciplinary action, as there was no record relating to the dismissal of Adams. It is clear that Adams wanted to get out of Texas after this unfortunate experience, however, as she wasted no time in moving to Louisiana.

With her credentials and experience, Adams had no problem in finding another position, and she joined the staff at Central Louisiana State Hospital in Pineville June 1954 where she was described as the "lone woman psychiatrist". This proved to be the right decision because her efforts were finally appreciated by peers, patients, and supervisors, and she was even "awarded the Christian Service Cross presented each year by the Episcopal Chaplaincy at the hospital." She was cited for "her deep personal concern with her patients and their problems," and she directed and trained staff "into a smoothly functioning treatment team." The hospital superintendent reported that her dedication to duty was "an inspiration to all of those with whom she served."[86] After putting in thirteen productive years at the state hospital in Pineville, Louisiana, Adams retired in 1967 and returned to Texas. She passed away in November 1986 at the age of eighty-four. [87]

Elizabeth Lynn Bryan was the second in a large family which consisted of seven girls and one boy. She was born 1 December 1898 in Dallas, Texas, but she later moved to Baltimore, Maryland, and New York City with her family. She received her BA from Goucher College (then a women's institution) in Baltimore, Maryland, in 1921 and her MD from Johns Hopkins Medical School four years later. As was the case with several of the other women doctors, she acquired experience with seriously disturbed patients early on as she interned at Western Pennsylvania Hospital, commonly known as West Penn Hospital, in Pittsburgh, Pennsylvania, and the Manhattan State Hospital, Ward's Island, New York City. She followed up with a residency at the Children's Hospital in Oakland, California 1928-29 and the Indiana State Board of Health, 1929. After this, Bryan took postgraduate training at the New York Psychiatric Institute and the Montefiore Hospital in the Bronx, New York. She was a very active woman since she also held positions as the senior assistant physician at the State Hospital, Ward's Island and Wingdale State Hospital 1931-43, was a clinical assistant in the Vanderbilt Clinic at the Presbyterian Hospital in New York City during 1941-43 and again in 1949-1955; and later she would return to be an assistant attending psychiatrist there in 1955-57.[88]

Like many gifted and talented people, however, Bryan was often pulled in different directions when it came to making career plans. This was evident when she started taking postgraduate courses in New York because she was uncertain about her future in psychiatry. When a new opportunity presented itself in January of 1944, however, she left the city to accept a fellowship at the Institute for Juvenile Research (IJR) on Chicago's South side. Bryan felt that the appointment not only carried a great deal of honor and prestige, but that the experience would enable her to something else other than direct psychiatric treatment with patients. Unfortunately, it took her less than two months to conclude that she had made the wrong decision, and she decided to apply for a commission in the AMC and take the physical to see if she qualified. In April she moved back East to join the staff at Rockland State Hospital in New York as a psychiatrist "with the understanding that it may be only temporary, so she can still join the Army if she hears from her application." She also wrote her sisters telling them that she was not happy with the electrotherapy work that they had put her on with chronic patients at the hospital.[89]

One week later, on 27 April 1944, Bryan was notified that she had been commissioned in the Army as a captain and she was ordered to report to Lawson GH, Atlanta, Georgia, for her basic training. On 12 May 1944, Velma, the eldest sister wrote: "This is just to let you all know that our Elizabeth is now Captain Elizabeth Bryan of the U. S. Army (not the WAC)... Naturally we are all very proud of her...We don't know what kind of work will be assigned to her, or where she may be sent [as] she signed up for being quite willing to be sent overseas! She looked very well indeed in all her uniforms winter, summer, 'dress pinks,' etc. and is in the best of health and spirits."

Bryan loved being in the Army. "This is a new life...a strange new existence, satisfying because it is in the line of duty and because Uncle Sam provides so very well for us. I attended a Retirement Board, and Monday go to a Court Martial." She continued: "I live in a white clapboard one story building kept clean by our colored maid. We have 50 cent breakfasts and dollar lunches and dinners for only 35 cents apiece…I have learned that only two women doctors in the U.S. Army have ranks about that of Captain. There are about ten women doctors here now…We also have three or four WAC officers in this cottage…We all feel we have a long war ahead and are glad to be helping."[90]

By the end of May, Bryan learned that she was to be trained "to be a chief of neuropsychiatric service." She hadn't been quite sure what a chief of NP did, but she wrote later: "My new job will undoubtedly have to do with getting undesirables out of the Army: passing on the sanity of [others], helping to ease out mental defectives and epileptics and insane, trying maybe to rehabilitate those whose headaches and weakness are too severe to do calisthenics but not to go on passes to Atlanta… So far my favorite patients have been WACs and believe me they are mostly game little girls, brighter than average and good little things. None seems to deserve the mildest slur." In June she was suddenly ordered to Camp Blanding in Florida, a transfer which she found somewhat confusing. "I'll confess I had an attack of bewilderment myself, "she wrote. "I'm supposed to be N.P. and I haven't finished the lecture courses they usually give women indoctrination or whatever. I had been there only five weeks, really quite enough but some girls had been there for months: a younger girl Ramos really only twenty-five, was passed over for me. It might have to do with my being a good American, or with my being a Captain… Well, I am a Captain because I'm [a] Neuropsychiatric specialist; however, as usual, the N.P. cases are slightly less attractive than our suffering heroes and a new specialty would thrill me.[91]

Towards the end of June 1944, Bryan was assigned to Wakeman General and Convalescent Hospital at Camp Atterbury, Indiana. Wakeman was the largest convalescent hospital in the U.S. Army, it housed a new technical school for WAC training that was under construction, and it contained a prisoner of war camp which held

German and Italian soldiers. At first Bryan was assigned as a ward officer, but that same month the Army decided she would make an excellent instructor for the technical school. This was not a welcome change. "The real news which is extremely disappointing to me, but which I am trying to take alike a solider," she wrote to her father, "is that the WAC school finally got me…I flatter myself that they like my personality, and that the little WACs need me. As for advancement I haven't any hope of it if I stay with them. Once they clamp down with permanent orders I'll never get to Europe or elsewhere."[92]

Bryan was correct in her assessment as she never made it overseas. She had two more postings after this, and her last station was Mason General Hospital where doctors treated psychological casualties from the battlefield. Overall, she was glad she had been in the Army except for being a teacher at the WAC School, work which was "too elemental for a specialist" and where she was also "required to do patrols at night." When it came to describing conditions there, she said candidly: "At WAC School…our table was next to the swill pails used by WAC privates and officers alike." She was also convinced that there was "prejudice against women physicians" in some quarters.

> We did not as a rule get either the rank or responsibility our experience entitled us to. Drs. should not receive ratings from psychologists and WAC officers…A major in N.P. who is unscrupulous, and probably the most inexperienced N.P. officers of lower grade, are getting by with very shoddy judgments: they have too much power over the lives of their patients and under officers. There are many injustices, probably more attributable to poorly systematized thinking in the psychiatric profession as well as to poor organization in the Army…I feel that being merely a Capt. has harmed me professionally and I feel

that many other women in the Medical Corps have been tricked below their deserts.[93]

As was true for many of the other women medical officers, the war left a lasting impression on her, and she made up her mind to devote herself to veterans' health care in 1945. Bryan accepted a position in 1947 as a staff psychiatrist at the VA Regional Office, Baltimore, Maryland, and that same year switched to the VA Regional Office in Brooklyn, New York where she remained for many years while she continued to maintain close contact with her large family. She retired in 1965, but sometime in the late 1960s she started to lose her grip on reality and "she began seeing little people in her house and started calling the police to insist they force the little people out." She was admitted for psychiatric evaluation but on 5 January 1970 she passed away in the VA hospital where she had worked. She never married and she had no children, but she is still remembered in the "sister letters" that were circulated during her lifetime as her elder sister, Velma, recalled once: "Her devotion to the family and her pride in us have been a major influence in all our lives." She volunteered with the AMC "to render a service to our country in a time of great need. We are all very proud of her."[94]

Dr. Mary Jane Walters, like Bryan, had many years of experience in civilian life before the Army, and she too worked in a state institution prior to the outbreak of the war. Born 1 January 1894 in Langley, Virginia, she received her Bachelor's degree from Goucher College at Baltimore, Maryland, in 1917. She took three jobs in rapid order as an assistant or instructor in physiology at various colleges, and then in 1925 attended the University of Pennsylvania in Philadelphia where she was awarded her MD four years later and remained to do her internship at the hospital connected with the medical school. For the next two years, she continued on at the University as an instructor of pediatrics and then as a researcher in pathology, but then she decided to head East to serve as an assistant physician at Vassar

College, Poughkeepsie, New York, from1933-38. By 1938 she was in private practice in Clifton Heights, Aldan, and Delaware County, Pennsylvania. But after three years, she was ready for a different kind of challenge and from 1941-44 she accepted a position as a psychiatrist at Norristown State Hospital in Pennsylvania, formerly known as the State Lunatic Hospital at Norristown. It had been established in 1880 to help alleviate the crowded psychiatric wards of other nearby institutions and it was said to be the first state institution that recognized female physicians. Choosing Norristown seemed a natural choice in her professional career as Walters had strong feelings about women's rights. She had pointed out on her alumni form, for example, that since it required the "wife's maiden name" on the blank, it should also have space for "a husband's name."[95]

In the fall of 1943 when she was age 49 years old and still on the staff of Norristown State Hospital, Walters made inquiries about the possibility of a commission in the AMC. (At this time, she was already a member of several professional groups and had passed her Boards in Neurology and Psychiatry). Craighill gave her a reassuring answer: "The Army is particularly anxious to have trained psychiatrists such as you in the service. I hope you will decide to come in and can be freed from your present appointment...You would probably qualify for a Captaincy or a Majority, but no one can say positively which until your credentials are all in." Because of her age, she had also advised Walters: "The physical examinations are fairly rigid, but some exceptions are made in the case of medical officers. Your chief problem might be the matter of eyes. The requirements are that you must have a .21 in each eye, correctable with glasses to 20/20 in one eye and 20/30 in the other, without organic disease in either eye."[96]

Once she accepted her commission 18 February 1944, Walters traveled to three different hospitals during her service, not counting her initial training at Lawson General Hospital. First she went to O'Reilly General Hospital in Springfield, Missouri, where the post commander Colonel George B. Foster Jr., emphasized health care to such a degree that the hospital was considered a model for other Army hospitals. Afterwards she left for Clinton, Iowa, at Schick General Hospital which was named in honor of First Lt. William Rhinehart Schick, one of the first U.S. Army medical corps to be killed in action in WWII. Walters worked here from September 1944 to May 1945, a time when the patient census reached a high with 1,681 cases that January.[97] Her last duty station was at the US Army General dispensary in Kansas City, Missouri.

In reflecting on her overall accomplishments during the war Walters reported: "I have been pleased to be assigned to psychiatry, my specialty. However, I had hoped to be able to see and study more neurological cases for my own training." She had been the least satisfied at the US Army General Dispensary, however, where she was put in charge of the Eyes, Ears, Nose, and Throat (EENT) office. "[I] like the present one a bit less than the others," she admitted, "because not so much psychiatric work." She also elaborated that her work had been almost exclusively with men patients. "Rapport has been good. [I] have had almost no embarrassing situations. Many times I have felt that I was able to help the patients more just *because* of being a *woman* physician." Walters also stated: "I would not care to continue long in the service, however, unless I were able to get more neurology."

While Walters had reservations about continuing in the Army, she had none when it came to working with soldiers, and after her discharge in March 1946, she decided to continue to work with them. She accepted a position on the staff of the Lawson Veterans Administration Hospital in Atlanta, Georgia, which had one added advantage—she could share a house with her brother who was living nearby. Unexpectedly in December 1946, she became very ill. Her mother wrote: She never told any of us she was ill. But we did know that her hours and work were very long and hard. She kept on with her arduous duties until December 27, 1946, when *she* became a *patient* in Lawson Gen. VA Hospital where she had been working so faithfully. She seemed to be getting better very fast and on January 21, 1947 we celebrated her 53*rd* birthday...but on February 21*st*... she had to have a second operation and her surgeon told us it was a cancer of the intestines. She gradually became weaker and passed away March 7*th* at 8:30a.m." Although Walters could have been buried in Arlington National Cemetery, her family preferred to have her interred in the family plot with a simple military service.[98]

There was some difficulty with the classification system when it was applied to Julie Etta Olentine, the daughter of Dr. Fred B. Olentine. She was referred to as a psychiatrist in one list and a generalist in another list.[99] Born 28 November 1915, at the age of twenty-seven, she became the first Chicago woman doctor to be commissioned in the AMC. She was accepted on 15 July 1943 with the rank and pay of a first lieutenant having received her Bachelor of Science (BS) degree from Northwestern State Teachers College in Tahlequah, Oklahoma, in 1936, and her MD from Rush Medical College (then part of the University of Chicago) in 1940. She also remained in her hometown to complete an internship at St. Anthony de Padua Hospital in Chicago—which turned out to be an important decision as she was to return there to work in postwar years. Although she had no classification number, she was referred to as a neuropsychiatrist and posted to four stations. She did general duty and was also assigned to work in psychiatry where she took care of women neuropsychiatric patients at Darnall General Hospital in Kentucky during the war. In 1945, she returned to St. Anthony's and practiced as a physician and surgeon while also maintaining a private practice with her father in Chicago, Illinois. She died 2 February 2005 at the age of eighty-nine.[100]

There were just two women born in China who served as medical officers in the AMC, and only one neuropsychiatrist, Poe-Eng Yu. (The other officer, Theresa Ting Woo is discussed in a later chapter). Yu was born in Foochow, China, 28 April 1899, and received her secondary school training at Girls' High School in Kulangsu,

Amoy, China. She spent two years in the Kulangsu Normal School, received her teaching certificate from that school in 1916, and then taught high school for ten years at Amoy before coming to the United States to further her education and train as a nurse at the University of California. After four more years of study, she received her BA in psychology along with highest honors in the Department of Psychology, and then continued on to receive her MA at the same university in 1934. She decided, however, to follow in the footsteps of her parents, both physicians, and she enrolled in the University of Michigan where she received her medical degree in 1939. It was further reported that she was "awarded scholarships for every year of her education in this country."[101] Dr. Yu interned two years at Johns Hopkins where she specialized in psychiatry, and then she moved to New York and served as an assistant resident in neurology in Montefiori Hospital. She had two offers after that for another residency and a fellowship, but she decided to volunteer instead, listing Cambridge, Massachusetts, as her home address.

It is not always clear why a woman doctor volunteered or even how she felt about it, but in Yu's case, she had an "usually urgent reason for joining the Army [as] Japanese oppressors have destroyed her home in Amoy, Fukien, China." And if there was still any doubt about her motivation, she once stated: "I was given the commission of Captain in the Medical Corps of the U.S. Army the first of October [1943], and was sworn in on October tenth, which was our National Holiday. I am glad to be the only Chinese woman doctor in the Army, and the first Chinese women to be commissioned." Capt. Yu also believed she was lucky because early on she got her wish to go overseas. In December of 1943 she was assigned to the North African Theater of Operations, U.S. Army (NATOUSA), following Major Margaret Janeway who had gone overseas with the first WAAC contingent to North Africa nearly a year earlier on 13 January 1943. At one time she wrote how much she enjoyed working with patients returning from overseas. "They often say to me when they see my overseas ribbon, 'You have been overseas, you know the situations, etc.' I feel quite flattered to be recognized that way, but I have to admit to these heroes that I was nowhere near the front lines."[102]

Dr. Poe-Eng Yu. Courtesy private collection.

Yu was one of the few women medical officers who had a longer than average service record during WWII. She entered service as a civilian contract surgeon 4 November 1942, and was stationed as a lieutenant to the First WAC Training Center at Des Moines, Iowa; and the following month she was "authorized to wear a uniform similar to those worn by men with the bar of 1st lieutenants on their shoulders."[103] In March 1943 she, along with a handful of other women contract surgeons, became part of the WAAC for a very short time when all were named as second officers while they waited to transfer to the AMC as commissions become available.

(See Table 1, preceding chapter). Finally, Yu was named a captain and classified as a neuropsychiatrist.

In February of 1944, Yu was posted back to Ft. Des Moines, which she was "sorry to leave, being used to it" when she was reassigned to the ASF Regional Hospital at Camp Crowder, Missouri at the end of the year. Here she was the only woman doctor and she worked exclusively with men patients; but at least she was finally practicing her specialty which more than made up for the difference in leaving Iowa behind. "This part of Missouri is not as cold as Iowa," she confided, "all winter here I never had to use my winter coat. I live in the nurses barracks and they have all been very kind to me...I am given the same privilege and responsibility as the men doctors. I take the duties of O.D. (officer of the day) and sleeping in the regular O.D. room, where, as a rule, only men O.D.s sleep there." It is apparent that she also managed to keep her sense of humor in situations that might have troubled someone else. The first night she was on O.D. duty, a line officer from the camp called and wanted to speak to the medical officer of the day. "So the phone was switched over to me," Yu related. "He asked me twice if I were the medical O.D. and I answered him twice that I was, then there was a silence of unbelief, I guess, for his next question was 'Are you an M.D.?' After I reassured him that I was, he told me his problem."[104] Yu's last station was at Valley Forge GH in Pennsylvania where she was assigned once more to her specialty, psychiatry, before she was discharged in 1948.[105]

Like other women Army doctors, Yu worked at a state institution in postwar years, and she spent about ten years in the same facility. After leaving the service, she accepted a position at Connecticut State Hospital, which underwent several name changes from the General Hospital for the Insane to the Connecticut Hospital for the Insane—and lastly, Connecticut Valley Hospital. In the 1950s, the patient population was over 3,000 when Yu was employed there. As a staff physician, "she had directed the 600-bed continued treatment service known as Weeks Hall... and she was perhaps best known for her intense interest in gardening and her work with patients in this respect." After a short illness, Yu succumbed to cancer 28 July 1958 at the age of fifty-nine. The hospital trustees voted to set aside her garden area "as a memorial to her work with patients in that area."[106]

Two former WWII women medical officers give new meaning to the phrase "Army strong" because they were both alive and in their nineties at the time of this manuscript in the fall of 2011. Dr. Teresa McNeel and Dr. B. Joan Harte (referred to as Bernice in Army records) retired from their private practices many years ago, but they still recall why they joined the AMC. McNeel was an intern who was working with male colleagues who had "shortened" internships so they could enter the Armed Forces as soon as possible, and she wanted to have the same opportunity to serve her country like any of them. Harte said: "I signed up because I was against Hitler and what he stood for." She emphasized the fact that unless you were around at that time you couldn't understand the strong feelings that were aroused in you with the Nazis' rise to power.[107] In several important ways these two women were very much alike: They were patriots; they served as Army neuropsychiatrists, they both practiced their specialty in postwar years, and they have had long productive lives.

Teresa L. McNeel was an only child born 24 December 1918 in Herman, Missouri. She never knew her father who had served in WWI and "died in France of gas gangrene after being struck by shrapnel the night before the Armistice." When she was sixteen years old, she moved to Milwaukee with her widowed mother who worked as a teacher to support them both. She attended St. Mary College in Wisconsin graduating in 1939, and then entered medical school at Marquette University in Milwaukee, Wisconsin, where she received her MD in 1943. Her internship was completed in two phases: She spent three months at St. Mary Hospital in Milwaukee and nine months at Cincinnati General Hospital in Ohio.[108]

At the age of twenty-six she was determined to "join up" but her mother became distraught over the idea because she had already lost one member of the family to war. Nevertheless, McNeel was commissioned 21 June 1944 as a first lieutenant and went for basic training to Lawson General Hospital and then on for special training to the School of Military Neuropsychiatry. Still it did not take her long to realize that Army life had its own rules and regulations. She was housed, for example, in the barracks with the nurses at Lawson. When she was called to the hospital one day for an emergency, she had to rush out of the barracks and leave her bed unmade. As luck would have it, there was an inspection afterwards and she was subsequently "ousted" for not following regulations, and from then on she had to find her own quarters off the base. Some male officers were naturally inquisitive about serving with a woman doctor, and one superior officer even inquired if she had "enough education" to do the job.

At another time during drill practice, the women (seven of whom were doctors) had difficulty with formation and they were "very awkward spreading out in all directions." She remembered exactly what an exasperated sergeant called out: "Stand up straight with your thumbs in line with the seams of you pant—ies!"

After she left Lawson she was sent to Wakeman General Hospital at Camp Atterbury, Indiana, the largest military hospital in the nation during World War II which also specialized in neurosurgery, plastic surgery, and bone reconstruction. When McNeel first reported, the Commanding Officer said to her: "I don't like women doctors and I don't like Catholics, but I think I can get along with you." He was right as she spent six months as a ward officer in neuropsychiatry and four months in tropical diseases with no problems. She also treated men patients exclusively while she was there. Her work also provided her with the opportunity "to see many interesting cases of tropical and contagious diseases, including malaria."

As soon as McNeel was discharged, she chose to use the G.I. Bill to take advanced courses in neuropsychiatry, and while taking classes, she met and married her husband, August Joseph Haschka.

He had also served in the Army during the war and had decided to study medicine on the G.I. Bill as well. In the meantime, she completed a psychiatric residency and then from 1948-51worked as a staff psychiatrist at the Milwaukee County Hospital.[109] In 1951, she acquired her license to practice in California and was also certified by the American Board of Psychiatry and Neurology. From about 1951-1980 she continued to work in various settings in California and engaged in private practice.

While she was working in the late 1970s and early 1980s there was a great deal of controversy going on about the use of certain drugs for patients, specifically laetrile, which was considered an alternative treatment for cancer at that time. McNeel recollected: "I did physical examinations and signed affidavits for patients to receive amygdalin or laetrile from Mexico which supposedly was a cure for cancer. I did not find it to be a cure though it may have been helpful for the patients." In 1980, however, the National Cancer Institute began a study to evaluate the use of laetrile in cancer patients, and they found that while some patients reported they better while taking laetrile, there was no definitive proof that the drug could fight or destroy cancer cells.[110]

By the 1990s, however, it was time for another change and Mc-Neel picked up stakes, moved to Nevada, and was employed in the State Mental Hospital and the Nevada State Prison System until about the early 1990s. After she retired by 2000 she moved back to California and she has been living in Seal Beach, California, ever since.

Bernice Joan Harte was born 18 January 1915 in Waterbury, Connecticut, and records indicate that she was of German descent on her father's side. She graduated from Hunter College in New York with a BA in 1935 and received a BS from Dalhousie (Halifax, Nova Scotia, Canada) the following year. Around this time, however, she knew she wanted to be a psychoanalyst, and she was determined to enter medical school so she could achieve her goal. In 1939 she was admitted to the third-year class at Middlesex University in Massachusetts, and she graduated in 1941, completed an internship at Swedish Hospital, Brooklyn, and was licensed in Massachusetts in July 1941.[111]

Harte, who preferred to sign herself B. Joan, was twenty-eight, single, and claimed Brooklyn as her residence when she volunteered for the Army Medical Corps.[112] In explaining her reason for joining, she said: "I signed up because I was against Hitler and what he stood for, and I felt I wanted to do my part in the war." After her commission, she was sent to the school at Mason General Hospital to get training in neuropsychiatry, and she served at six different hospitals. "I got bounced around quite a bit," she explained, "but after all, it was the Army." In spite of all its rules and regulations, she settled into Army life. "I didn't mind because that is why I joined." She added: "People were very nice to me and I made many good friends. I was usually housed with the nurses although I sometimes lived off base."

Harte also felt she did not experience any bias as a woman doctor in the Army, but she did "run into a WAC officer who seemed jealous." For instance, she recalled, "I once walked past a WAC colonel and did not salute her, so she reported me. When I spoke to the commanding Officer he told me she was a secretary before the war and I was a doctor, and I would return to being a doctor when it was all over, so I shouldn't worry about it."

In her remarks on her Army Questionnaire, Harte noted: "While at Ft. Leonard Wood and Camp Carson, I felt that, while I was not forging ahead in my profession, I was doing a needed job as far as the war effort was concerned. After my transfer to Ft. Des Moines, my special training was of no use and a great deal of my work was paper work and that which could be done by an administrative officer. The rest could have been done by an intern with no special training."[112]

After her discharge, Harte sought a residency at Newberry State Hospital in Michigan, but then it got so cold there she resigned after a year and returned to New York where she worked at the Stony

Lodge Sanitarium in Ossining. From 1947 on she was at the Karen Horney Clinic and she did some teaching, consulting, and lecturing while she also had her own private practice until about 2000.[113] In New York, Karen Horney was first her mentor and then her colleague and they remained friends at the institute of Psychoanalysis until Horney's death. In private practice Harte devoted herself to psychoanalysis and she was a member of the American Academy of Psychoanalysis and the Association for the Advancement of Psychoanalysis. She also traveled around the world speaking about various topics in psychoanalysis, and she went to France, China, Japan, and Bermuda—to mention a few of the places she visited.

In 2000 Harte retired to Clearwater, Florida. She married and divorced in postwar years and has one adopted daughter who lives with her. She continues to be active at age 96 although she had a couple of surgeries on her hips and knees. Harte said that she is a practicing Catholic and attends services every Sunday, but she still finds time to counsel other church members if they seek out her advice.

—⚏—

Many of the characteristics displayed by female neuropsychiatrists were likewise seen in all the women doctors in terms of qualifications and training, age, and marital status. Similar to their male colleagues in the Army Medical Department, all the women, whether specialists or not, had the appropriate credentials and training to work as doctors. Indeed, they had practiced several years and so were out of their twenties which was "a far cry from the teenage college boys who had entered Harvard Medical School during the war."[114] Women neuropsychiatrists also shared other commonalities with the men: Many worked in state institutions before they volunteered, they were sent for further training to the Army's specialized school in neuropsychiatry, and they found their time consumed with duties other than medical. Finally, after the war ended, a few of them went back to work in state institutions like Clyde Adams, Teresa McNeel, and Poe-Eng Yu.

With one exception, the women neuropsychiatrists were single when they volunteered, most likely because they had to be extremely dedicated to pursue a residency and then secure and maintain a position in civilian life. In discussing WACs who served in 1943, however, Campbell contends that 70 percent were single, 15 percent married, and 15 percent divorced, widowed, or separated. She believed this was the case because "wives in general and mothers in particular were not welcome, and no dependency allowances were given for children or for husbands." Women doctors, regardless of specialty, were also often underused, misassigned, or unable to go overseas. Again Campbell noted that the same scenario was also true for WACs, and that such factors further contributed to "low morale".[115]

In looking at the women psychiatrists as a group, two surprising facts emerged. First, what cannot be explained is why roughly one-third of these women were foreign born, although as individuals they all believed the United States had better opportunities for them than they might have had abroad. In any event, four out of the five women would have been living in war torn countries had they remained in their native countries so their decision to emigrate proved to be a sound choice in the end.[116] Secondly, eight of these women doctors, which constitutes fifty percent of the group, went to work in VA facilities in postwar years.

In contrasting the careers of these women with their male colleagues, Army women doctors had to deal with unique situations and circumstances because they were women. They never saw combat, and they were frequently met with suspicion because of their gender. At the same time, they were all volunteers, and they were optimistic that their wartime record would ensure other women "the right for consideration for entrance into the country's finest medical schools and acceptance for training" at war's end—which was a dream that did not become a reality for many more years than any of them could have guessed.[117]

~ NOTES ~

1. The issue is much more complicated than space permits here as there are many more factors that influence a woman's choice of a specialty such as marriage, children, husband's job, household help, length of work day, scheduling, pay, etc.

2. Quotes in Lopate, *Women in Medicine*, 126, 127.

3. Moore, *Restoring the Balance*, 52-56; quote, 111.

4. Trends, *Women in Medicine*, 121. General and Family practice did not appear as a separate specialty in the survey of 1966.

5. Thus, the AMA survey noted that internal medicine moved to first choice followed by pediatrics and family practice appeared for the first time in third position. Obstetrics/gynecology, psychiatry, anesthesiology, and pathology followed next in that order. (Radiology remained in the top ten but moved to ninth place). See "By the Numbers: A look at Physician Characteristics", *Women in Health Sciences*, Washington University in the St. Louis School of Medicine, Bernard Becker Medical Library Digital Coll.

6. "Speech of Dr. Margaret Craighill at the Luncheon for the 94th Commencement of the Woman's Medical College of Pennsylvania 16 March, 1944", speech, MDC Coll., Box 10.

7. *Neuropsychiatry in World War II*, Vol. 1 (Office of the Surgeon General, Dept. of the Army: Washington, DC, 1966), 42; Chief, 41; total officers, 46. Many of these doctors were referred to as "90-day wonders" as they were mostly young doctors who volunteered for or were assigned to an intensive 90-day course after which they were reclassified as psychiatrists.

8. Peck strength, *Personnel in World War II*, 14.

9. The number fourteen for those with a primary classification in neuropsychiatry is found in Craighill's records, but number may vary depending on when the count was taken.

10. Male doctors in McMinn, *Personnel in World War II*, 290.

11. Classification system, *Personnel in World War II*, 271.

12. *Neuropsychiatry in World War II*, 44.

13. See Questionnaires for Thomas, Bremner, and Shirlock, Box 30, MDC Coll.

14. NP school and first class: *Neuropsychiatry in World War II*, 43. Mason General Hospital consisted of the buildings that comprised Edgewood State Hospital as well as three buildings from Pilgrim State Hospital and other temporary buildings that were established during the war.

15. Basic training: "Women Medical Officers, AUS," Histories, Box 29. Also see Lt. Col. Craighill's "Memorandum for Director, Historical Division: (Subject) Logistics of World War II, 26 September 1945, Official Correspondence: Memorandums from the Women's Health and Welfare Unit, Box 3, MDC Coll.

16. Bryan to family, two letters, 16 May 1944; from a private collection of Bryan family letters. The author is grateful to Dr. Bryan's niece, Lynn Swenson (known as Elizabeth Lynn Bryan II) who supplied the letters and gave permission to quote freely from them; hereafter referred to as Bryan family letters.

17. Training noted on their Questionnaires submitted to Craighill. Foreign born: "Craighill to Brig. General William L. Sheep, 7 July 1944," letter, Histories, Box 29, MDC Coll.

18. See McGregor Questionnaire, Box 30, MDC Coll. Also see *Neuropsychiatry in World War II*, 43.

19. Quote in Kempker questionnaire, Box 30; also see DUCM Archives & Special Coll. which has a brief clipping, "In Memoriam" for Deceased Alumnae 1991-92. Her thesis from the WMCP was entitled, "A Study of Cases of Intracranial Hemorrhage in the Newborn from the Standpoint of Their Prevention." Also see *Bio. Dir. APA*, 1968 ed., 372.

20. See Questionnaire for Harte, Box 30, MDC Coll.

21. See Bryan Questionnaire, Ibid.

22. Rost entry in *Bio. Dir.*, 1977 ed., 1132. Records note that she was living in Chicago, Illinois when she was twenty-one, so it appears that she left Germany, came to the USA and then went back to Europe for extensive medical studies. Her father was listed as being born in America. See Fourteenth Census of the United States, 1920, Records of the Bureau of the Census, RG 29, NARA microfilm T625, NARA, Washington, DC. Reference to work at the Sanitarium in "Ambulance and Car Collide" and Dr. Alice Rost is slightly injured, *Kingston Daily Freeman*, Kingston, New York, 19 January 1939. Rost received her Diploma in N & P, Archives of Neurology and Psychiatry, 1940: 43(2): 423-424. She also had a brother who was a physician and practiced in New York, and it was probably because of him and his family that she left Europe. The *Kingston Daily Freeman*, Kingston, New York, 15 January 1944. Quote and duty stations listed as Lawson General Hospital, Ft. Oglethorpe Station Hospital HQ 2nd Service Command, and Mason General

Hospital in Rost Questionnaire, Box 30, MDC Coll. Army historian Campbell quote in "The Regimented Women of WWII", 118.

23. "Testimony of Capt. Alice E. Rost, ANC,"Taken at Ft. Oglethorpe, Georgia on 26 June 2944, by Lieut. Col. Birge Holt, IGD " (declassified document 735033), RG 159, entry 26f, box 17, National Archives, MD. Rost was not in the ANC as noted, however, but the AMC. For more on Rost testimony, see Berube, Allan, *Coming Out Under Fire: The History of Gay Men and Women in World War Two* (New York: the Free Press, 1990), 170; and Hampf, M. Michaela, *Release a Man for Combat: The Women's Army Corps during WWII*, (Koln; Weimar Wien: Bohlau, 2010), 267-68.

24. The American Academy of Forensic Sciences is a multi-disciplinary professional organization that provides leadership to advance science and its application to the legal system. Quote on discharge in Rost Questionnaire; VA position noted in "Club News", The *Kingston Daily Freeman*, Kingston, New York, 13 May 1946. See Rost Social Security Death Index.

25. Koppel biographical information in *Biographical Directory: Fellows and Members of the American Psychiatric Association* (New York & London: R.R. Bowker, 1977), 721; hereinafter referred to as *Bio. Dir. APA*. Also see membership file, New York Psychoanalytic Institute (NYPSI), New York, thanks to Dr. Nellie L. Thompson, curator for providing information.

26. She emigrated 1 April 1938, Passenger and Crew Lists of Vessels Arriving at New York, NY 1897-1957; NARA Microfilm Publication T715; Records of the Immigration and Naturalization Service, NARA, Washington DC. Hospital quote: "Gerda's Long Quest for the Truth: Who Sent My Family to Their Deaths?" *The Independent*, 17 July, 2011, independent.co.uk (Email newsletter). Also see Index to Petitions for Naturalization Filed in Federal, State, and Local Courts located in New York City, 1792-1989, NARA, Northeast Region.

27. Station assignments on Koppel's Questionnaire, Box 30, MDC Coll. "Bushnell Has Two Women Doctors, *Box Elder News Journal* (BENJ), 13 October 1943 [in Brigham City, Utah]. Overseas: "Women Physicians in the Army of the United States," *Women in Medicine*, 90 (October 1945), 9. Japan service for 1945-46 noted in her membership file/listing provided by NYPSY, New York; also see *New York Times*, 24 November 1945 article supplied by WIMSA, which indicates she arrived in Japan with Capt. Mae Josephine O'Donnell. The adjusted service rating (ASR) score was based on a point system whereby a soldier was awarded points for months of service, overseas duty, and other factors. The higher the score the higher the probability of being sent home for demobilization and discharge. Campbell quote, "The Regimented Women of WWII", 118.

28. Koppel in postwar: Jewish Board of Family and Children's Services today: "The JBFCS Story: Our History," *JBFCS Report Newsletter*, Home page online: http://www.jbfcs.org/about/agency-history. Koppel Obituary, *JAMA*, 1985; 253(6):869-874. Information on training at NYPSI from AA Brill Library/NYPSI, Archives Sp. Coll., New York, NY.

29. Quote in *Personnel in World War II*, 289; see Walters and Bryan Questionnaires, MDC Coll.

30. Bryan quote in her Questionnaire, Ibid.

31. State institutions and men, *Neuropsychiatry in World War II, 49*.

32. Morantz-Sanchez, *Sympathy and Science*, 155.

33. Shirlock's married name was Foery; See a small head shot about her commission in the *Philadelphia Evening Bulletin*, 31 August, 1943. Information provided by Alex Miller, DUSM Archives & Special Coll.

34. *Neuropsychiatry in World War II*, 53.

35. Bremner Questionnaire, Box 30; Harte, letter attached to her Questionnaire, Box 30, MDC Coll.

36. Adams Questionnaire, Box 30, MDC Coll.

37. Koppel's Questionnaire, Ibid.

38. Hurianek's information in Social Security Death Index; New York Passenger Lists, 1820-1957; *JAMA*, Vol. 235. No. 26, 28 June 1976, p. 2348. At Darnall: *The Medical Department: Hospitalization and Evacuation, Zone of Interior, United States Army in World War II* (Washington, D.C.: Office of the Chief of Military History, Depart. of the Army, 1956), 73. Also see "Neuropsychiatric activities at Darnall General Hospital," *Mil. Surg.*, May 1948; 102(5): 365-73. Thanks to Arizona State Library, Archives and Public Records, with locating and providing information on Hurianek.

39. "Psychiatrist Follows Own Advice with Sunny Attitude Toward Life," Unidentified Sun City, Arizona, newspaper clipping, 4 August 1971, supplied by DUCM Archives and Special Coll.

40. Quotes from Hurianek Questionnaire, Box 30, MDC Coll.

41. Quotes from "Psychiatrist Follows Own Advice."

42. Internal medicine and married women quotes, "Psychiatrist Follows Own Advice," marriage quotes from "The WMCP Alumnae Questionnaire, 25 July 1960", DUCM Archives and Special Coll. More points out that even today the greatest

obstacle still facing women practitioners is "the need to accommodate the demands of childbearing and child rearing", in *Restoring the Balance*, 248.

43. Initially the hospital was going to be known as the Ogdensburg State Asylum for the Insane, but the name was changed to the St. Lawrence State Hospital before the first patient was admitted in December of 1890. It was based on the cottage plan, and it was a self-supporting community that produced its own food. It was also progressive in having an occupational therapy program for its patients in 1908. In the late 1970's, it was re-christened the St. Lawrence Psychiatric Center. For more, see *History of St. Lawrence State Hospital* (New York: St. Lawrence County Historical Assoc., December 1965); *St. Lawrence State Hospital* (New York: The State of New York Department of Mental Hygiene, 1954).

44. See Hurianek Questionnaire where she writes "No!" in response to getting an allowance for dependent son and underlines the word twice in addition to the exclamation mark.

45. Integration Act and barriers, Holm, 119. Also see Morden, *The Women's Army Corps*, 56.

46. Information provided in "Questionnaire of the Alumnae Association of the WMCP, 9 April 1953" and "The WMCP Alumnae Questionnaire, 25 July 1960."

47. Death notice also provided by DUCM with a notation that they received the news of Hurianek's death by telephone from her son in California.

48. She spelled her name de Aguiar on her Questionnaire, although Craighill referred to her as D'Aguiar, Box 30, MDC Coll. Also see "Women Physicians in the Army of the United States," *Women in Medicine*, 90 (October 1945), 9.

49. Birth and death in Social Security Index. Arrival in "List or Manifest of Alien Passengers for the United States, 1 December 1925", Records of the U.S. Customs Service, RG 36, NARA Microfilm Publication T715, Roll T715_3766, Line 3, p. 72; U.S. Naturalization Record Index 1794-1995. She listed her occupation as "physician". Because her name was spelled various ways (D'Aguiar and Deaguiar) it was difficult to track her records. Apparently she traveled back and forth to Portugal as there is another sailing entry for her in 1932. Also see De Aguiar, *Biographical Dictionary: Fellows and Members of the Amer. Psychiatric Assoc.*, 1977 ed. (New York: R. R. Bowker, 1977), 295.

50. Position in Rome State School in "Changes in the Personnel of the Medical Service", Psychiatric Quarterly, Vol. 4, No. 1, 1929; Vol. 6, Supplement 1, 1932. At Wrentham: *The New England Journal of Medicine*, 24 October 1940, 688. In the mid-1940s, the Wrentham School was one of several state schools in Massachusetts involved in a scandal related to the government-sanctioned practice of put-

ting fluoride in the drinking water of school-age patients without their knowledge. Trustees at Wrentham voted in 1954 to stop this practice as there was growing concern in regard to receiving a toxic overdose. See Statement of Miss Florence Birmingham, President, Massachusetts Women's Political Club, Boston, Massachusetts, in "Fluoridation of Water", Hearings before the Committee on Interstate and Foreign Commerce. House of Representatives, 83rd Congress, 2nd session, May 1954, p.45. This practice would have occurred while de Aguiar was working at Wrentham.

51. Hospitals, Records of the Office of The Surgeon General, Record Group (RG) 112.5.15, Records of miscellaneous hospitals and medical facilities, NARA, Washington, D.C.

52. All quotes from de Aguiar Questionnaire, Box 30, MDC Coll. Also see *Bio. Dir. AMA*, 1968 ed., 157.

53. Raven's observation "hocus pocus": Lt. Col. Clara Raven, MC, USAR, "Achievements of Women in Medicine, Past and Present—Women in the Medial Corps of the Army," *Military Medicine*, February 1960, 110. Raven served with de Aguiar in Japan as a pathologist.

54. See Henry M. Hurd, MD, ed, *The Institutional Care of the Insane in the United States and Canada*, Vol. 2 (Baltimore, MD: Johns Hopkins Press, 1916), 718. There had also been a long period starting in the 1880s when senior students from the Boston University School of Medicine went there for a course of clinical instruction in mental diseases.

55. Social Security Index for de Aguiar.

56. Mention of Thomas is made in four sources: *Who's Who in the West*, 20*th*, 21*st*, 22*nd* Editions; *Who's Who in the World*, 8*th* Edition; *Who's Who of American Women*, 15*th* Edition. Also see Bio. Dir. APA, 1968 ed., 719. Thanks to USC, Archives and Manuscripts, Doheny Memorial Library, for supplying biographical information on Thomas.

57. Assignments noted in Thomas Questionnaire, Box 30, MDC Coll.

58. Quotes from Thomas Questionnaire, Ibid.

59. Majors in "Women Medical Officers, AUS", Histories, Box 29, MDC Coll.

60. Sick leave quote in her Questionnaire, Box 30, MDC Coll. Thomas indicated that two other women doctors (Lt. Virginia L. Wright, Capt. Dorothy Scarborough) in the VA Service become ill in the line of duty, both while assigned to the Tuberculosis Service. She was implying that due to the overwork at the VA Facilities, the women were prone to becoming sick or succumbing to other illnesses.

61. Thomas as staff psychiatrist: California State Hospital System 1937-42, Glenside Sanitarium 1943-44.

62. Other positions included: Directors of psychiatry, Mississippi State Hospital, Jackson, 1955; Stark County Guidance Center, Canton, Ohio, 1956-58; Huron County Guidance Center, Norwalk, Ohio 1958-61; Arrowhead Mental Health Center, San Bernardino, California, 1962-64; Mendocino County Mental Health Services, 1964-65; Tuolumne County Mental Health Services, Sonora, California, 1966-1970; Emanuel Hospital Mental Health Center, Turlock California, 1970-71.

63. Thomas Social Security Death Index. She had listed widow on her Army Questionnaire, but her former name and length of marriage could not be determined at this point.

64. Nersessian in "War Service," *MWJ*, February 1945, 39. Because the Army referred to her as Aznive, it was difficult to locate information about her until it was learned she called herself by another first name.

65. Immigration from Armenia: "Fourteenth Census of the United States, 1920, Records of the Bureau of the Census," (NARA microfilm pub. T625) RG 29, NARA, Washington, D.C. Graduation, *New England Journal of Medicine* 20 February 1975, 292: 425-26. Birth and death, Social Security Death Index. For occupational history, see *Bio. Dir. APA*, 1968 ed., 518.

66. Foxborough State Hospital: "Annual Report of the Commissioner of Mental Diseases for Year Ending 1936—37", *Massachusetts Department of Mental Diseases*, Vol 1, 1936-37, 118-120. This institution is closed today like so many of the other state facilities which were overhauled starting in the 1960s.

67. Private practice listing, *New England Journal of Medicine*, December 1940, 223:999-1000.

68. Nersessian: Obituary, *New England Journal of Medicine*, February 1975, 292:425-426.

69. Obituary for Nersessian, JAMA, 12 May, 1975, 232 (6):666. Alumni records note her estate made a bequest to Temple following her death; Bequests: Temple University's Online Community, 2011.

70. Bremner Questionnaire, Box 30, MDC Coll. Records do not list her previous married name, but her birthdate was determined to be 27 January 1910.

71. Bremner: "Columbia Briefs", *The Chronicle Telegram*, Elyria, Ohio, 9 July 1935. When the hospital was built in 1898, it only took male patients, but women were accepted around the turn of the century. Like many of the other early asylums, it was built on the cottage plan.

72. Bremner Questionnaire, Box 30, MDC Coll.

73. Belmont, Herman S., Mitchell Dratman, Elizabeth Bremner Kaplan, et al., *A Handbook of Child Psychoanalysis* (NY: Basic books, 1968). Also see Elizabeth B. Kaplan: "Reflections Regarding Psychomotor Activities during the Latency Period," Psychoanalytic Study of the Child, 1965, 20:220-238; and "Manifestations of Aggression in Latency and Preadolescent Girls," *The Psychoanalytic Quarterly*, 1979, 48:523, 63-78.

74. Bremner marriage: This was also a second marriage for Dr. Albert J. Kaplan and he married a third time after Elizabeth died in 1981.

75. Social Security Death Index lists her as Elizabeth Kaplan and notes she died November 1981; also noted in *Bulletin of the American Psychoanalytic Association*, Vol. 38 No. 1, December 1981. Quote from "In Memoriam Albert J. Kaplan, MD," *Journal of the Violin Society of America*, 1981, Vol. 6, Issue 3, 112.

76. "Shirlock Commissioned," *Philadelphia Evening Bulletin*, 31 August 1943. She graduated from the WMCP in 1927 and her thesis was entitled: "The History and Control of Small Pox." Thanks to DUCM for supplying biographical information from their alumnae files. Also see WIMSA brief biographical file.

77. Vineland State School was built in 1888 and alternately referred to as The Training School at Vineland. It started accepting "feeble-minded" boys to train them on a state farm so they could learn skills that would support them outside the institution. (It is now demolished). Shirlock's contributions are mentioned in Chapter 17 on the feeble-minded child, Doll, Edgar A., *Manual of Child Psychology* (Hoboken, NJ: John Wiley & Sons Inc., 1946). She was also one of several authors in various published studies on mental deficiency in the 1940s, all associated with the Vineland School.

78. Duty station and quotes from Shirlock Questionnaire, Box 30, MDC Coll.

79. See "In Memoriam", Medical Women's International Assoc., Report of the XXVth Congress, Sydney, Australia, 19*th*-23*rd* April 2001, No. 37, May 2002; Shirlock: Social Security Death Index. Also see "Find a Grave Memorial" for Margaret S. Foery, on-line.

80. Biographical information on Adams in her vertical file and from article, "Native on Staff of Hospital," *Daily Sentinel*, 21 May 1962, East Texas Research Center, Stephen F. Austin State University, Nacogdoches, Texas.

81. After 1 September 1943 when the WAC became an integral part of the Army of the United States, WAC officers and warrant officers had to buy their own military clothing, initially using a one-time uniform allowance given them by the Army,

but enlisted women continued to receive their uniforms free; Morden, Betty J., *The Women's Army Corps 1945-1978* (Washington, DC: Center for Military History, 2000), 437. Quote regarding Adams in "Dr. Elizabeth L. Bryan to Mother and Father, 25 May 1944", Bryan family letters.

82. Quotes from Adams Questionnaire, Box 30, MDC Coll.

83. Work places in directories for the various years listed by The Texas State Board of Medical Examiners with a summary provided by Betsy Tyson, archivist and exhibits coordinator, Texas Medical Association, Austin, Texas. Also see *Bio. Dir. APA,* 1968 ed., 4.

84. Description and quotes in *Journal of the House of Representative of the Regular Session of the Fifty-third Legislature of the State of Texas, Austin,* 13 January 1953. Also see The Texas Department of State Health Services, State Hospitals: on line dshs. state.tx.us/mhhospitals/rusksh/rsh_about.shtm.

85. "Three Are suspended At Rusk Hospital Pending State Probe," *The Rusk Cherokeean* (Rusk, Texas), Vol. 106, No.22, 26 November 1953.

86. Hospital quotes, "Native On Staff of Hospital." *Daily Sentinel,* 21 May 1962.

87. "Obituary: Dr. Clyde Adams", *The Daily Sentinel,* 23 November 1986.

88. While there was no biographical file for Bryan, there was a student record from 1925 with sparse information, supplied by Alan Mason Chesney Medical Archives, Johns Hopkins. Birthdate and death from Social Security Death Index.

89. Occupational information supplied by Elizabeth Lynn Bryan II, and the Bryan family letters. The Bryans were a close-knit family and they circulated the "sister letters" to update everyone about what was going on. Fortunately relatives kept the letters which included the ones that Bess wrote from March 1943 to October 1944. Quotes from Bryan family letters, 20 April 1944; 12 May 1944. IJR had formerly been known as the Cook County Juvenile Psychopathic Institute. In 1917 it began to serve as a research center and to coordinate statewide activity in child guidance and delinquency prevention. For records regarding IJR, see Illinois State Archives, Office of the Secretary of State. Her work history is from *Bio. Directory APA,* 1968 ed., 93. That directory gives her birthdate as 17 December 1998 rather than 1 December as noted in the family letters.

90. Dr. Bryan's Account, 12 May 1944, Bryan family letters.

91. Dr. Bryan's account, 25, May 1944 and 20 June, 1944, Bryan Family Letters. Ramos was a lieutenant who had graduated from the medical school at Tulane and her specialty was orthopedics.

92. Dr. Bryan's account 1 October 1944, Bryan Family Letters.

93. Quotes from Bryan Questionnaire, Box 30, MDC Coll.

94. Final days and death: From the account of Elizabeth Lynn Bryan II and Velma's accounts, Bryan Family Letters.

95. Thanks to the University of Pennsylvania Archives and Vassar College Special Coll. for providing biographical information for Walters. Also see "Association News" The Sixty-third Annual Meeting of the American Public Health Assoc., *American Journal of Public Health*, 1934. Her birthdate is noted in her handwritten record for the "Alumni Folder: Biographical Files," University of Pennsylvania, Philadelphia, 26 September 1936; also see their copy of "News Release" (undated) from the Public Relation Office, Ft. Des Moines, Iowa, 7 November 1944 for Walters which summarizes her various career choices. For Norristown State Hospital, see the Pennsylvania State Archives, RG 23, Records of the Department of Public Welfare; there are a series of annual reports dating back to 1902. Walters photo courtesy of the University of Pennsylvania Archives.

96. Major Craighill to Dr. Mary Jane Walters, 13 October 1943, letter, Official Correspondence, Women Medical Officers, Box 5, MDC Coll. Walters was a member of the Philadelphia Pediatric Society, New York State Medical Society, American Public Health Association, and Fellow of the AMA, and she was Board certified in Neurology and Psychiatry.

97. See Michael Glenn, "O'Reilly General Hospital of Springfield, Missouri: A Brief Introduction", Springfield-Greene County Library District, on-line. For Schick GH, see "91st General Hospital Unit History," WWII US Medical History Centre, on-line. Duty stations and quotes from Walters Questionnaire, Box 30, MDC Coll.

98. "Letter of Katharine H. Walters, 10 May 1947", handwritten, supplied by Vassar Special Collections from her alumni file. Also see Walters's obituary, "Deaths", *JAMA* 24 May 1947, 390.

99. There was no Questionnaire available for Olentine in Craighill's files. Olentine is discussed briefly in "Uniforms for Women Staff Corps Officers," *MWJ*, October 1943; biography also in "St. Anthony Hospital's 2006 Report to the Community", as she made a bequest to the hospital upon her death. Duty stations are noted as part of the "Status of Women Commissioned in AMC as of 1 September 1945," Histories, Box 29, MDC Coll; Darnall service is noted in *Women in Medicine*, 90 (October 1945) where is also referred to specifically as a neuropsychiatrist, p.9.

100. Also see Social Security Death Index for Olentine. Thanks to Nathalie Wheaton, assistant archivist, Rush Univ. Med. Ctr. Archives, Chicago, Illinois, for providing notes and picture.

101. Poe-Eng YU in the *MWJ*, September 1943, 233. Her master's thesis in May 1934 at the University of California was: "A Personality Study of Two Groups of Psychotics." Biographical information summarized from necrology file supplied by the Office of Alumni Records, University of Michigan, Bentley Historical Library (BHL). She was also the sister-in-law of Lin Yu-Tang, famous Chinese philosopher.

102. Poe-Eng Yu to Major Craighill, 20 February 1945, letter, Box 1, Personal Papers, MDC Coll. Oppression quote in "Chinese Physician Captain in WACs," *Oswego, NY Palladium-Times*, 8 February 1945; glad quote noted in Yu's alumni record, both provided by BHL, University of Michigan.

103. Quote from "Women Contract Surgeons in World War II," Box 29, Histories, MDC Coll. The other medical officers waiting with her were: Drs. Gutman, Garber, and Hayden. Dr. Janeway, who had also been a contract surgeon at Ft. Des Moines, had already sailed with the first WAAC Contingent to North Africa in January of 1943.

104. Quotes in Yu to Craighill, in preceding note #102.

105. See Yu's file, Historical files, Women's Memorial Foundation (WIMSA), Arlington, Va.

106. Quotes from "Garden Area at Hospital to Honor Dr. Yu," *The Hartford Coronet*, 31 October 1958, 81. Also see obituary "Dr. Poe-Eng Yu, 61, Dies; Native of China," *The Hartford Coronet*, 29 July 1958, 4.

107. Phone Interviews were conducted with Drs. McNeel and Harte, August 2011.

108. All information from McNeel's phone interviews August 2011 and written transcripts she provided. Quotes are from interviews unless indicated otherwise. Occupational history, *Bio. Dir. APA*, 1968 ed.

109. The Milwaukee Country Hospital was known then as the Milwaukee County Hospital for the Insane.

110. Laetrile is a chemically modified form of a compound called amygdalin which is found in the pits of many fruits, raw nuts and plants. The freedom to use laetrile became a civil rights issue as many felt the government did not have the right later to forbid its use. Interstate shipment of laetrile was later banned. H. Tristram Engelhardt Jr. and Arthur L. Caplan, *Scientific Controversies: Case Studies in the Resolution and Closure of Disputes in Science and Technology* (Cambridge & New York: Cambridge University Press, 1984); S. L. Nightingale, "Laetrile: The Regulatory Challenge of an Unproven Remedy, *Public Health Report* 1984 July-August,

99(4): 333-38, PMCID: PMC 1424606; Rutherford v. United States, 424 F Supp. (W.D. Okla. 1977); "Illegal Laetrile" [Editorial], *The New York Times*, July 29, 1975.

111. Biographical information was provided by Brandeis University Archives, as records from Middlesex University were transferred there in the past. Quotes are from oral interviews conducted with Dr. B. Joan Harte in August 2011.

112. See her entry, *Bio. Dir. APA*, 1968 ed.

113. Harte Questionnaire, Box 30, MDC Coll.

114. Quote in Walsh, *Doctors Wanted: No Women Need Apply*, 233.

115. See Campbell, *Women and War with America: Private Lives in a Patriotic Era* (Cambridge, Mass.: Harvard University Press, 1984), quotes 23 and 35.

116. Only de Aguiar came from a Spanish state which remained non-belligerent throughout World War II; Poe-Eng Yu was from China, Nersessian from Armenia, and Koppel and Rost were from Germany.

117. Quote in Walsh, *Doctors Wanted: No Women Need Apply*, 234. Such optimism seemed justified at first, but Walsh pointed out is was short-lived as one year after the war a number of women interns and residents were removed from hospital staffs to make room for the veterans who were returning.

Table 2.
WWII Women Army Neuropsychiatrists

Name	Age/Rank at Appt.	Medical School
Clyde Adams	42, Capt.	Texas
Elizabeth C. Bremner	34, Lt.	Ohio State
Elizabeth L. Bryan	46, Capt.	Johns Hopkins
Alcinda Pereira de Aguiar*	45, Lt. to Capt.	Oponto University
Bernice Joan Harte	28, Lt. to Capt.	Middlesex (Mass.)
Zdenka Hurianek	42, Capt.	WMCP
Adele C. Kempker	40, Capt.	WMCP
Hilde G. Koppel*	31, Lt. to Capt.	University of Bern, Switzerland
Teresa McNeel	26, Lt.	Marquette
Aznive Nersessian*	41, Capt.	Temple
Julie E. Olentine	28, Lt.	Rush
Alice E. Rost*	45, Capt.	Breslau
Margaret E. Shirlock**	44, Capt.	WMCP
Grace Fern Thomas	47, Capt.	Southern California
Mary J. Walters	50, Capt.	Pennsylvania
Poe-Eng Yu*	35, Capt.	Michigan

Note: Craighill said there were 14 women with a primary classification of NP; she might not have had the total count depending on the date the count was taken.

*Designates the woman was born in another country.

**Dr. Margaret E. Shirlock had dual classifications in Gen. Duty (primary) and neuropsychiatry.

***Name in bold indicates work in a VA facility in postwar years.

MERCEDES GRAF

CHAPTER FOUR:

"Specialization as a Mark of Expertise": Women Doctors in Internal Medicine, Pathology, Anesthesiology, and Orthopedics

The specialty in internal medicine seemed to be a natural extension of the medical role for women, and its development went hand-in-hand with the story of female physicians during the beginning of the twentieth century. Women doctors had been used to fighting for what they wanted and early on they demonstrated this by embracing public health initiatives such as maternal and child care, hygiene, and the prevention of venereal disease—thus craving out their role as patient advocate. During this time, the definition of internal medicine as a specialty was constantly being redefined because of changing professional standards, the growth of professional organizations, and the emergence of modern "scientific" medicine. As the emphasis on specialties increased, the field of internal medicine offered the most promise to women as it provided training at an advanced level on primary care issues.

One medical historian maintained that internal medicine cannot be considered to attract women through either its "feminine image" or its possibilities for scheduling their time. It is, after all, a highly competitive and very demanding specialty which requires Board certification with the usual length of time being three year for residency training. As late as 1987, for example, Duke University Medical School has had an active women's committee in its Department of Medicine which addresses issues such as maternity leave, child care, professional development, mentoring, and other concerns related to maintaining the balance between home life and work for women internists. This, of course, is true for other fields where women choose to specialize even today.

The Internists

Eight women medical officers were classified as internists during WWII making this specialty the second most popular one for women medical officers after neuropsychiatry, although there were many more women officers serving as General Duty Officers. One possible explanation is that "with the disappearance of the general practitioner, specialists in internal medicine have taken over much of their work in addition to the regular specialty practice." Since internists, then, could also be assigned to general duties as ward or dispensary officers, the Army needed them.[1]

Of the eight women internists in the AMC, one was divorced and six were single that we know of for sure (one woman did not list her status), and four of them managed to get shipped overseas: Drs. Connor, Janeway, Loizeaux, and O'Donnell. Although women internists constituted a narrow group within the medical officers, one commonality existed—all of them performed ward/dispensary duties at various times in addition to working in their specialty. This was also true for Dr. Marion Loizeaux (discussed in Chapter Two), who was assigned as special medical consultant to the ETO. One odd fact was that half the women internists claimed mothers as dependents. Three women who specialized in internal medicine, Angie Connor, Jean Henley, and Margaret Janeway are profiled in detail here, but since less information was available about the others, they are only discussed briefly. (See Table 4).

Angie Connor was born 24 November 1912 and lived in Marsh-field, Wisconsin. When she decided to study medicine, she left the state to attend the Woman's Medical College of Pennsylvania (WMCP). Determined to get her degree in spite of her lack of money, she did what many of the pioneer women doctors had done before her—she supplemented her funds with outside work. Thus, she started to cook for a faculty member, recalling that "students seemed always pressed by work and sometimes hungry."[2] Connor graduated in 1937 and in July of 1940, she accepted a six-month appointment to the staff of Grenfell Missions, a medical and religious mission, in Labrador, Canada, where she was to be in charge of one of the hospitals there at Harrington. No sooner had she finished her appointment when the American troop ship *Edmund B. Alexander*, arrived at the capital, St. John's, with the first American troops in January 1941.[3] It is not clear how long she stayed in Labrador or what she did right after this, but it is reported that she was next "in New Guinea", probably at another missionary station, before she volunteered with the Army Medical Corps in 1944.[4]

Connor was thirty-one years of age when she was commissioned a lieutenant, and she listed herself as divorced on her Army Questionnaire. Early in her career, she had displayed an interest in childhood illness and she was able to capitalize on this in the service because she wrote: "At every station except Fort Oglethorpe, Georgia, I was given a choice as to wards and when Pediatrics or Contagious Wards were available I received them. If I desired Male Medical Wards, all I had to do was ask and they were given to me." At the various stations, she worked in Dispensary Service "exclusively women" about four months, "male patients exclusively" five months, and the rest of her time was given over to "mixed" work.[5]

Like many Army doctors, she did not complain about her quarters, but simply pointed out that she was frequently housed with the nurses—a common enough practice when it came to women doctors. Lt. Elizabeth Khayat, an Army pathologist, believed this was the case because "the female officers are too few to have separate quarters and they are sometimes the only one at a time in general hospital." Housing problems, however, produced mixed feelings in other doctors. Lt. Martha Crandall, a recent graduate from the University of the Indiana Medical School who was assigned duty in contagious diseases, believed that while housing was generally satisfactory, her present barracks assignment was "the poorest" she had had. "During the 13 months that I have been here," she said, "I have been personally responsible for the care and cleanliness of my room despite the fact that $5 is paid monthly to the Nurses fund for maid service." Lt. Anna Patton (later Russell), a graduate of the WMCP assigned to general duty, stated bluntly that the camp at Fort Oglethorpe "lacked adequate quarters" for women medical officers. Thus, accommodations varied greatly depending on the assignment; and nowhere was this more evident than overseas. Lt. Evira C. Seno, for example was quartered with nurses in tents in a Redeployment area in France; while at the other extreme, women medical officers were generally content when they were housed with WAC officers, allotted "Quarters" allowances or, in one instance, even provided with a three-room house on the post.[6]

In June of 1944, Connor was not concerned in the least with her quarters as she was posted to the 120th General Hospital at Santo Tomas, Manila. She "served on a hospital ship off Corregidor [and] went into Manila shortly after our troops and started work under adverse circumstances." On one occasion, a bomb landed close to her, but fortunately "it was a dud."[7] In March of 1945 she was promoted to captain, and she was functioning as Chief of the Contagious Disease Section at the 120th General Hospital. At the same time, the WACs had reached Manila in the same month where the working conditions were deplorable for both men and women who, nevertheless, stayed until they left under demobilization rules in December 1945. Connor found herself working long hours given the extremely high medical evacuation rates in Manila for WACs. One military historian observed: "It was ...something less than a happy experience for the women involved." In her remarks on her Army Questionnaire, however, Connor simply said: "I have been well treated in all my assignments by Chiefs of service, Commanding offices, and fellow medical officers."[8]

The 1950s found Angie Connor living in Hawaii. She had acquired a great deal of experience in childhood illnesses and contagious diseases through her missionary duties and her Army work, and she knew she was ready to set up her own practice as a pediatrician. On top of this, she completed a Master's Degree in Public Health. Among her accomplishments, she became Chief of the Bureau of Maternal and Child Health and Crippled Children's Services in Honolulu, found time to work in the Psychology Department at the University of Hawaii, published several articles on child and family concerns, and wrote a chapter for a medical book.[9] When she died at the age of 94 on 2 August 2007, money from her estate went to Planned Parenthood of Hawaii.

Aurelia Rozov, who was born 16 May 1904, is the only internist in this group who was born abroad. She graduated from Komensky University Medical School in Czechoslovakia in 1929, came to the United States sometime in the 1930s, and was licensed in New York in 1941, later becoming Board certified in Internal Medicine.[10] She was commissioned a lieutenant 25 April 1944 and classified as an internist and a cardiologist.

According to her Army record, she had several assignments as a ward officer, ward surgeon on a cardio-vascular-renal section, and as an instructor and supervisor at the Enlisted Women Medical Technicians School, 3d WAC Training Center, Fort Oglethorpe, Georgia. In July of 1945 Rozov was even sent to the Army School of Tropical Medicine in Washington DC for specialized training.[11] In regard to her assignment as an instructor, however, she observed: "From March 1945 until end of June 1945, I was... [the] supervising medical officer in charge of the 5*th* week of training, consisting of orthopedic nursing and orthopedic technical procedures. With regard to the fact that as an Internist I did not see this type of work the last 15 years, I felt I was of no use to the war effort and my time as medical officer was wasted, as there were 4 very competent sergeants and 2 nurses in charge of the 13 instructors of this section."

When Rozov considered her experiences overall in the Army, she was convinced that she had good relations with patients, nurses, and other medical officers. The only time she encountered any difficulty was with one Chief of the Medical Section "who did not seem to have much use for women in the profession." She attributed this to the fact that she "was the first woman medical officer on duty at that installation." After she left that post, however, she learned: "I was given a N.S. (not satisfactory) rating throughout the 9 months tour of duty, while I have been convinced I was excellent at Battery General Hospital" in Rome, Georgia.

After the war, Rozov returned home and became a life member of the American College of Physicians in 1951. She was active in the New York County Medical Society, the American Society of Tropical Medicine, and the American Heart Association. In 1983 she was listed as being on the staff of the New York University School of Medicine. She passed away 8 May 1993.[12]

Like Rozov, the next woman doctor also learned that the Army did not have much use for women in certain situations. In addition to this, she was one of the few female Army doctors to grow up and attend medical school in the South. Gertrude R. Holmes was born 27 February 1903 in South Carolina, and she lived in Greenville, South Carolina, when she volunteered.[13] She graduated magna cum laude, was a member of Phi Beta Kappa from the University of South Carolina, and was also a graduate of the medical school there at Charleston. She interned at Warren Chandler Hospital in Savannah, which was Georgia's oldest hospital, and then went on to the University of Pennsylvania to study diagnostic radiology and allergies.

After commissioning 16 March 1944, she was appointed a captain at the age of forty-two. She claimed her mother as a dependent and later received a dependency allowance for her. She was classified in two specialties: as an internist and as a gastroenterologist. Holmes assumed a variety of assignments, not always in keeping with her specialty: as an assistant ward officer in an allergy ward for women, in a gastroenterology ward, and in a surgical ward for both men and women patients. In August of 1944 she was appointed Chief of a Gastroenterology Section, and then bounced around to five other stations. At two of these posts she was a surgeon in a WAC Dispensary and later a ward officer in a Tropical Disease Ward. While she was at Lawson, "she was assigned to a combat unit three times and each time orders were withdrawn when they discovered the officer was *a woman.*" She made no negative remarks on her Army Questionnaire.[14]

Holmes was a hometown girl at heart because following her discharge, she returned to Greenville, South Carolina, and practiced there for the next thirty years. She served on the staff of Greenville General Hospital, Greenville Memorial Hospital, and was a physician to the Sisters at St. Francis Hospital. She also found time to teach nurses and interns at these hospitals, was active in research and writing, and had several publications to her credit in the Journal of the American Medical Association, among others. With her specific interest in gastroenterology, many of the articles were focused in this area.[15] She died at the age of ninety-two 15 February 1996.

Considerably more is known about Jean Henley who grew up in Chicago, Illinois. An only child, she was born 3 December 1910, to parents who were both professionals.[16] Her father emigrated from Hungary and her mother came from Germany. The family name was actually Heller, but the father decided to change it—and thus Jean Emily Heller became Jean E. Henley. As the family made many trips abroad Jean had the opportunity to practice her language skills, and she became fluent in both German and French.[17] While she did not know it at the time, her knowledge of German was going to have a profound effect in the field of anesthesiology at a later time.

As a young woman, medicine did not seem to be Henley's first choice. She attended both Vassar and Barnard Colleges in the 1930s, received her BA, and afterwards left for Paris to study sculpture. In the 1930s Paris attracted many intellectuals, including Sylvia Beach, who established a famous Shakespeare and Company Bookshop which became a hub of international literature. Henley lived at a student hostel and since she needed a job, she soon found herself working for Sylvia half-days as a salesgirl and general helper from 1932-33. Sylvia described Henley as "a large, fine looking German girl, very anxious to help me all she can, and not deceitful…she is intelligent in the college girl way, though knowing nothing of books, and seems rather too susceptible falling in love …" Henley was also enterprising, and when the bookstore was not doing well financially, she suggested to Sylvia that they sell the erotic books that customers were asking for, such as *Fannie Hill.* Jean Henley returned to the States by 1934 and she resumed her artistic work. From 1 February to 8 March 1934, there was an exhibit at the Art Institute of Chicago in which she was credited with the sculpture of "Mademoiselle M. Bruineton".[18]

That same year, however, Henley decided on another course of action, and she wrote: "I had always thought of studying medicine but the long term of preparation rather frightened me. Then after having been on my own for several years in Paris, I think I must have attained to a greater measure of maturity; so that by the summer of 1934 there was no longer any doubt or conflict." She also stated that she had always been interested in the human body. "The earlier form of this interest expressed itself through work in sculpture. Later I realized that the study of medicine and surgery offered me a greater challenge and I realized that I showed prefer to work in this field…I hope that I can eventually qualify as a plastic surgeon."[19] After entering Columbia University, she graduated from the College of Physicians and Surgeons in 1940, followed-up the next year with an internship at Santa Barbara Cottage Hospital in California, and then went on for a residency in internal medicine. In 1942 she moved to Boston to complete her training at the Peter Bent Brigham Hospital, one of the principal teacher hospitals associated with Harvard Medical School.[20]

Henley's biographers maintain that she was brought up to deny her Jewish heritage and that she did probably did not volunteer this information to Harvard because as far as admission of Jewish students was concerned, there was a "strict but secret quota of 10%."[21] It was also true, however, that a similar policy existed at the College of Physicians and Surgeons at Columbia, where she received her M.D. earlier. This medical college was the first to adopt a policy of "selective admissions" in 1918. In fact, there was "a decline of Jewish admissions to the College of Physicians and Surgeons from 14 to fewer than 4% between 1920 and 1948."[22]

In 1944, Henley volunteered with the Army Medical Corps and on 26 July 1944, she was commissioned a lieutenant and promoted to captain 25 June 1945. According to her service record, she served as a ward officer in general medicine and arthritis in two different locations, starting with Thayer General Hospital in Nashville, Tennessee, from August of 1944 to April of 1945. From there she went to the ASF (Quartermaster Corp) at Camp Beale in California that housed a 1,000-bed hospital, and was also a large staging area for Army personnel who were being assigned overseas. Sometime in 1945 she was sent to the South Pacific with the 8th General Hospital in New Caledonia in Melanesia where the inhabitants, who are predominantly Melanesian and European, are all French citizens.

Lt. Henley was one of the few women medical officers who took care of "predominately" male patients, and she described her duties as routine ones. "Besides taking sick call, saw all the French civilians who were treated at the hospital. Did complete work-ups and carried the patients through to treatment." In her impressions of her Army service, she maintained: "I have not been used in the most effective way for which my training has prepared me and would surely have been able to render far greater service had my ability to speak French and German and my training for relief work been taken into account."[23] Her dissatisfaction stemmed from not engaging in more challenging medical tasks than that of a general ward office. While we know nothing of the relief work to which she referred, we do know that Camp Beale contained a POW camp which held German prisoners. Given her fluency in German, she might have felt she could have served as an interpreter or liaison for medical needs at the camp. Apparently she did not feel that her fluency in French was a good enough reason to treat civilians in Caledonia.

After Jean Henley left the Army she decided to undertake training in anesthesia, rather than plastic surgery, and she became the "Assistant Resident Anesthetist" 1 March 1947 at Presbyterian Hospital which was associated with Columbia. It seems likely that she acquired her interest in anesthesiology when she was in medical school at Columbia. The noted anesthesiologist, Virginia Apgar, was chief then, and one focus of the department was on teaching medical students. Apgar was a dynamic teacher and one of the very few women role models at the time. When Henley became a resident under Apgar, roughly half of the department's faculty was female, and this was at a time when women were only about 5% of the MD population.[24] in 1952, Henley became an instructor in anesthesiology at Columbia, and quickly moved up the academic ladder to associate and assistant professor by 1972. At the same time that she held academic appointments, she also practiced as an anesthesiologist at Delafield Hospital from 1952 until 1958 when she also became the director of Service at Delafield, remaining until she resigned 31 December 1972 from there and also at Columbia.[25]

In 1949, Henley visited Germany, which was underdeveloped in its approaches to modern anesthesia compared to the United States and Great Britain. She noticed, for example, that the University

Hospital in Giessen owned only two Heidbrink machines that they had obtained from the American Army, and no one was trained on how to use them.[26] She spent four months in Gissen teaching her techniques "in physiology as it related to anesthesia" to two surgical residents who volunteered to work with her. She continued to teach and demonstrate in various places "all over the German Federal Republic" until "the American Military government (High Commission for Germany) heard about her activities, hired her as a consultant, and gave her the use of a car" so she could drive to various places to demonstrate her methods.[27] Following this tour, she prepared a report on her observations and made recommendations to institute more modern practices in German anesthesia.

Perhaps one of Jean Henley's greatest contributions to anesthesia in Germany was a textbook she wrote in English that was translated into German in 1951. This work was considered the "first modern textbook of anesthesia to be published in Germany after the war." Her text stressed aspects of American anesthesia "that were hardly in use in Germany in 1950. Henley returned to the United States in January 1951 to assume the position of director of Anesthesia at the Francis Delafield Hospital in New York. Her biographers concluded: "The available evidence supports the thesis that Dr. Jean Henley made a significant contribution to the growth of modern scientific anesthesiology as a separate discipline in Germany in the years immediately after the Second World War."[28]

Jean Henley retired in 1972 from teaching and practice in anesthesiology, and she was able to devote her time and interest to preserving the environment. Those people who knew her described her as "a very good teacher, a forceful personality who imposed herself on the operating team. She was energetic, clear in expression, and expounded original ideas, and she developed a good working relationship with her surgical colleagues...The general opinion of those who knew her was that she was a 'very private person.'" She died 19 August 1994 at the age of eighty-three.[29] Two obituaries note that she was survived by her companion of forty years, Barbara Jones. By the time of her death in the 1990s, it was acceptable to make mention of a domestic partnership with a person of the same gender. It also appears that Henley was able to maintain a public professional life and a private one at the same time; and one writer adds that such domestic partnerships were often mutually supportive in the medical community for women.[30]

As was mentioned earlier, few women doctors came from the South, but Like Gertrude Holmes, Louella Hudson Liebert was another medical officer who did just that. She received her undergraduate degree from the University of Louisville and graduated from the School of Medicine there in 1940 and went on for a residency at Louisville General Hospital. At the time of her commissioning 5 August 1944, she was single and living in Louisville, Kentucky. Born 17 May 1916, she was the youngest of the internists at age twenty-eight.

Liebert worked mostly with women patients and served at various times as ward officer or assistant chief of either the out-patient service or medical section while stationed at Lawson General Hospital in Atlanta, Schick General Hospital in Clinton, Georgia, and at the Station Hospital in Ft. Des Moines, Iowa. In regard to her status as a medical officer while in the Army, she was very disillusioned, and she maintained: "I have not been afforded an opportunity to utilize the special training I have had." With the exception of Schick General hospital she observed: "A large part of my working time has been consumed in monthly physical inspections and participation in meetings of boards...At the time I entered the Army I was doing a great deal more for both the war effort and for the alleviation of human ills than I have one at any time since being in the Army. In fact, I accomplished more in one day of practice, hat I have in any week since in the Army."

Like several of the women doctors, Liebert acknowledged that she had a mother who was dependent on her. Another medical officer, however, was concerned about the personal toll this was taking on Liebert, and she wrote: "She has been in practice there [Louisville], seems capable. Has a dependent mother, and though she said little I know the dependency problem was a shock to her and she has been missing meals, perhaps to save some money, as she is sending practically her whole check home." After her discharge, Liebert returned to her private practice in Louisville, Kentucky. She had a short-lived career as she passed away in a Veterans Hospital in 1963.[31]

Four women medical officers graduated from medical school at the University of Wisconsin, but Mae Josephine O'Donnell, was the only one who served as an internist in the Army. She gave her place and date of birth as 23 August 1909, Janesville, Wisconsin. At the point she entered medical school in 1937, she stated that both her parents were deceased.[32]

She accepted a commission as a lieutenant 23 November 1943 and after basic training was immediately sent for the next nine and one-half months to the Blood Donor Service in St. Louis, Missouri. This was a routine, if not a boring assignment, and O'Donnell was glad to be posted next in her specialty at the Beaumont General Hospital in El Paso Texas, formerly used as a WWI hospital, and later expanded to 174 buildings with a crowded capacity of 4,064 beds in WWII. After almost five months in this setting, she was promoted to captain and shipped to the Southwest Pacific Area (SWPA) and made Chief, Cardiovascular Section, 318*th* General Hospital in Honolulu, Hawaii. She was also assigned to the 307th General Hospital in Osaka, Japan, late in 1945 to care for soldiers in the Army of Occupation. When asked to consider the value of her military service to her own professional experiences, she wrote: "Time will tell."

In postwar years O'Donnell moved to Oklahoma and then to Wadsworth, Kansas, and in 1964 she was still practicing medicine. "Time" did reveal, however, that her military service had had an impact on her career because she accepted an appointment as an internist with the Veterans' Administration in Leavenworth where she remained for many years until she retired in 1976. She was a member of the Association of Military Surgeons, and as a devout Catholic, she attended chapel services at the VA Hospital in Leavenworth. She died 25 November 2000 at the age of ninety-one in a Leavenworth hospital and she was buried in Janesville, Wisconsin. Her service, however, demonstrates the multiple roles WWII internists held in blood banks, general hospitals, and overseas.[33]

Margaret McAllister Janeway, who was born in Trenton, New Jersey, 3 May 1896, was the second women physician to be commissioned behind Margaret D. Craighill although she had started out by being a contract surgeon on 21 September 1942. She was one of four women medical officers who had graduated from the College of Physicians and Surgeons at Columbia—the others being Eleanor Peck, Jean Henley, and Jean Henderson. (Barbara Stimson had also graduated from there but she declined a commission and remained with the RAMC). Janeway did not have an easy first year in medical school because she became ill and her grades suffered for it. The teaching staff was very sympathetic and advised her to "repeat the work of the first year with the first year class" which started in 1923. Another student might have become discouraged and dropped out, but it was typical of her to accept a challenge and forge ahead. As a result, she spent five years in school, instead of four, and received her medical degree in 1927. She proceeded to intern for a year and a half at Bellevue Hospital, New York City, worked at the gynecological clinic at St. Luke's Hospital for ten years, and was on the attending staff of Lenox Hill Hospital where she was attached to the cardiac clinic and served as physician for the nursing school.

Like Margaret D. Craighill, Janeway came from a military family as her grandfather was a surgeon in the Union Army in the Civil War. Although we don't always know the motivations of these women Army doctors, it was said that she left a good practice in New York "to follow in his footsteps." She was also willing to take a strong stand for the position of women in the military—for as soon as she became a contract surgeon, she filed a protest with the War Department stating that she hoped this would led to a regular commission. As soon as she volunteered, however, she began to carve out a path of her own which led her to the WAAC training center at Des Moines, Iowa, where for three months she was on different services at the station hospital, receiving what she called "excellent" training. When the WAACS were to be sent overseas, she was asked to go with them, but since there were no female medical officers in the WAAC at the time, she had to go through a series of maneuvers to make this possible: Her contract was terminated on 16 December 1942, the following day she was enrolled as an auxiliary (the equivalent of a buck private), discharged the same day, and then appointed a third officer WAAC. At the time of the first mass promotion of WAAC officers the next month, she was promoted to the grade of second officer and sailed with the first WAAC contingent as their medical officer to North Africa on 13 January 1943.[34]

Janeway was the first woman doctors overseas at the North African Theater of Operations, United States Army (NATOUSA), and then in the next fourteen months her work was expanded to all WACs in the Mediterranean Area—which meant the responsibility for the health of nearly 2000 women soldiers in North Africa and Italy. When she first arrived in Algiers, she and the WAACS were quartered in an old French convent outside the city with no heat and no running water—and the weather was cold and wet and remained that way until May. She elaborated how the women carried all their water upstairs in their helmets, and had to wear their clothes to bed to keep warm, then suffered from sunburn. "Despite the rugged conditions—and they were rugged—we were lucky," reported Janeway. "Nobody developed any of the strange tropical maladies I was afraid the girls might pick up in Africa. There was no venereal disease and few serious illnesses of any kind. I was kept busy most of the time practicing preventive medicine and acting as a sanitary inspector...Although the WAACS worked under terrific pressure at all times, their health was excellent. Luckily no one got hurt in the nightly bombings although a shell fragment landed in one bed beside a girl's leg one time." She believed, however, that the incessant loud noises contributed to shattered sleep and frayed nerves—all this on top of the fatigue the women endured because of working twelve hours a day and seven day a week on their assigned tasks. Despite these hardships, only twelve of the entire 1,800 women soldiers in the Mediterranean had to be returned to the United States because of physical disability.[35]

In June of 1943 she heard that the Army was commissioning women doctors and she applied for one in the Medical Corps. She received her majority in July and by January of 1944, four other women medical corps officers were assisting her in the Mediterranean Theatre—Drs. Eleanor Gutman, Poe-Eng Yu, Elizabeth Garber, and Belle Shedrovitz. As part of her responsibilities she also inspected the medical facilities of all WAC installations in Africa and Italy, and one of her last tours took her within four miles of the Italian fighting front. After nearly eighteen months overseas, she was sent back to the States and appointed Assistant Consultant for Women's Health and Welfare, in the SGO in Washington, DC. Towards the spring of 1945, she was a guest lecturer along with Craighill at the School for WAC Personnel Administration established at Purdue University at West Lafayette, Indiana.[36]

Following her discharge, she served as one of the first women doctors with the VA in 1946 attached to the New York branch office, and eventually returned as a physician on the staff of Lenox Hill Hospital where she remained until her retirement in 1973. She also married and assumed her husband's name, thereafter signing herself as Margaret Janeway McLanahan. She died in her home in Manhattan at the age of eight-five in 1981. In 1983, one of her stepsons set up a scholarship at Princeton University from a bequest from her estate in memory of "his mother".[37]

The Pathologists

According to Army records, four women were classified as pathologists: Clara Raven, Elizabeth Khayat (later Bouton), Machteld Sano, and Joyce S. Morris. (Cornelia Wyckoff did not appear on the official Army Specialty List for women doctors, possibly because she died in service, but she had completed an internship in pathology and worked for six months in X-Ray). The women performed a wide range of duties in diagnostics, laboratory and blood work, forensics, research, and consultation. As a matter of fact, pathology is one of the few specialties that allows for such diversification, and a doctor can develop subspecialty expertise through formal fellowships or experience. This can lead to additional certification in areas such as cytopathology, pediatric pathology, forensic pathology, microbiology, chemistry and even transfusion medicine.[38] As we shall see, these women pathologists had subspecialties which they practiced in and out of the Army.

Dr. Clara Raven was born in a small Russian village of Staraya Palana on 6 April 1905. She was the oldest of nine children, but only six survived. In 1912, the family immigrated to Canada and then moved to Youngstown, Ohio. Against her father's wishes, Clara Raven headed to the University of Michigan after high school. She received both a BA and MS in bacteriology and the sciences in 1927 and 1928 respectively, but she elected to stay on for two more years of graduate work. In 1930-31 she completed another year of graduate studies at the University of Chicago.

Dr. Clara Raven. Courtesy of WIMSA.

By now, it had become very clear to Clara Raven that she wanted to pursue a medical degree, and she entered Duke University Medical School where she was the only female student in the freshman class in 1932-33. As a sophomore, however, she decided to transfer to Northwestern University Medical School under a quota system that allowed only four female students into the Medical School.[39] At the end of her sophomore year, however, she was still having problems supporting herself, and she "was unable to get any work for the summer." She confided to one of her mentors: "I do hope, however, that something materializes in Chicago that will make my return to school this fall a surety."[40] As it turned out, Raven did receive a research grant at NUMS for 1934-36. A letter from the Dean of NUMS noted that, "Dr. Clara Raven received her M.D. degree in 1938. In spite of financial difficulties while in school, she carried on research work in the Department of Bacteriology both at the school and at Cook County Hospital and graduated with a very respectable grade point average."[41] She opted for an internship at the Women and Children's Hospital in Chicago, Illinois, next and then decided she would like to study abroad in England 1938-39.

At the end of her Fellowship at the University of Liverpool, she wrote: "It has been a most interesting year here in Liverpool and actually I have liked it better than I had hoped. It is too bad that the international situation has been occupying the medical profession recently—meetings of all kinds are going on all the time. Actually I am looking forward to coming back home even though apprehensive about everything including for my own future, since so far I have nothing definite to return to."[42] Americans were also being warned to leave England, and Bertram Raven, her brother pointed out: "The war was just about ready to break out and Clara began hearing rumors about what was happening to Jews in Germany. She went to the American Embassy and tried to sign up, but was told that women physicians weren't being accepted. She returned home just as England declared war on Germany."[43]

She arrived in New York "just two days before the declaration of war," but she did not go home. One of the deans at the WMCP in Philadelphia learned of her return and asked Raven to help fill in an emergency vacancy on the teaching staff there. Raven said, "I had, therefore, no time even to go back to Chicago and have been working hard since September 20th. In addition to bacteriology I am also in charge of a small junior dispensary section in medicine. So I feel even though this is temporary it is additional experience."[44] And it was a wonderful opportunity for the next year, but when it ended she had to switch gears again and, this time, she entered private practice in clinical and laboratory work. After two years, she was hunting around again for a new challenge, and she became the Pathologist and director of Laboratories, Scranton State (General) Hospital in Pennsylvania from 1941-43.[45]

It is not widely recognized that Clara Raven was active in promoting the bill to secure commissions for women doctors as part of her work with one of the AMWA committees. Dr. Nellie S. Noble, president of AMWA before Barringer, had asked her help in gathering information to promote the passage of the Equal Rights Amendment, hoping that once the bill was passed, women doctors would be in a better position to promote their platform.[46] Somehow Raven found time to engage in this valuable work even as she tried to volunteer long before commissions became available to women. In June of 1940 she wrote to Julia C. Stimson, President of the American Nurses' Association, for her assistance in helping those women who wanted to join the Armed Forces. Stimson wrote back: "[I] am afraid that there is very little that I personally can do to help you or other women doctors to secure a place in the Medical Department of the Army. You will understand that I am very much interested when I tell you that I have a sister [Barbara] who is a doctor who has talked to me about this matter a great deal...My sister is older than you are but she too feels that she could be of real use in the Army."[47]

Raven was not one to be discouraged easily and even though she had been unsuccessful in England, she wrote to the Surgeon General of the U.S. Navy in February 1941 asking if were possible to volunteer in the Navy. She received a letter back which said: "You are advised there is no provision in existing Navy Regulations whereby it is possible to offer a commission in the Medical Corps of the regular Navy, or of the Naval Reserve, to other than male citizens who are graduate Doctors of Medicine".[48] As soon as women doctors were able to be commissioned in the United States Army, however, she knew she still wanted to be part of that pioneer group of medical officers. In August of 1943, Raven wrote: "I have joined the Armed Forces."[49] Thus, she entered a new phase in her career, which was to last until 1948.

Capt. Raven was among the first five women commissioned in the Army Medical Corps, and her service included duty in the States as well as France and Germany during WWII. She officially received three classifications in the Army Medical Corps: tissue pathologist, medical laboratory officer, and bacteriologist. She also received special training at the Army Institute of Pathology in Washington, D. C. and at the School of Tropical Medicine.[50] When speaking of her Army experiences, she said: "Assigned as a pathologist, I was sent to the Army Medical Museum in Washington, and later to a general hospital and overseas." This Museum "had the largest depository and consulting service in pathology in the world... [and] she reviewed and consulted on specimens submitted from military and civilian sources from over the world."[51] At one of the general hospitals she was in charge of the laboratory that included two junior sanitary corps officers and 20 enlisted laboratory technicians. Her work consisted "of pathology (surgical ad morbid) and supervision of clinical pathology." At last she went overseas with the 239*th* General Hospital, which saw service in France (1944-45). "I was assigned as chief of Laboratory Service. The 239*th* General Hospital while in France was distinguished by being chosen as an Infectious Hepatitis Center. The results of the clinical and laboratory studies were the subject for subsequent publications."[52]

At the end of the war, women physicians were discharged despite the fact that the demobilization process created a severe postwar physician shortage for both the Army and Navy Medical Corps. Towards the end of 1945, however, the Army had sent three women physicians to the Far East, but within eighteen months all were recalled to the States and relieved from duty. Four other women including Clara Raven, who was working as chief of laboratory service at Tripler General Hospital in Hawaii, were still in the Army by 1947. Army Surgeon General Raymond Bliss wanted to keep these highly skilled doctors, and he hunted for loopholes in the military regulations that would allow him to do just that. He was unsuccessful, and the Army Medical Corps was forced to release its last four women medical officers. After she was demobilized, Raven started to work as Chief Pathologist for the Veterans Administration in Dayton, Ohio, but she remained in the reserve in the event the Army needed her again.[53]

With the passage of the Women's Armed Services Integration Act in 1948, the Navy quietly started to commission women doctors into the Naval Women's Reserve (WAVES) as opposed to the medical corps. "The 1948 act made no specific provision for the commissioning of women doctors in the services; it simply did not expressly forbid it, probably because Congress had not considered the possibility."[54] As soon as the Korean War started, there were three women doctors in the regular Navy and twenty in the Naval Reserve, and none in the Army or the Air Force. A month into the war, the Army and Air Force petitioned Congress to allow them to admit female doctors for extended active duty in the reserve. Because of the severe shortage of physicians, lawmakers finally passed the legislation (which included the Navy) in 1950 although it was not until 1952 that permanent legislation enabled women physicians to enter the service with the same rights and privileges afforded their male colleagues.

With the new legislation in place, Clara Raven was one of three women physicians recalled to active duty in the Army, and she was sent to Japan where there was a need to treat soldiers from the Korean battlefields.[55] While stationed in Tokyo, Osaka, and Hiroshima, she noted:

> I had the rare opportunity to come in contact with many Japanese physicians, present papers, and organize lectures and meetings with the Japanese. I was also invited to speak to the 38th Parallel Medical Association in Korea in the spring of 1952. As a result of my contacts, I as made an honorary member of the Japanese NationalSociety of Pathologists and later co-authored a Japanese Textbook of Histopathology, published in Tokyo in 1956. In 1951, I had a chance to review the materials from the early deaths

of Epidemic Hemorrhagic Fever and compare the pathology with what I had previously known...I was also given
the opportunity to study the liver biopsies taken in a nu-
tritional study of Infectious Hepatitis. While in Osaka in
1942, my laboratory made a survey of the incidence of
parasites in the casualties evacuated from Korea. While in
Japan I also had the opportunity to observe the work done
by the Atomic Bomb Casualty Commission in Nagasaki
and Hiroshima.[56]

For the next several years, Clara Raven continued to work as
an Army pathologist. From 1954-56, she was assigned as Chief of
Laboratory Service at the U.S. Army Hospital Aviation Center, Fort
Rucker, Alabama. Besides being Chief, she set up an organizational
and training program which satisfied the requirements of the Joint
Commission on Accreditation of Hospitals in less than a year of the
opening of the hospital. One source held that she had "the distinction of being possibly the first woman to command a medical unit,
when in 1959, she was assigned as post surgeon at Camp Brecken-
ridge, Kentucky, during the summer training of U.S. Army Reserve
units." In 1961, "she was the first female U.S. physician promoted
to full colonel in the Army Medical Corps."[57] She was also the first
woman accepted to membership in the Military Order of World
Wars and the Association of Military Surgeons.

Raven returned to Detroit after retiring from the Army. For twelve
years she was Deputy Chief Medical Examiner of Wayne County. In
this highly visible position "she dealt with ongoing investigations related to homicides, suicides, accidents...and crime in general...She
also gave testimony in court of law in the above cases and has attained a record of honesty, integrity, and reliability in the legal, medical and lay community of Wayne County." One subject of particular
interest to her was the investigation of unexplained sudden deaths
in infants (SIDS). She was considered a national and international

expert on this topic, and she guided bereaved parents to found the Michigan Sudden Infant Death Study Association. She retired from being Deputy Chief Medical Examiner in 1970. She was inducted into the Michigan Women's Hall of Fame in 1987. She died at the age of 89 on 2 May 1994, and the Raven family asked that tributes be sent to the Sudden Infant Death Syndrome Alliance in Lansing, Michigan.[58]

Like many physicians, Machteld Sano made her decision to study medicine early in life. Born 21 February 1903 in Antwerp, Belgium, she attended public schools and graduated from high school there in 1919. After taking and passing the University of Cambridge entrance exam the same year, she left for England for further studies. Subsequently, she attended MIT in Boston, 1925-1926, where she studied chemistry. While at MIT she started to work at the Boston Dispensary as the chief laboratory and research assistant.[59]

In 1929 she accepted an appointment at Willard Parker Hospital located on the East River on Manhattan's lower East side in New York. Because Willard was one of three infectious disease hospitals at the time, the wards were constantly filled with children who were admitted with diphtheria, scarlet fever, measles, and pertussis (whooping cough) as well as a variety of other ailments. Diphtheria, however, has always aroused worldwide concern and it was unusually prevalent in the winter of 1932-33 in New York. Sano was one of three researchers who investigated the problem of the control of diphtheria bacillus carriers, and by the time she left Willard in 1933, she was an expert in contagious diseases.[60] Somewhere in this time frame she went to Columbia University for further studies, but she eventually returned to Belgium where she received her MD from the University of Brussels in 1939. She followed up with an internship in Brussels and then returned to the United States and Temple University Medical School and Hospital in Philadelphia for a fellowship. She remained at Temple from 1940-43 teaching pathology, and during the same period, she entered private practice in 1942-43.

The position at Temple gave Sano the opportunity to carry on an extensive research program where she conducted experiments in the refrigeration of living tissue, which had major implications for cancer cells. In fact, she "was acclaimed" for this work as she was "the first person to reduce the temperature of mammal heart tissue to actual freezing and then revive it." The significance of her work was "the fact that cancer cells stop growing at temperatures of 68 degrees." Another one of her important contributions was a new skin grafting technique she developed. By 1941, she began to experiment on hastening the healing of grafted skin, a process that surgeons normally expected to take five days before the grafted portion began to adhere. A year later, she used her method on humans "so that the patient was walking upon a graft on the heel within a week." Her method was widely used in civilian hospitals throughout the country, as it required one-fourth of the operation time necessary than the usual skin graft in which stitches were used. Basically the method consisted of making an extract from human blood mixed with a substance to prevent clotting, and painting the area to be covered and the graft with the "glue". Within 48 hours, the new skin is "glued on" without stitches or dressing. Sano explained that the method "has also been used successfully in healing of injuries to the liver, spleen and other delicate organs that heal better without bloody stitches."[61]

When she accepted a commission 5 January 1944, she was described as "a petite, bright-eyed woman wearing the bars of captain in the United States Medical Corps... [who] took pride in her Army uniform." She said her days were filled with work and in learning how an "Army doctor" lives.[62] During her Army career, she was assigned as chief pathologist at Kennedy General Hospital, Memphis Tennessee. When Capt. Sano arrived there in 1944, the original bed capacity of the hospital had been expanded from 1,500 to over 4,400. The role of the hospital also changed as it was enlarged, and it grew from a regional hospital whose mission had been the care of patients who lived in the region, to a center for research, evaluation, psychiatric and surgical care.[63] When she talked about her work at Kennedy, Sano noted that she gave demonstrations and lectures to surgical and medical staff and examined and diagnosed all surgical specimens in addition to consulting with surgeons before and at the time of operations. She conducted postmortems for the hospital and adjacent camps—the postmortems performed on military personnel "whose deaths were violent or where there was suspicion of foul play"; and when called upon, she testified in court in regard to these cases.[64]

On her Army Questionnaire, Sano had claimed her parents as dependents, and while she was at Kennedy, Machteld requested to be assigned overseas. "Today I received news through the Red Cross of my father's illness and the loss of their home in Belgium," she wrote. "I am more than ever anxious to be sent there so that I may help them as much as possible." Her request was denied as there were no requests for women officers at that time and she was told: "[I]t is not possible in the Army to make assignments on the basis of the individual's wishes." By 1945, however, Sano felt her parents' situation in Belgium was desperate and she asked to be transferred to a position for a physician that had opened up at the American Consulate in Antwerp. "My parents are going rapidly downhill. The troubles, which the war brought on, the anxiety, and the disruption of the family as a whole seems to have taken away their very reason for existence." And she was prepared to leave the Army, as she explained: "If I should not be able to be transferred to Antwerp either as an officer or a civil service officer, I shall ask for my discharge…on the hardship claim."[65]

It is not known what happened to her after that, but by 1950 she became a faculty member with the WMCP, and for the next two years she once again began to conduct research and teach in the United States. Then followed a series of different appointments at two hospitals in New Jersey where she worked as a pathologist and at Hahnemann Medical College in 1962 where she remained until 1968. In recalling the work of pioneer women in cytology, one researcher recalled Machteld Sano as a woman who "had done good work in tissue culture at Temple before she joined me at Hahnemann to get more experience in cytology."[66] By the time she retired, Sano was a member of many medical organizations such as the American Society of Cytology, the International Society of Cytology, and she was a founding fellow (emeritus) of the American College of Pathologists. For her research work she also received an award from the Tissue Culture Association.

In summarizing her Army experiences, she believed that "the Army has not made use of my real qualifications which are those of research in the field of surgery and medicine. Especially in war surgery, my past work has been widely made use of by the English Army and Navy and by some American surgeons… Suggestions were made at multiple times to consulting surgeons for me to do research on such vital problems as nerve grafting and lesions of the spinal cord but to no avail. In the latter especially it would seem that any suggestion would have been received in view of the hopelessness of most cases. In my original applications I asked for research work but at no time was I given any cooperation, such co-operation at no time requiring any expenditure exceeding 100 dollars."[67] She never married, but as one medical scholar pointed out, "The most 'successful' women physicians from the perspective of their profession were more likely to be single." She died 28 Nov 1993.[68]

Elizabeth Khayat was born 17 December 1910.[69] She was a native New Yorker and one of nine children. Her father was an archeologist who took his family with him on his many excursions and, as a result, she attended a convent school in Cairo where she learned to speak several languages. She was a talented painter, so it was no surprise that she wanted to live and study in Paris where she attended Le Sorbonne and remained to acquire her medical degree from Toulouse and a Ph.D. from the University of Paris. She chose to return to the States after that, and she completed a residency in pathology at the New York College of Medicine.[70]

Sometime before the outbreak of WWII, she married Alfred Bouton, a member of the French Underground, but she did not assume his name until years later.[71] On her Army Questionnaire, she stated that she was thirty-four years old and married, but she did not supply her husband's name. She volunteered 19 March 1944 with the rank of lieutenant and was promoted to captain 25 September 1945.

Lt. Elizabeth Khayat was assigned to Lawson General Hospital and then to Finney General Hospital in Thomasville, Georgia, which had a capacity of 1994 beds.[72] Finney was only about 350 miles away from Kennedy General Hospital in Tennessee, so both facilities were located in the southern part of the United States where traditions and prejudices were more deeply rooted. It will be recalled that another pathologist, Machteld Sano, served at Kennedy where she was given no cooperation as a medical officer when she asked to conduct research. One writer felt that although Kennedy benefited patients and the medical community in Memphis during and after the war, "local and social racial and gender beliefs and customs blocked sweeping changes during wartime mobilization because of racial segregation and the *subservient role of women in medicine and the military*."[73]

It would not be surprising, therefore, that in nearby Finney Hospital, Khayat should experience her share of problems. "Being the only female medical officer there," she pointed out, "I had to contend with many difficulties and sometimes have had humiliations." She detailed the difficulties this way: "[M]y opinion was never asked for or listened to in Finney General Hospital. During medical conferences I was entirely disregarded as a medical officer...I was called a WAC laboratory technician." As to the living conditions at Finney, they were "unsatisfactory for quarters. The female officers are too few to have separate quarters and they are sometimes the only one at a time in general hospital and are housed with the nurses. If the Chief of Nurses had a personal liking for the female medical officer," she went on, "things were just about satisfactory. If, the contrary was true, living conditions were most unsatisfactory."

Khayat tried to be equitable in evaluating the value of her Army service. As far as the war was concerned, she held that "Female officers, in general, and owing to the prevailing prejudice in the medical profession, have not been fully utilized in their particular field. In my own case, I happened to be a pathologist, besides my training in general surgery, and was used to fully capacity in this particular field." Overall she believed these experiences were not professionally satisfying, although on a personal level she gained experience "in dealing with individuals of all categories." She could only conclude, "My experience in the Army has been a keen disappointment, medically speaking. I do not regret, however, having had the opportunity to serve my country. I also feel that whatever disagreeable incidents I have had to contend with, have made me stronger and better equipped for my medical career, later on, in civilian life."[74] While in service, however, she learned to fly an airplane and she got her pilot's license.

After WWII, Khayat returned to New York and sometime later, her husband joined her. She accepted a position in the department of pathology at Mary Immaculate Hospital for two years, and then became a staff member of the Jamaica Hospital where she served as chairperson of the department and also as director of laboratories and residency training in pathology. She helped expand the facilities at the hospital so that Jamaica eventually produced one of the finest laboratories in Queens County; and she found time to serve as president of the medical board there. She was a consulting pathologist for Creedmore State Hospital, Queen's Village in New York in 1965. Like many women physicians, she devoted herself to worthy causes, and she was involved with planning for the Ship of Good Hope, which furnished medical supplies and services to the poor of South and Central America. When it came to subspecialties, she was certified in anatomic and clinical pathology as well as nuclear medicine.

Alfred Bouton preceded his wife in death, and he was buried in Calverton National Cemetery in New York 28 April 1983. Khayat passed away twenty-two years later and was buried next to Alfred 17 January 2005. There they lie as they had lived in life—two patriots side by side.[75]

Of the four Army women pathologists, Joyce Springer Morris was the most elusive. Little is known of her early life, but she was born in 1905 in Elmendorf, Texas, and her medical degree was awarded from the University of Texas in 1927. She was appointed an intern in 1930 at the Hudson River State Hospital in New York, after which she sought out a residency in pathology from 1932-33 and then worked as an assistant pathologist, both at Grasslands Hospital Valhalla, New York. By 1939 she was back to New York where she accepted an appointment as a pathologist at Binghamton State Hospital, which was the first institution designed and established to treat alcoholism as a mental disorder. That same year she was also called on to testify on problems related to the delivery of services to patients at the Norwich State Hospital in Connecticut.

She was thirty-nine years old when she was commissioned a captain 23 February 1945, and she indicated that she was a widow on her Army questionnaire and claimed her father as a dependent. She always signed herself as Springer Morris after she married Dr. William E. Morris who had served in the Navy during WWI. (He had entered private practice, was a member of the American College of Radiology, and he conducted research in deep therapy for the treatment of cancer). The couple lived in Mount Kisco, New York, until his death in the late 1930s.[76]

Once in the service, Morris was classified as a pathologist and assigned to the Army Institute of Pathology where her duties consisted of a "review of autopsy and surgical material from all Army hospitals." She had no patient contact, which often turned out to be the case in her field, but she believed that her overall contributions were worthwhile to the war effort. After she was discharged, she returned to her specialty and by 1958 she was employed at the Greenwich Hospital in Greenwich, Connecticut.[77]

The Anesthetists

As was the case in WWI, there was a continuing need for qualified women anesthetists (used interchangeable with anesthesiologists) in WWII although not to the same extent as the emphasis shifted to finding more qualified women neuropsychiatrists. Nevertheless, the Army was clear in outlining the duties and relation of the anesthetists to the surgeon. (See Table 5 for listing). It was recognized, for example, that they should assume the responsibility for more than the administration of anesthesia. Not only must they relieve the surgeon of all concern for anesthesia, but "they assumed the responsibility for shock therapy during operation, and, when it was practical, before operation." Thus, the anesthetist carried "a large part of the responsibility in treating severely wounded men." It was held that "the more competent the anesthetist the less the burden on the surgeon. With a well-qualified anesthetist at the head of the table the surgeon can give his undivided attention to the operative procedure itself." In fact, military surgeons agreed that the anesthetist could "support an inexperienced surgeon better than a brilliant surgeon [could] maintain an inexpert anesthetist."

Before WWII, anesthesia was generally conducted by nurse anesthetists or partially trained practitioners who were considered to have lower status in the medical field; but because of the shortages of physician anesthetists, nurse anesthetists dominated many medical departments. Still a survey conducted during WWI of women physicians interested in being part of the military noted that anesthesia was their second choice of specialization, following behind gynecology.[78] It continued to be a popular choice through World War II for women doctors as between 1920-1948 they made up 11 to 13 percent of the professional anesthesia organizations while representing only 3 to 4 percent of the physician population.[79] In tracing the history of the female wartime physician, eleven women were employed on contract as anesthetists during WWI and all of them were sent overseas to Europe. The Army's need for physician anesthetists, it seemed, finally overcame its reluctance to place women in danger.[80]

In WWII, six women were classified as anesthetists (See Table 5), but only two of them saw duty overseas. They were ranked as lieutenants when they volunteered, with the exception of Capt. Katherine Jackson, who was also the oldest and most experienced of the women. Nell Reiley and Margarete Erna Kotrnetz and were the only two married officers. Reiley, who came from Auburn California, had a brief career as she was appointed in May of 1944, was released 6 November because of pregnancy, and gave birth the following month.

Kotrnetz, who listed her home as Herkimer, New York, was married to another physician, Hans A. Kotrnetz, and both of them had come from Austria to the United States in the 1930s , no doubt to escape the turbulent conditions in Europe at that time. The couple became American citizens in December 1943, and she was commissioned 9 March 1944, and assigned to only one location, Lawson General Hospital, during her military service. She served as an assistant to the Chief of Anesthesia, worked with predominantly men patients, and reported that her duties consisted of "administering, teaching, and supervising anesthesias." She was the only one in the group who claimed any dependents—both of her parents, for whom she started receiving dependency allowances starting 1 November 1944. After discharge, she returned to New York where she continued to practice until her death in 1993 at the age of eighty-five.[81]

Since there were not enough qualified physicians to serve in anesthesiology, the Army provided short and intensive training for its medical officers that usually consisted of twelve weeks at various institutions across the country. Often these courses were "all the training in anesthesia many physicians had before practicing and supervising anesthetics in a variety of military operating rooms."[82] Three of the women doctors received such training: Audrey Allerton Bill, Jean L. Dunham, and Katherine Jackson.

Audrey Bill, who had graduated medical school from Boston University in 1941, was sent immediately for training in anesthesiology at Tilton General Hospital at Ft. Dix, New Jersey. Lt. Bill commented: "I did sincerely try to learn what I could from these various duties, believing that any additional knowledge, whether or not of primary interest, is grist for the mill of an individual so relatively young in medicine as I am." She served at five different Army hospitals in Massachusetts with varying duties related to being the dispensary officer who took care of sick call, and as outpatient officer who took care of all female personnel and civilian dependents on the post. At another hospital she was an assistant obstetrician and anesthetist assigned as a ward officer to female patients on the Surgical Service. Since the obstetrician "was an excellent teacher," she felt she learned a great deal in gynecology and obstetrics. The drawback was that she was expected to set up a central supply for the hospital and was also put in charge of the operating room property, "which responsibility had considerably nuisance value at times." When she was at Cushing General Hospital in Framingham, Massachusetts, she was made the Assistant Chief, Anesthesia and Operating Room Section. Here she was expected to give a course for nurses in anesthesia and spent a great deal of time relieving the Chief of "paper work." Lastly, she was placed at the SGO in the Division of Preventive Medicine. She seems to have disappeared from view after the war, but she eventually moved to Ontario, Canada, and set up practice in general medicine.[83]

At the time of her commissioning 28 June 1943, Jean Dunham lived in Washington DC, and at age twenty-four she was the youngest of all the women medical officers. She was a graduate of George Washington University School of Medicine and Health Sciences, and came straight from her internship to be sent for Army training in anesthesiology to Bellevue Hospital in New York. Afterwards she was posted to four different hospitals, and at all of them she served as an anesthetist. After finishing up at the first medical installation, she was sent to the ETO and assigned to the 182*nd* General Hospital in England; and just as her tour of duty was ending in July of 1945, she was promoted to captain. There can be no doubt that the Army impacted her career choices, as she continued to practice her specialty in postwar years and she was certified by the American Board of Anesthesiology after her discharge.[84]

Katherine Jackson was forty-three years of age when she was commissioned a captain. She was born 16 October 1901 in Wren, Ohio, but her family later moved to Indiana where she graduated in 1920 from high school in Fort Wayne, Indiana, attended the university there, but transferred to the University of Wisconsin in Madison in 1922 and worked as a part-time physical education teacher at a Wisconsin high school in 1923. After transferring, she originally started out as a physical education major, with her advisor, Margaret H'Doubler, considered to be the founder of dance education in the United States. H'Doubler used skeletons a great deal in her teaching to talk about movement, and when Jackson stayed on after receiving her undergraduate degree, she became an assistant in anatomy in medical school. (She was on the Medic Hockey Team in 1931). Jackson also stated that she could read French and German.[85] After receiving her MD in 1932; she interned in Flint, Michigan in 1932-33 and continued next with a residency in Logansport, Indiana.

Jackson was lucky in two ways—she got special training in the Army and she managed to be shipped overseas. After being commissioned 2 February 1944, Jackson was sent to Walter Reed Hospital for further training in anesthesia, and then stationed in November of 1944 at Camp Barkeley, Texas, where there were about 900 German POWs. (This was also the same camp where the first two Chinese-American men were commissioned second lieutenants in the Medical Administrative Corps Officer Candidate School). In January of 1945 she was shipped overseas to the ETO where she served as Chief, Anesthesia and Operating Room, with the 240*th* General Hospital unit. She earned two Battle Stars for serving in two cam-

paigns—the Battle of Ardennes and the Battle of Germany. Jackson
made no comments on her Army Questionnaire.[86]

After the war, Jackson returned to practice medicine, but her
Army experience left a lasting impression on her and she undertook
further training in anesthesiology in 1947-48 at the Hospital for
Special Surgery in New York City. She proceeded next to become
Chief of the Department of Anesthesiology at St. Mary's Hospital
in Troy, New York; and she also started researching the psychiatric
effects of anesthesia—which led her to becoming a member of the
American Psychiatric Association. In 1951 she set up private practice and engaged in psychotherapy. By 1964, she listed herself as a
psychiatrist in Albany, New York, and indicated she was practicing at
a VA Hospital full-time. She died 29 December 1994 in Fort Wayne,
Indiana.[87]

Gwendolyn Taylor, commissioned a lieutenant 28 August 1943,
was single and a graduate of the medical school at Colorado University. She was stationed in four General Hospitals within the United
States as an anesthetist and later as Chief of Anesthesia and Operating Section where her patients were predominately men. In contrast
to Bill and Dunham who were in their twenties, she was older and
more experienced at the age of thirty-six. She maintained: "My impression, both from my own experience and from other women medical officers I have talked to, is that we are treated a little less than
the male medical officers. There is a tendency to give to us the work
nobody else wants, and a failure to give due recognition to our work.
In this respect my experience in the Army has been disappointing."
She did acknowledge, however, that she had been "very fortunate" in
being assigned to her specialty as she "derived a great deal of satisfaction" from her work. She returned to Colorado to practice medicine
after the war.[88]

In considering Taylor's experiences, it is clear that there were still
some lingering doubts about the contributions of the women doctors in the Army, but this became less and less as more military sur-

geons encountered them in the hospitals and operating room. When it came to the anesthesiologists, however, between the two world wars they waged a campaign to increase their numbers and their visibility. The outcome was seen in the founding of the American Board of Anesthesiology in 1937 as an affiliate of the Board of Surgery "and as an independent board to pass on the qualifications of trained anesthetists in 1941." Also, the American Society of Anesthetists, a physician organization, grew out of the New York Society of Anesthetists which later became the American Society of Anesthesiologists.[89]

Several important advances occurred in the medical field following WWII. First, anesthesia, like neuropsychiatry, emerged as a physician specialty; and this, in turn, was the impetus for further growth in this field after 1946. More important, the training courses in anesthesiology sponsored by the Army, however limited, provided physicians with a new set of experiences. "Wartime training exposed neophyte physician-anesthetists to role models who showed the potential of anesthesiology and to the richness of practicing anesthesia. Wartime anesthesia required dexterity, imagination, and pluck, and surgeons and other physicians were suitably impressed."[90] While many male physicians maintained that they did not desire a career in the military at war's end, many of them were drawn to anesthesiology in postwar years despite their initial reservations.

In her article on women and the history of anesthesiology, one medical historian maintains that World War II produced changes that greatly shifted dominance in anesthesia towards men. Many of them had been drafted into the armed services and forced to become anesthetists, which increased the numbers of male physician anesthetists—whereas women physicians did not have the early benefits of such training opportunities as they were not commissioned officers until 1943 and there were very few of them by comparison. Furthermore, in postwar years, anesthesia was financially rewarding as it provided workers with health insurance benefits that allowed payment to anesthesiologists, thereby attracting even more former Army doctors to the field.[91]In the case of the women medical officers, only a small handful of them specialized in anesthesia in post-war years.

Orthopedic Surgery

In considering the career of an orthopedic surgeon, few women chose this specialty in the past although the numbers are increasing as of late. Many experts believe that this field has been plagued by negative stereotypes and misconceptions. "Orthopedic surgery seems to have somewhat of an image problem," Dr. Thomas Sculco, surgeon-in-chief at the Hospital for Special Surgery in New York City, reported, and there is a strong feeling that "orthopedic surgery requires a strong back and weak mind." There has also been the long-standing problem with adequate role models, and when women don't see many others in the field, they are frequently discouraged from considering this specialty.[92] While it is not known why Dr. Trinidad Margarita Ramos, the only women medical officer in orthopedics, chose this specialty in the late 1930s given that few women were in that field, she continued to dedicate herself to this work in postwar years.

Trinidad M. Ramos was born 6 March 1919, and she listed her home as New Orleans, Louisiana, when she volunteered. She graduated from Tulane University School of Medicine, New Orleans, 1942, interned at the Methodist Hospital in Dallas, Texas, and served a residency at the Shriners Hospital for Crippled Children in Chicago, Illinois, in 1943.[93] Commissioned 22 April 1944 at the age of twenty-five, she was classified with a specialty in orthopedics, the only woman Army doctor with this designation. Next she was assigned briefly to the Army Headquarters in South Carolina and then sent on as a ward officer to Mayo General Hospital in Galesburg, Illinois, and Vaughan General Hospital, Hines, Ill. Her duties consisted of taking care of predominately male patients and she felt that her status as medical officer was satisfactory. In her remarks regarding her military service, she observed: "Complaints those of all medical officers—most of work is paper work that could be done by administrative men with practically no actual medical work."[94]

Following discharge, Ramos returned to New Orleans was married twice, and changed her name each time (Edwards and Nagel), making it difficult initially to track her postwar career. She was awarded a fellowship at Charity Hospital of New Orleans 1946-48, and she was certified by the American Board of Orthopaedic Surgery in 1950 as Trinidad Ramos Edwards Nagel. She went on to serve on several medical staffs as an orthopedic surgeon in and around New Orleans for the next decade. She met an untimely death at the age of forty 18 January 1960.[95]

—∞—

Women specialists were the most satisfied when they were assigned to their area of expertise. Conversely, morale was low when they had to assume responsibilities not related to their training and interests. This could be exacerbated by engaging in routine duties that were beneath them such as setting up a central supply in a hospital. In this sense the women doctors were no different than their male colleagues. Furthermore, living and working conditions in the Army were sufficiently different from those in civilian life as to require a great deal of adjustment on the part of any medical officer, male or female.

Women doctors, however, seemed to have had to make more adjustments because of their gender. This was often true when it came to accommodations as well as job expectations which required that most of them worked predominantly on female wards or with WACs. More often than not, they were the first female Army doctor to be sent to a hospital or ward; and while they might have expected to be met with indifference or even suspicion, they preferred to avoid the open hostility displayed by the Chief of the Medical Section who did not have much use for women in the profession or the Army. Surely their reactions were tinged with disappointment as they had hoped that they would find more equality as a medical officer having already fought so hard for the right to have the MD after their names. At the same time, being referred to as a laboratory technician was demeaning, but being totally disregarded as a medical officer at meetings because of gender seemed unconscionable. It was no wonder that the women sometimes felt disgruntled although it was also pointed out that male Medical Department officers were just as likely to get a "fed-up" attitude after serving a year overseas in unfamiliar surroundings—with some of the men showing "loss of interest in routine duties, irritability and general inefficiency."[96]

In postwar years, all four of the Army pathologists returned to their specialty with Morris and Khayat working in state hospitals at one time or another. The women who had been classified as internists went back to hospitals, established their own practices, or even assumed an administrative position like Connor who became Chief of a Maternal Bureau in Hawaii. Five out of eight of these doctors also worked at VA settings following their return home: Connor, Janeway, Loizeaux (among the first to be appointed in 1946, See Table E), Holmes and O'Donnell—thus affirming the influence the AMC had on their career paths. Jean E. Henley, however, accepted a residency in anesthesiology.

The Army anesthesiologists were harder to track in postwar years as less is known about some of them, but it appears that none of these women seem to have made their way to VA facilities. Scanty records indicate that Bill practiced general medicine later on while Dunham returned to her specialty in anesthesiology. Jackson profited from the special training in anesthesiology she had received in the Army, and became the Chief of a Department of Anesthesiology. While both Henley and Jackson did advanced training in anesthesiology, this was also a popular career choice for many male Army doctors following their return home where they found there was a growing need for anesthesiologists in civilian hospitals. After 1945, more anesthesia was administered by doctors than nurses and anesthesiology became recognized as a bona fide national specialty.

~ NOTES ~

1. Quotes in Lopate, *Women in Medicine*, 124; Program for Women in Internal Medicine, Duke University, Durham, North Carolina. Also see Stevens, Rosemary, "The Curious Career of Internal Medicine: Functional Ambivalence, Social Success.," in *Grand Rounds: One Hundred Years of Internal Medicine*, eds. Russell C. Maulitz and Diana E. Long (Philadelphia: University of Pennsylvania Press, 1988), 339-64. Women physicians were often conflicted over the rise of specialties, and some were even opposed as they were concerned that their profession was becoming "less human". See Morantz-Sanchez who chronicles problems in specialties for women in *Sympathy and Science*, 1985.

2. Records for Connor were provided by DUCM Archives & Sp. Coll. Quote from Steven J. Peitzman, M.D., A New and Untried Course: *Woman's Medical College and Medical College of Pennsylvania, 1850-1998* (New Brunswick, NJ: Rutgers University Press, 2000), 16. He had interviewed Dr. Connor 23 May 1997. Teaching as frequently cited as a way to earn and/or save money for medical school.

3. During the war, more than 100,000 American troops were stationed in Newfoundland and Labrador.

4. Connor in New Guinea, "Women Physicians in the Army of the United States," *Women in Medicine*, 90 (October 1949), 9.

5. Quotes from Connor Questionnaire, Box 30, MDC Coll. Connor Thesis on rheumatic fever in children, provided by DUCM Archives. In personal correspondence with the DUCM archivist, it was learned that her married name was Mrs. Charles Henry.

6. Accommodation comments and quotes from Questionnaires, Box 30: Connor, Khayat, Crandall, Patton, Seno, and Dr. Eleanor B. Hamilton (3-room house), MDC Coll.

7. Hospital ship and bomb quotes: "Women Physicians in the Army of the United States," *Women in Medicine*, 90 October 1949, 9.

8. Conditions at SWPA: Major Gen. Jeanne M. Holm, ed., *In Defense of a Nation: Servicewomen in World War II* (Washington, DC. Military Women's Press), 1998, 52-53. WAC problems noted in Holm, *Women in the Military*, 88-89; quote, 86. Connor quotes in her Questionnaire, Box 30, and MDC Coll. Publications with co-authors, Connor wrote: "Communitywide Pregnancy Reporting in Kauai, Hawaii," *Public Health Reports*, Vol. 73, No. 1, January 1958; Reproductive and En-

vironmental Casualties: A Report on the 10-Year follow-Up of the Children of the Kauai Pregnancy Study," *Pediatrics*, Vol. 42, No. 1, July 1968. She also wrote a chapter on pediatrics for the *Cyclopedia of Medicine*, a book published in 1949 by the F.A. Davis Company in Philadelphia.

9. "In Memoriam", Connor obituary, was printed 2 August 2007 by the DUCM Alumni Association.

10. Rozov in the *American Medical Directory*, 19*th* Ed. Also see *Bulletin*: Volume 85, Medical Women's Association, 1944.

11. Rozov Army assignments and quotes from her Questionnaire, Box 30, MDC Coll.

12. Rozov in the Social Security Death Index. Life member: *Annuals of Intern Med* March 1, 1951 34:826-848.

13. Biographical material was gleaned from the Holmes Obituary, 24 February 1999, *The Greenville News*, and South Carolina, supplied by the Greenville County Library System. Numerous stations noted in Holmes questionnaire, Box 30, MDC Coll.

14. "Combat unit assignment" quote, from McNeel's oral history, in which she specifically recalled this incident. Also see the Social Security Death Index for Holmes.

15. Many of Holmes' publications appeared in the Journals of the American Medical Assoc.: "Gastrointestinal Allergy Associated with Organic Disease," Aug 1941; 117: 641-656; "Chronic Conditions of Gallbladder", Dec 1940; 115: 2309-2318.

16. Henley's parents were both said to be lay psychologists but later went back to school to acquire degrees. Her father was thought to be a friend of Carl Jung. Biographical information in Gerald L. Zeitlin and Michael Goerig, "Dr. Jean Henley, Author of the First Modern German Textbook of Anaesthesia," International Congress Series 1242 (2002), 277-281.

17. 17 After her mother died, her father reportedly became depressed and tried to kill himself, but his failed attempt left him paralyzed instead. He later married the nurse who took care of him. Information from Zeitlin and Goerig in note above.

18. See Noel Riley Fitch, *Sylvia Beach and the Lost Generation: a History of Literary Paris in the Twenties and Thirties*. New York: W. W. Norton & Co., 1985, 329-330; 333. Also see Chicago Art Institute Catalog, Dated February 1 to March 8, 1934.

19. Quotes are from Henley's application to medical school, in her alumni folder; supplied by College of Physicians & Surgeons, Columbia University Archives.

20. Zeitlin and Goerig note that she started out studying internal medicine at University College in San Francisco and then at the New York Hospital before finishing

at Brigham, 278. The point out that doing a residency at three different places was highly unusual.

21. Zeitlin and Goerig, Ibid.

22. See Leon Sokoloff, "The Rise and Decline of the Jewish Quota in Medical School Admissions," *Bulletin of the New York Academy of Medicine*, Vol. 68, No. 4, November 1992, 500. Sokoloff, pp. 500-501. One scholar noted that in addition to asking for the required background information, the applicant might be asked to supply a statement concerning his "religion and place of birth of father and mother". Later, another requirement was that the applicant furnishes a photograph. "Some of the schools, apparently because of criticism concerning the requirement that the applicant state his religion, substituted a question concerning the 'racial origin' of the applicant. Thereafter, this question was dropped and applicants were required to state their "mother's maiden name."

23. Service record and quotes in this section are on her Questionnaire, Box 30, MDC Coll.

24. Information from Henley's Employee Card, Archives & Special Coll., Augustus C. Long Health Sciences Library, Columbia University Medical Center; hereafter CUMC Archives. Notes on Apgar were provided in communication from Dr. Selma Harrison Calmes, University of California, Los Angeles. Dr. Apgar designed and introduced the Apgar Score, the first standardized method for evaluating a newborn's transition to life outside the womb. When she started the department in 1938 she could accept only two residents, and while she slowly increased their numbers, she was prevented from accepting more because the hospital had no available resident rooms in which to house them. Her papers are housed at the National Library of Medicine.

25. Henley's CUMC Employee Card is most specific: "Asst. Visiting Anesthetist 1/1/52-10-31-1953; Assoc. Visiting Anesthetist 11-1-53-6-30-1958; Visiting Anesthetist and Director of Service, 7-1-1958—resigned, 12-31-1972."

26. In the early half of the 20th century, Heidbrink machines were used, which incorporated gases, nitrous oxide in particular. In the United States in 1913, J. Heidbrink attained a refinement of anaesthetic machines, which formed the basis on which the present technology is based.

27. Gerald L. Zeitlin and Michael Goerig, "An American Contribution to German Anesthesia," *Anesthesiology*, August 2003, Vol. 99, No. 2.

28. Techniques "included tracheal intubation, controlled ventilation, the use of nondepolarizing muscle relaxants, proper intra- and post-operative monitoring, detailed

record keeping, and the application of known physiologic and pharmacologic prin-
ciples." All quotes from Zeitlin and Goerig, 2003.

29. See Social Security Death Index; obituary, *Journal of the College of Physicians and Surgeons of Columbia University*, v. 15, no. 2. spring 1995.

30. "Henley Obituary", *Journal of the College of Physicians and Surgeons of Columbia University*, Volume 15, No. 2, spring 1995. Zeitlin and Goerig note that this was a forty-year relationship in the obituary they provide. Also see Hansen, Bert, "Public Careers and Private Sexuality: Some Gay and Lesbian Lives in the History of Medicine and Public Health," *American Journal of Public Health*, January 2002, 92(1): 36–44. He makes a plea for historians to provide readers with a more frank acknowledgment of the possible relevance of personal life to intellectual work, even in the sciences. He discusses the private lives of Dr. Sara Josephine Baker and Dr. Ethel Collins Dunham.

31. Quotes from Liebert Questionnaire. Obituary, *JAMA*, 1963; 185(12):994-998. See Extract from Adele C. Kempker, 13 August, 1944, letter, in Histories, Box 29, MDC Coll. Liebert's picture is available at Digital Coll. Univ. of Louisville, Ekstrom Library. Thanks to Manuscript Collections, University Archives and Records Center, Kornhauser Health Sciences Library, University of Louisville, for providing information.

32. O'Donnell's Registration Form, Univ. of Wisconsin, 20 September 1937. The other Wis. Graduates: Drs. Katherine Jackson, Christine Martin Wood, and Elvira C. Seno.

33. Information and quotes on O'Donnell from her Questionnaire, Box 30, MDC Coll. For service in Japan, see "U.S. Women at Nagoya," *New York Times*, 24 November 1945, p. 21. O'Donnell Obituary, *Topeka Capital-Journal*, 27 November 2000. Upon her Death it was requested that donations be made to the Leavenworth County Infirmary in Leavenworth, Kansas.

34. The Augustus C. Long Health Sciences Library, Columbia University Medical Center (CUMC), supplied some biographical materials for Janeway. School quote: Dean William Darrach to Margaret M. Janeway, 29 May 1923, letter, Janeway Alumni File, CUMC; protest quote in Walsh, *Doctors Wanted: No Women Need Apply*, 227; "Dr. Janeway Joins Army; Ex-Wac Is Made Major," *New York Times*, 3 July 1943, p. 16; excellent training quote: "Major Margaret Janeway, M.C., AUS," *Women in Medicine*, January 1945, 15. See also "First Woman Army Doctor in Africa," (Section on War Service), MWJ, March 1944, 33.

35. Janeway's account and quotes in, "Major Margaret Janeway," 16. See also "Wac Doctor Finds Health Good in Overseas Corps Despite Rigors," The *New York Times*, 30 May 1944, p. 16.

36. See Treadwell, *The Women's Army Corps*, 716.

37. Janeway obituary, "Dr. Margaret McLanahan, 85, Formerly on Lenox Hill Staff," The *New York Times*, 19 November 1981, p. B8. Also See "Princeton Scholarships" on-line.

38. Cytopathology is the branch of pathology that deals with abnormalities of cells.

39. "Summary of Qualifications and Experiences of Clara Raven", Dated 21 June 1943, supplied by Northwestern University Medical School Archives, hereafter NUMSA.

40. Raven to Dr. Irving S. Cutter, Dated 8 August 1934, letter, NUMSA.

41. Dr. Richard H. Young, Dean, NUMS, to Dr. TR. L. Harvey, Veterans Administration, Lake City, Florida, 17 December 1954, letter, NUMSA. Another writer believed that since this was in the 1930s, "a medical degree for a young Jewish woman was no ordinary achievement." See Unidentified article with no author and date entitled "She Wouldn't Take No for an Answer: Remembering Dr. Clara Raven" photocopy of newspaper clipping, n. d. Clara Raven File, Historian's Files, WIMSA, Arlington, VA.

42. Raven to Dr. Cutter, 14 July 1939, letter, NUMSA.

43. "She Wouldn't Take No for an Answer: Remembering Dr. Clara Raven," WIMSA.

44. Raven to Dr. I. S. Cutter, 19 October 1939, letter, NUMSA.

45. "Summary of Qualifications and Experiences of Clara Raven", 21 June 1943, NUMSA.

46. Raven to Hon. Edward R. Burke, chairman judiciary sub-committee, United States Senate, Washington, DC, 15 April 1940, letter, NUMSA.

47. One of the assets of early women doctors is that they knew how to network with other women. It will be recalled that Julia was the older sister of Barbara Stimson who who would later join the RAMC.

48. Capt. W.J. C. Agnew, U.S. Navy, Bureau of Medicine and Surgery, to Raven, letter, 5 March 1941, Raven Family Papers.

49. Raven to Alumni Association, 5 August 1943, letter, NUMSA.

50. Schools of training (Pathology, July-October 1943; Tropical, July-September 1944) noted on her Questionnaire, Box 30.

51. The Army Medical Museum evolved into the Armed Forces Institute of Pathology. Quote from "News Release: Blackwell Chapter, the AMWA, April 1978," Raven Family Papers.

52. 52.Quotes from Raven, Clara, "Achievements of Women in Medicine, Past and Present—Women in the Medical Corps of the Army," *Military Medicine*, February 1960, 109; and from her Questionnaire, Box 30.

53. Three women in the Far East: Mae Josephine O'Donnell (cardiovascular specialist), Hilde J. Koppel (psychiatrist), and Pauline Garber (chief of laboratory services in Korea). Last four women in service: Clara Raven, Genia Sakin, Poe-Eng Yu, and Eleanor Hamilton. VA position: Raven to NUMS Alumnae Association, Dated 8 May 1951, letter, NUMSA.

54. Bellafaire and Graf, *Women Doctors in War*, 120-21.

55. Two other women doctors recalled: Alcinde de Aguiar and Theresa T. Woo.

56. Quote in Raven, Achievements of Women in Medicine, *Military Medicine*, February 1960, 110.

57. Quotes in "News Release: Blackwell Chapter", the AMWA, April 1978.

58. Description of work from 1954 to 1961 in "News Release", the AMWA, April 1978. Raven "Obituary," *Detroit News*, 12 May 1994.

59. Biographical Data for Machteld Elisabeth Sano, 1950, WMCP, DUCM Archives. Also See MIT Museum Coll., People; Marilynn A. Beaver, "The Women of MIT, 1871 to 1941," June 1976, thesis.

60. Lawrence W. Smith, Machteld E. Sano, and Josephine J. Jerema, "Diphtheria Bacilli," *The Journal of Infectious Diseases*, The University of Chicago Press, 1934.

61. See "Dr. Sano Lauded for Experiments in Refrigeration of Living Tissue," n.d. unidentified newspaper article supplied by DUCM Archives. On grafting, see "New Skin Grafting Technique Developed", *The Atlanta Constitution*, 23 January 1944. Her work is also described in "Medicine: Blood Glue", *Time Magazine*, 27 December 1943; and in "Head Wounds Rise in Present War," n. d., *Philadelphia Evening Bulletin* News Clipping Coll., Temple University, Urban Archives.

62. Quotes, "New Skin Grafting Technique Developed," *The Atlanta Constitution*.

63. After the war it became Kennedy Veteran's Administration Hospital. See Paul W. White, Kennedy General Hospital: Its Impact on Memphis in War and Peace, diss., the University of Memphis, 2007.

64. Quote in her Questionnaire, Box 30, MDC Coll.

65. Quotes from: Capt. Sano to Major Craighill, 3 July 1944, letter, Box 5; Major Janeway to Capt. Sano, 8 July 1944, letter, Box 5; Capt. Sano to Capt. Mills, 7 November 1945, letter, Box 5, MDC Coll.

66. Irena Koprowska, Women in the Early Days of Cytology: A Personal Recollection, *Diagnostic Cytopathology*, Vol. 10, no. 2, 183. Hospitals in New Jersey: Newton Memorial and Morristown Memorial.

67. Quote from Sano's Questionnaire, Box 30, MDC Coll.

68. Regina Markell Morantz, Cynthia Stodola Pomerleau, and Carol Hansen Fenichel. *In Her Own Words: Oral Histories of Women Physicians.* New Haven: Yale University 34.Press, 1982. Also see Sano's Social Security Death Index.

69. Khayat's Social Security Death Index.

70. Summarized from: "Tribute" to her by Jamaica Hospital, unidentified newspaper clipping n.d.

71. Bouton's date of birth is given as 25 December 1911 in the Social Security Death Index.

72. Information from Khayat's Questionnaire, Box 30, MDC Coll.

73. Italics, mine. See, Paul W. White, "Kennedy General Hospital", diss., Univ. of Memphis.

74. Quotes in Khayat's Questionnaire, Box 30, MDC Coll.

75. Khayat "Tribute" by Jamaica Hospital; both death dates Social Security Master File Index.

76. Morris: Dir. of Med. Specialists, Vol. 4, 1949; "News of the State Institutions," *Psychiatric Quarterly*, Vol. 13, No. 1, 128, DOI: 10.1007/BFO1575549; *New York State Journal of Medicine*, Vol. 37, Issues 1-12, 1937.

77. Quotes from Morris Questionnaire. Date of death could not be verified.

78. For quotes and summary of anesthetist role, see *Medical Department United States Surgery in World War II, Thoracic Surgery*, Vol. 1., 1963, 261.

79. Esther Leonard Papers, Missouri Historical Society, St Louis, Missouri. Also see Calmes, Selma Harrison, M.D. "Virginia Apgar M.D. At the Forefront of Obstetric Anesthesia. *American Society of Anesthesiologists Newsletter*, October 1992.

80. Bellafaire and Graf in *Women Doctors in War* note that there were fifty-six women contract surgeons in WWI although official records noted only fifty-five.

81. Margarete was listed with Hans A. Kotrnetz in the American Medical Directory, 1986 Ed. Sadly, Margarete and her husband died within months of each other. Hans born 23 August 1903 died at the age of 89 in New York 9 September 1992; she died 25 January 1993, in JAMA, 1993; *70(24):2987-2992.doi:10./ JAMA*.1993.03510240103047 Also noted in the Social Security Death Index for both. Hans produced many publications, both in German and English. Citizenship in "*Otsego Farmer,*"17 December 1943, p. 1.

82. See Laurie Wright, M.D., Douglas Bacon, M.D., and David Waisel, M.D., "Anesthesiology's Response to the Needs of the Armed Forces in World War Two." *Anesthesiology 2003*; 99: Abstract Archive 1283.

83. Credentials on-line: http:mds.servicerating.ca/Dr/Audrey_Allerton_Bill. Quotes in Bill Questionnaire; also see "Women Physicians in the Army", *Women in Medicine*, 9.

84. Dunham in "Women in Medicine,"8; stations noted in her Army Questionnaire.

85. School records and alumni information supplied by the University of Wisconsin, Madison. Dance information was supplied by David Null, archivist, who speculated that H'Doubler may have influenced Jackson's choices. Univ. of Wisconsin also had the first major in dance in the country. Also special thanks to David Null for his help with locating information and obituaries on Wisconsin women doctors.

86. Anesthesia training noted in "Women in Medicine," 7. Camp Barkeley is frequently misspelled as Barkley. There is also a picture of the two male *2nd* lieutenants at the Library of Congress Prints & Photographs Division Washington, DC, call number, LC-USE6-D-007368.

87. Jackson, in B*io Dir. Of the Amer. Psychiatric Assoc.*, 1968 Ed. Also see Jackson Social Security Death.

88. Quotes from Taylor Questionnaire.

89. Mary Ellen Condon-Rall, *A Brief History of Military Anesthesia*, 873.

90. David B. Waisel, "The Role of World War II and the European Theater of Operations in the Development of Anesthesiology as a Physician Specialty in the USA," *Anesthesiology* 2001, May; 94(5):907-14.

91. The author is grateful for notes, personal correspondence, and draft of chapter "A History of Women in American Anesthesiology," provided by Selma Harrison Calmes, MD.

92. "Experts Say Women Still Underrepresented in Orthopedic Surgery," 1 August 2005, Medscape Medical News. There still is that general perception that orthopedics is physically demanding and requires a lot of strength. With proper tech-

niques, new technology and devices, brute strength is not a requirement for the highly competitive field. Still, that perception is one reason women represent just 4.3 percent of board-certified orthopedic surgeons, according to the American Academy of Orthopaedic surgeons. A lack of role models is another. See *Chicago Tribune*, 17 November 2010.

93. "In Memoriam", The *Bulletin* of the Orleans Parish Medical Socʻety, 14 March 1960.

94. Ramos Questionnaire, Box 30, MDC Coll.

95. "Deaths", *JAMA* 9 April 1969, p. 180; also see *Times-Picayune*, 20 January 1960, p. 2, col. 1, and p.7, col. 2. She was listed on the orthopedic staff of the Charity Hospital, Louisiana State Unit for 1945-46 in "Reports of the Charity Hospital of Louisiana at New Orleans", 1 July 1945 to 30 June 1946; and again 4 January 1946 to 30 June 1947.

96. Quote "fed-up" in *Personnel in World War II*, 329. Some qualified women were not even accepted as contract surgeons. While one woman with an MD was not only classified as a special technician at one Army camp, they refused to grant her the required living expense allocation paid to doctors, see Walsh, *Doctors Wanted: No Women Need Apply*, 227.

Table 4.
Women Doctors Classified as
Internists in the AMC

Name	Rank at Assignment	Age/Status at Assignment	Dependents	Ward Duties
Angie Connor	Lt.	Div./31 single	No	Yes
Jean E. Henley	Lt.	Single/34	No	Yes
Gertrude Holmes	Capt.	Single/41	Mother	Yes
Margaret Janeway	Major	Single/47	Mother	Yes
Louella H. Liebert	Capt.	Single/28	Mother	Yes
Marion Loizeaux	Capt.	Single/39	Mother	Yes (See Chapt. 1)
Mae J. O'Donnell	Lt.	Single/34	No	Yes
Aurelia Rozov	Lt.	?/40	No	Yes

Table 5.
Six Women Doctors Classified as
Anesthesiologists in the AMC

Name	Rank/Age at Appointment	Medical School	Overseas
Audrey A. Bill*	Lt./27	Boston Medical	
Jean L. Dunham*	Lt./24	George Washington	Yes
Katherine Jackson*	Capt./43	Wisconsin	Yes
Margarete E. Kotrnetz	Lt./37	Vienna University	
Nell R. Reiley	Lt./25	Louisiana State	
Gwendolyn E. Taylor	Lt./35	Colorado	

*Received special anesthesia training in the Army

CHAPTER FIVE:

"Narrowing the Field": Women Doctors in Radiology, Preventive Medicine, Surgery, and Other Areas

Radiology was one of the few male-dominated scientific professions in which women gained a foothold and eventually went on to outnumber the men. This first happened in the context of X-ray technology during the first two decades of the twentieth century when both men and women practiced as radiologists and took X-rays and also interpreted them. Although radiologists professionalized in the early 1920s, "a division occurred between the radiologists, who could interpret X-rays for doctors, and the radiographers, who were proficient at taking patient X-rays." Male radiographers maintained that they needed only technical skills not nursing skills to take X-rays, but female radiographers, most often nurses, valued the importance of patient care and contact from dealing with broken bones, anesthesia, and injections to operating the equipment itself. Eventually the male radiographers were pushed out and females were able to advance as more positions became available to them.[1]

Radiology as a separate medical specialty has always had considerable appeal to the woman physician. "Almost any working arrangement is possible, ranging from full-time to part-time positions... short or long maternity leaves to temporary retirement." One important point is that "though there is emergency work in modern radiology, the woman who so desires can generally find a position that will involve little or no night and weekend call." It is also an expanding field since it has been subdivided into diagnosis and therapy. Within each division "there is room for further specialization" although a radiologist can still cover the general field if that is preferred. One researcher corresponded with twenty women who were either residents or in different types of practice of radiology. She learned that these women generally agreed that "acceptance by their colleagues and the variety of positions were part of their decision to enter the specialty."[2]

Pioneer women in radiology practiced their specialty at great personal costs. The risks of X-ray work for the operator and patient included the danger of getting radiation burns and radiation poisoning.[3] The long-terms side effects for the radiologist could also lead to cancer or even death. Marie Curie, for instance, contracted leukemia as a result of her continued exposure to radium. Elizabeth Fleischmann-Ascheim, another victim, was one of California's earliest radiographers. She was a bookkeeper who became interested in medical X-ray because of her physician brother-in-law. With his encouragement she took courses at the Van der Naille School of engineering and Electricity. In 1897, she was also the first person to open an X-ray laboratory in the state. "She radiographed many casualties of the Spanish-American War in order to locate metallic foreign bodies and fractures." In order to convince patients of the safety of the equipment, she frequently exposed herself to the X-ray beam. However, the equipment she was using at the time was also unshielded. By 1903 she developed skin irritation of her hands which she felt was related to the chemicals she used, but a year later she developed a skin carcinoma which claimed her life at the age of 46.[4] Two other cases demonstrated what could occur when dealing with radiation. Dr. Mary Monica Donovan lost the fingers on one hand because of the frequent radium insertions she performed for cancer of the cervix at St. Mary's Hospital in San Francisco. Dr.

Anna Hamann, from Germany, had no fingerprints due to radium damage so she was unable to prove to the government's satisfaction that she might not be a spy. This lack of proof kept her out of the Manhattan Project, an experience that her other colleagues at the University of Chicago shared.[5]

Radiology or roentgenology was still a very limited specialty by 1917.[6] When the United States entered World War I in April of that year, it continued as a separate division in the Surgeon General's Office throughout the war and until 1 December 1918, when it became the Section of Roentgenology under the Division of Surgery. Only the larger of the military hospitals were equipped with X-ray apparatus. Also, no effort had been made to maintain a selected group of officers who specialized in roenterology.[7] It was not surprising, then, that the fastest advances in radiology occurred in WWI when one of goals of the Army Medical Corps was to improve the portability of the X-ray machine. The United States had a total of five mobile X-Ray machines mounted on four-mule wagons before WWI, but after fifteen months of fighting, there were over seven hundred automobile units.[8] Another important goal for the Army was the recruitment of physicians, surgeons, and others who could operate the equipment such as X-ray technicians, electricians and photographers. Of the fifty-six women contract surgeons appointed in WWI, however, only one claimed roenterology as her specialty.[9]

The Radiologists

The Army Medical Corps classified only two women as radiologists in WWII although there were other interested applicants. When Dr. Dorothy Bell of Massachusetts inquired of Major Margaret Craighill if there were an opening for a woman medical officer in radiology, she received this response: "The Army Medical Corps needs medical officers, particularly those trained in special fields. In order to qualify for a responsible position as a Radiologist, one must be a Fellow of the American College of Radiologists. If you can meet these, as well as the qualifications for age and physical fitness, there is opportunity for you, although of course no one can promise you a definite assignment in advance."[10] Since Bells' name never appeared later on the list of commissioned officers, it can only be assumed that she decided to remain in civilian practice rather than take her chances with the Army.

Unlike Dr. Bell, the other two women radiologists were willing to gamble on getting an assignment in their specialty with the Army. One of these physicians was Dr. Melson Barfield-Carter, who one colleague described "as a hard worker, dedicated, firm in convictions, stern but fair, a challenger, an encourager, and easy to work with. She went out of her way to do for others."[11] One of the few Army women doctors to graduate from a southern medical school, she was the first female to graduate from Tulane Medical School in Louisiana in 1921, and she had to be firm in her convictions if she were to win a residency in radiology after that. Still single when she applied at Massachusetts General Hospital in Boston, she submitted her credentials under the name of M. Barfield. Although she was elated when she secured the position as the hospital's first female resident, the supervising physician was not; in fact, he became "upset" on learning that 'M. Barfield' was a woman.[12] When the administration learned they had hired a female, she had to be housed in the nursing school dormitories. "The embarrassment led to personal interviews for selection of future radiology residents at Massachusetts General Hospital."[13]

Dr. Melson Barfield (Carter). Courtesy Dept. of
Radiology, Univ. Alabama at Birmingham.

In contrast, Margaret Elizabeth Howe attended schools in the
Eastern part of the United States. A graduate of Bryn Mawr College in 1924, she completed work in physics, biological and physical
chemistry at University College, University of London, before entering medical school. She was awarded her medical degree in 1929
from the Woman's Medical College of Pennsylvania (WMCP), finished an internship in 1930 at Woman's Hospital of Philadelphia,
and did post-graduate work in Vienna in anatomy, clinical pathology, and cadaver surgery.[14]

Howe was just as strong in her convictions as Barfield-Carter. For her whole life she was convinced that women should have the right to be educated in separate institutions from men. After the WMCP decided to become coeducational in 1970 and admit six men in 1971, Howe protested as one of its loyal alumnae. She was opposed to the passing of Woman's Medical: "It would seem to me totally impractical and unwise to try to maintain the WMC as suggested and admit men students... Also it would seem almost inevitable that the men who might apply for admission would likely be the least desirable of the...men applicants to all medical schools both scholastically and otherwise."[15]

Both Howe and Barfield encountered many changes in the years preceding WWII. Melson Barfield married Dr. Henry Rose Carter, a cardiologist, on Feb. 18, 1928.[16] She returned to Birmingham in 1929, and began to practice radiology at Hillman Hospital, which had been the major hospital in Birmingham at the turn of the nineteenth century and gradually evolved into a large medical center and was renamed University of Alabama at Birmingham (UAB) Hospital in 1964.[17] While Barfield-Carter remained in the South, Martha E. Howe practiced in the East. From 1931 to 1934 she was in private practice in Philadelphia and also served on the staff of the Woman's Hospital and taught at the WMCP, which was associated with the hospital. She spent the next three years as Clinical Research Fellow at Memorial Hospital in New York City where she began another private practice. She held several hospital appointments as an assistant attending surgeon and as a consultant in oncology. She never married, but she did celebrate a golden anniversary. Having received her medical degree in 1929 from the WMCP, she received a congratulatory letter on the occasion of her fiftieth anniversary in 1979.[18]

These two women joined the Army Medical Corps only a month apart. In August of 1943 at the age of forty-eight, Barfield-Carter was commissioned a major, making her the third woman to be commissioned behind Craighill and Janeway. Certified by the American

Board of Radiology, all her Army assignments were in that specialty and all were in the Zone of the Interior. Howe's appointment was effective in September of 1943 when she received her captaincy. Like Barfield-Carter she was Board certified in Radiology (radiation therapy) but she was also a Fellow of the American College of Surgeons. The Army utilized her skills in both areas and assigned her at various times to radiology and the surgical services both in the United States and in two theaters of operation abroad.

Dr. Barfield-Carter was assigned first to Oliver General Hospital in Augusta, Georgia.[19] In August 1945 she was posted to Camp Grant, Illinois, and then in September to the Dante Annex of the Letterman General Hospital. Because of its location in San Francisco on the Pacific coast, Letterman became one of most critical Army hospitals for receiving sick and wounded from all over the Pacific Theater and eastern Asia. It also served for the definitive care of cases requiring deep x-ray or radium therapy. In August of 1944, the Dante Station Hospital merged with Letterman, thus making a total of 2,338 beds available. It was at the last place with its staggering numbers of cases where Barfield-Carter was made head of the radiology department.[20]

By this point, however, Barfield-Carter had other plans and she wrote to Craighill asking to be "placed on the approved list for retirement."[21] While she did not state her reason for this decision, it is clear that she intended to resign in order to return to Alabama, as Craighill wrote back to her: "With all good wishes for you in your new undertaking."[22] The new undertaking was Barfield-Carter's appointment as the first chair of the Department of Radiology at UAB, a position she held from 1945 to 1955. During this period she started the radiology residency-training program and the School of Radiological Technology there. She also had a private practice, and she donated the money she made to the hospital, hoping it would be used to pay for new equipment.[23]

She retired from UAB in 1955 but her colleagues remembered her as "an efficient, capable radiologist and as a kind, caring chairman."[24] Later she was associated with the Baptist Medical Center in Birmingham where she served as chief of radiology. Dr. Barfield-Carter died in Birmingham on 26 May 1973 at the age of seventy-eight and was buried at Elmwood Cemetery in Birmingham.[25]

Martha E. Howe's first assignment was at Fitzsimons General Hospital in Aurora, Colorado, which was used heavily during WWII to treat returning casualties.[26] Here she was made Chief of the therapy division, radiology section, from October 1943 to September 1944. Following this assignment, Howe was shipped overseas to the Mediterranean Theater of Operations and then to the European Theater from November 1944 to February 1945.[27] Her assignments were as ward officer in surgical services and as surgical consultant to female patients.

In 1954, Howe moved to New Mexico where she practiced at the Espasalo Hospital. In February of 1969 she retired because "of severe angina pectoris". [28] Her exact date of death is unknown, but she was deceased by 1980 as some alumni association mail came back in 1980 stamped "deceased". While little is known of her personal life, she was a dedicated physician. When an alumnae survey was mailed out from the WMCP in 1960 asking how the college could make the study of medicine more attractive to women, she gave a very definitive answer. "Medicine seems to be no longer an art and a technique—only a technique. Marriage, for women, must be an art and a technique... I can devote myself to one 24 hours a day, prayed but could not do two. Divided allegiances are said by some... to be among the reasons for our current confusions and distresses."[29]

Specialists in Communicable Diseases and Tropical Medicine

While radiology made its biggest advances in WWI, there were other major advances in medical technology that also coincided with

WWII. Blood banks were established, which meant the greater availability of blood transfusions, and while penicillin was not invented during the war, it was mass produced for the first time so that troops had its benefits in treating diseases and wound infections. There was a major thrust in preventive medicine as seen in the "wide range of preventive measures including immunizations against yellow fever, cholera, plague, influenza, typhus, typhoid and tetanus" that were developed. One of the many results of these advances was "the lower death rate from disease markedly below the killed-in-action rate." Furthermore, "over 350,000 women served with a peak strength of 271,000 representing 2% of the personnel in uniforms."[30] While only a very small percentage of these women were medical officers, they made contributions in many areas to be discussed in this chapter, which include preventive medicine, plastic surgery, blood work, and radiology, and a few other narrow specialties.

In keeping with its goal of expanding preventive medicine, the Army Medical Corps classified women medical officers as specialists in communicable diseases and tropical medicine.(See Tables 6, 7) Since the largest number of women doctors were assigned to General Duty (See Table 8, next chapter), they might also rotate to other services, including the contagion section, for brief periods as was seen in the case of Elizabeth Garber Tate who was listed as one of several women assigned to general medical duties as well as preventive medicine. Only one woman, Dr. Agnes Hoeger, was classified as a specialist in Tropical Medicine although just three women were also sent to the Tropical School of Medicine in Washington, D.C. for training in this area, including one internist, Dr. Aurelia Rozov. At least three women medical officers served as an instructor in Tropical Medicine or were the Chief of a section at various times. Drs. Gertrude Cone, Martha L. Crandall, Theresa Ting Woo, and Elizabeth Garber (later Tate) were classified in Communicable Diseases. (See Table 7) Regarding their ages, Crandall and Garber were twenty-eight when they signed on and Cone and Woo were thirty-three years old. Crandall and Garber, the two youngest, were married with no children and Cone was the only officer who claimed a dependent, which in her case was her mother. When it came to their medical training, Cone attended Tufts University School of Medicine and Woo finished up at Michigan. Crandall and Garber were both graduates of the University of Indiana, but Garber started out by serving on contract as a medical officer with the WACs in 1942 before she was commissioned. Both Garber Tate and Woo had specialties in pediatrics in civilian life.[31]

Garber was commissioned 19 June 1943 and through November of 1944, she remained a medical officer with the WACs; and during all of her service up to that time, she was stationed at Ft. Des Moines, Iowa. In December, she was shipped overseas to the Mediterranean Theater, first to Africa and then to Italy. (She also got married to Tate while she was overseas). In looking back on her Army career, she reported that she was not given duties in keeping with her special training as she had been a pediatrician in civilian life. If she had any advice to offer, it was regarding the time she had put in as contract surgeon: "[I] believe that our assignment and duty as contract surgeons…be given credit for medical work similar to that done by commissioned officers."[32]

Dr. Martha Crandall had been working at Indianapolis City Hospital when she received a letter of congratulations on her appointment from Major Margaret D. Craighill. Apparently she had had some concerns over her uniform because Craighill, as Consultant for Women's Health and Welfare, had written:

> Women medical officers wear the same uniform as is worn by officers of the Women's Army Corps, with, however, two exceptions. They may wear the overseas cap, or the hat that has been authorized for women medical officers. This may be ordered from Knox the Hatter, Fifth Avenue, New York, for $7.50. Be sure to state your head size. Also, they

may use any sort of military design brown handbag, either with or without the strap. If the strap is used, the bag is suspended from the left shoulder...I advise you not to get more than one summer blouse (jacket)—that of tropical worsted. Officers, under the rank of Major, receive an initial uniform allowance of $250.00.

Craighill might have added that while women doctors wore the same uniform as the WAC because of endeavors to do away with the many different types of uniforms worn by the women in the Army, "they had some distinctive items, such as the off-duty dress, the yellow scarf and yellow gloves."[33]

When it came to formulating their impressions of the service, the women declared that everything had been generally satisfactory. Martha Crandall, however, was the only officer who offered information in any great detail. While she agreed with the women about her overall experience in the Army, she noted: "My assignment has been satisfactory except that many times there has been more work than could be capably and efficiently done by one person." For six months, for example, she and another medical officer were responsible for the monthly WAC physicals at her station, although during a three-month period she did "these physicals alone—an average of 425 women per month." During another month she had complete care of the contagion service, which consisted of 1-3 wards with approximately 90-100 patients. She recalled, "During that time there has been no other assigned medical officer." For six months she taught a class of 1-2 hours a week on "the Care and Control of Communicable Diseases" as part of the ANC training program. Crandall also served as Chief of the Contagious Disease Section at one station. She concluded, "because of the press of duties, mostly administrative, it has not been possible to study the cases thoroughly nor has it been possible to do any outside reading to any extent."[34]

Dr. Theresa Ting Woo was one of two Chinese women medical officers—the other being Poe-Eng Yu, a psychiatrist discussed in an earlier chapter. Woo, who was referred to as "a lady of many countries", was born 15 October 1911 in Peiping, China. She spent part of her childhood in Peru, but after coming to the United States she proceeded to enroll in school and received her BA from the College of the Pacific, Stockton, California, in 1930, and then her medical degree from the University of Michigan in 1934. She acquired her pediatric training as a resident at Children's Memorial Hospital in Chicago, Illinois and the Presbyterian Hospital in New York City.[35]

Woo's Army experiences expanded her interest in public health. Although her specialty was pediatrics, she was stationed as a ward officer in the communicable disease wards at Lawson General Hospital in Atlanta, Georgia. After that she received training in tropical medicine at the Army Medical Center in Washington D. C., and was posted next to the Analysis Branch, Medical Intelligence Division in the Preventive Medical Service, in the Surgeon General's Office. Following her discharge she gained further experience in the District of Columbia and the Territory of Hawaii Health Departments.

When the Korean War started, there was a pressing need for doctors once again. In August 1950, the Army reestablished the authorization for women physicians to serve in the Army since the law ended in 1947 that authorized the commissioning of women doctors. As soon as the enabling legislation passed, the Army recalled three reserve women physicians to active duty and Woo was among them.[37] She was commissioned a major and assigned to the Preventive Medicine Division of the Office of the Surgeon General along with Dr. Ruth E. Church in January of 1951—"not to roles that would have them treating or commanding men."[36]

After she left the service, Woo went back to school and received her Master's Degree in Public Health from Harvard University in 1955.[37] In August of 1956, she was appointed to a new position as director of the Ann Arbor public schools health services where she was responsible for implementing a new type of school health program. At the same time, she was an assistant professor of maternal and child health in the School of Public Health at the University of Michigan, and she was primarily responsible for supervising the medical staff of the school system—medical doctors and nurses who were provided under an arrangement with the University of Michigan's Department of Pediatrics. This was an exciting opportunity for her as it was the first time that there was a cooperative plan between public schools and a university program in terms of providing advanced field training for professionals in Ann Arbor. Eventually Woo also found time to engage in private practice. She passed away 22 November 1997 and was buried at Garrison Forest Veterans Cemetery, Owing, Mills, Maryland.[38]

While women doctors joined the Army for a variety of reasons, some volunteered because they had relatives in the Armed Forces. Dr. Gertrude Cone, for instance, wanted to be in uniform "because she had two brothers in the military." She graduated from Tufts Medical School in 1937, having received her BA from Radcliffe in 1931.[39] After receiving her commission in August of 1943, she was stationed at four different locations including the American Red Cross Blood Donor Center in San Francisco and the Bushnell General Hospital in Utah.[40]

Bushnell was a 60-building hospital and the fifth largest hospital on the United States mainland. It had several areas of specialization, which included tropical medicine, reconstructive medicine, neurology, and psychiatry. With Cone's classification in communicable diseases, it made sense that she should serve alongside Dr. Hilde Koppel, who was a neuropsychiatrist. When asked about her Army service, Cone reported that she treated both male and female patients and "everything was satisfactory" in terms of her assignments and status as an Army officer.[41]

The Army placed a great deal of emphasis on tropical medicine in WWII. The worldwide theatre of war and the shipping of troops to countries where tropical disease was endemic prompted this. Expanding air travel and transportation of military forces also made it easy to transmit disease from country to country. Of significant concern to the Army were such disease entities as malaria, dysentery, and to a lesser degree, sand fly fever, dengue, hookworm, etc. Malaria, however, remained the biggest problem of all, and "the numbers incapacitated were conjectured to be in the millions."[42]

During the war, the spread of the so-called exotic diseases was of such grave concern to the Armed Forces that "all military personnel were immunized against typhoid, paratyphoid, tetanus and smallpox. Those serving in endemic areas were also protected against cholera, plague, typhus, and yellow fever."[43] Early in the war, the Army School of Tropical Medicine at Washington selected groups of medical officers for an eight-week course of training in tropical medicine, and a few of these officers were women. (See Table 6). Agnes Hoeger, however, was the only woman Army officer classified with a specialty in tropical medicine. In fact, her experience was so vast since she had served as a medical missionary, that it is hard to believe that there were many male officers with similar expertise in the field. The fact remains, however, that The Surgeon General had been so active in finding qualified medical candidates to accept commissions that he had sought out and brought into the Medical Department "a number of returned medical missionaries, whose intimate knowledge of climate, sanitary conditions, and endemic diseases in strategic areas, such as Okinawa, later proved of inestimable value. Many of these men went into preventive medicine; others devoted themselves to medical intelligence work."[44]

The only woman specialist in tropical medicine was Agnes Hoeger who was born on 16 June 1910 in Arena, North Dakota. Her grandparents were both missionaries and her father was a Lutheran pastor, so it was not unexpected that she should follow in their footsteps and decide to become a medical missionary at a young age. She was one of six women to graduate from the University of Minnesota Medical School in 1935, and after completing her residency; she learned there was an urgent need for a doctor in New Guinea. By September of 1935, at the age of twenty-five, she completed all preparations to leave home and set off to fulfill her life-long dream.

After spending about two and one-half years in New Guinea, Hoeger was asked to leave in order to accompany a friend back home to the United States to seek medical care. Suddenly her days were filled with numerous requests from around the country to speak about her mission work in New Guinea. By the spring of 1938, she had grown weary of the demanding pace, and she took up residence in the Wartburg Hospice in Minneapolis, which was also near the University of Minnesota library. With time to think, she decided the best tropical medicine school in the world in 1938 was in London, England, and she applied and found that she was the first woman ever to be admitted. "She would attend their spring session from March 30 to July 6, a session specifically for medical doctors who either had been or were going to be practicing medicine in the tropics." On 24 June she attended her last classes—she had also accomplished one of her goals by becoming a "Fellow" in Tropical Medicine. Then she headed back to New Guinea where "her annual salary as a missionary medical doctor was between $200-$350 for almost 30 years."[45]

Back in New Guinea, Hoeger carried on her medical practice which included treating those suffering from malaria, leprosy, stomach disorders, and yaws (open sores that would not heal). But "her interest was greatest in the area of disease prevention. She constantly emphasized the fact that it was much easier to avoid illness than to cure it." One preventive measure she employed was to inject every single person in a community of 5,000 with a new vaccine for yaws, "eliminating disease that had once ravaged the country."[46] She also set up clinics stressing baby care and cleanliness, and she trained nurses and physicians' assistants, using classroom materials she wrote herself. Prior to World War II, she was known as "the walking doctor" because she would walk many miles to the scene of an accident or to the homes of sick or injured.

By the summer of 1940, Agnes was transferred to the tiny village of Finschhafen because the Allies were interning some German missionaries, including medical doctors, in Australia. The hope was that the allies and the Japanese would ignore such a small outlying area. On 13 February 1942, however, the American and Australian military ordered all missionaries evacuated from Finschhafen immediately in the event "that the allies needed to burn everything before the Japanese arrived."[47] Since Hoeger was the only doctor, she was allowed to remain, but within three days she was ordered to leave with a few other men who had also stayed behind. The small group was flown to another village, but when Japanese planes started dropping bombs, Hoeger and several men set out on foot for another village in a remote mountain area. When this was no longer safe, Agnes and her group were forced to cross directly through mountain jungles to avoid detection. "We were a party of six including the voluntary rifleman who escorted us," she wrote. "We were fortunate in having mostly dry weather so that we had to do very little slithering down mountain paths or wading through swampy country. It also made the work of carrying easier for the native men accompanying us."[48]

After a series of short stays in various places, Hoeger arrived in Australia 16 March 1942 and she decided to remain in Brisbane where she had many friends. After waiting two months, she obtained a position as a physician at Children's Hospital in Brisbane and then to Bundaberg Hospital where she remained for almost a year before she realized the war was going to last and it was best to return to the United States. She reached Fargo, North Dakota, 12 July 1943 and less than three weeks later she applied for a commission to the United States Army Medical Corps.

Hoeger was commissioned a first lieutenant in the Army Medical Corps 3 December 1943, and later promoted to captain 13 October 1944. She spent her first month at Lawson General Hospital and then went for a two-month training course in tropical medicine at the Army Medical Center, Washington, DC in March 1944. She had hoped to be stationed in New Guinea, but the Army had other ideas and sent her on to Lima, Peru, as a part of Nelson Rockefeller's Commission on Inter-American Affairs. After orientation in Lima she was assigned as a field medical officer in Peru "assisting in organizing small hospitals in the jungle along with a public health program with special emphasis on maternal and child health services."[49]

With her training and interest in disease prevention, this was a perfect assignment for her. In her first situation at Tingo Maria, the residents had come down from the mountains to work on a huge road construction project. "Unaccustomed to tropical living, they were easily susceptible to malaria, dysentery, ringworm, and hookworm. Hookworm was most prevalent among children as the parasitic hookworms entered through the soles of bare feet and travel upwards to the stomach where they eat most of the food their victims consumed. Thus, "Agnes understood that convincing the children to wear sandals would not be easy, since none had ever worn shoes." She began to hold classes for the children and began to train a few health care workers, who in turn trained others. "By the time she left Tingo Maria, "hookworm had been reduced to a minor annoyance instead of the leading cause of mortality in children."[50]

The next year, Hoeger (who was now a captain) was transferred to Chimbote, a small fishing port on the Peruvian coast.[51] She began to institute many of the same programs that had been successful in Tingo Maria, with similar results. Overall conditions of life in Tingo Maria and Chimbote were so greatly improved by her work that she "received many commendations and awards from the U.S. Army and special commendations from Nelson Rockefeller and from President

Harry S. Truman." When she left Tingo Maria, the newspaper carried this headline on the front page: "Our Savior Leaves Us!"[52]

Hoeger was one of the few women medical officers who were assigned only to her specialty area while in service. "I was particularly happy in my assignment to the Coordinator's Office of Inter-American Affairs, she recalled, "because it was based largely on my previous experience of 7 years as medical missionary in the Territory of New Guinea—that of dealing largely with tropical diseases, organizing small hospitals and training local personnel as sanitarians or nurses' aides."[53] In both places in Peru, she took care of women and children most of the time although she sometimes treated male patients.

In April 1945, the Board of Foreign Missions of the American Lutheran Church informed Agnes that they were sending missionaries back to New Guinea and requested that she resign from the Army. Agnes contacted her commanding officer on 29 April 1945 requested that she be able to return to her former missionary work. But her discharge did not come quickly and it was seven months before her separation papers arrived in December 1945. Once discharged, however, she returned home to Fargo, but it was nearly six months before she could sail again for New Guinea.

As she approached middle age, Hoeger was as active as ever. She remained in New Guinea from 1946-1953. Then she decided to return home for a year's furlough. By this time, "she had spent almost 17 years as a doctor in tropical settings." She returned to the mission field the next year and she remained until 1965 when her mother's failing health prompted her to leave her beloved New Guinea. Back in Fargo, she was now fifty-five years old and she had spent thirty years away from her homeland. For the next decade, Hoeger took care of her aging parents until their deaths. In 1966 she held a full-time job as the Director of Medical Services at the Good Samaritan Village in Hastings, Nebraska. In 1970 she completed school and qualified as a nursing home administrator, and she spent several months at a physicians' institute on Public Health at a university in

Denver, Colorado. She completed a medical records program next so "she could better assist" Good Samaritan facilities in resident care.[54]

At the age of 72, however, Hoeger surprised everyone when she told them she had been accepted by the Peace Corps and would be going to a South Pacific island, Tonga. She spent 16 months there before deciding it was time to take a leave of absence from the Peace Corps to travel and even make a return visit to New Guinea. After her traveling, she returned home where her life fell into a pleasant routine. By 1988, she decided to live near friends and relatives at the good Samaritan Village in Kissimmee, Florida, since her doctor felt she should no longer live alone. She met her death peacefully on 23 June 1992 and she was buried beside her father and mother in the cemetery on the grounds of the Arthur Good Samaritan Center. At a dedication service for the establishment of an Alzheimer's care unit in her name some years later, a good friend summed up her life this way: "For us, Dr. Agnes Hoeger will always be one of God's special saints who served her Lord with great dedication, perseverance, faith, love and kindness."[55]

Other Specialists in Surgery

When considering another field in medicine, such as surgery, it is generally conceded that this is the "most macho specialty." The doctor must win the approval of the head of the residency program in order to enter a specialty, and it is at this point in their career that women face the most barriers. In instances when there are few residencies in certain fields like surgery, combined with a high demand for such residencies, the bargaining power falls in the hands of the department heads who "feel that they would rather pick from the best male candidates than take a chance on a woman." Part of this thinking is related to the higher rate of mobility and even the temporary withdrawal of women surgeons to bear children which creates difficulties in the administration of the department in which the women serve.[56] Furthermore, the length of the residency in general surgery, like pathology, usually requires a residency of four or more years with regular duty in the hospital and on nights. Women doctors are more likely to consider how their choice of specialty and its demands will affect the balance between career and family and personal life, a fact which contributes to their underrepresentation in surgical specialties even today.

Dr. Alma Dea Morani, the first woman surgeon in the United States, believed that one of the major barriers for those seeking surgery as a specialty was the fact that there were no woman surgeons around who could serve as role models in the late 1920s and 30s— which, of course was between the two world wars. She maintained the reason the WMCP didn't encourage women to go into surgery at the time she was there, was very simple: "The men were the surgeons, and the men had never trained a woman in surgery." And there were practically no residencies in surgery in those days. "You became an assistant to an accomplished surgeon and took a preceptorship, which is exactly what I did."[57]

Dr. Genia Sakin was the only woman Army medical officer who was classified as a plastic surgeon and she was just four years older than Morani. Born in Lithuania in 1903 to Jewish parents, she was reported to be one of eight children, but she somehow managed to save enough money to go to Berlin where she was accepted as a medical student at the Friedrich Wilhelm University. She graduated with honors from a medical course which took six years, and she followed-up by working as an intern in government hospitals. Eventually Sakin opened her own office in Berlin where she practiced general medicine for a short time, but since she was interested in plastic surgery, she worked for two years as an assistant to one of her college professors. In this capacity she performed "many operations" until she was "pronounced qualified" by her professor.[58] Thus, like Dr. Morani, she, too, learned her craft in a preceptorship with a male surgeon.

Dr. Genia Sakin with Pres. Harry S. Truman.
Courtesy Sakin Family Collection.

Sakin's life was going smoothly until the Nazi government came into power and the anti-Semitic crusade started. Because of unwanted attentions from a prominent Nazi official, she knew she would have to flee Germany, as she feared "something terrible would happen" to her. "One cannot appreciate, I am sure," she said, "just how such a state of affairs will affect one's nerves, particularly when you see friends and members of your race beaten, killed, and imprisoned simply because they do not believe in a political party or happened to be born a Jew."[59] With the help of medical colleagues, she fled the country, supposedly to attend a plastic surgeons' convention in New York.

It is not known who or what organization helped her, but the AMWA was active in helping its women colleagues escape from Europe. The Committee for the Relief of Distressed Women Physicians had been created during the annual meeting of the AMWA in San Francisco in June of 1938. Through the efforts of the members of the committee, help was extended to women colleagues, who were obliged to flee from Austria and Germany "because of persecution, and because they were deprived of all means to earn a livelihood." The committee tried to remind its members: "One must always remember that these splendid and outstanding women formerly occupied important positions in their community, and were chiefs of various hospital departments, or were holding government positions in health, physical education, maternal welfare, etc."[60]

Sakin eventually made it to Boston, Massachusetts, where some of her relatives lived. She was admitted on a temporary permit as an alien, and it was said, "at first glance, she wouldn't impress new acquaintances as being a young woman with scientific degrees and professional responsibility."Her hair is too golden, her eyes too blue and wide, her lips too softly feminine." But she believed in her profession as a plastic surgeon. "It's been all she has had to cling to," one newspaper observed.[61] Congressman Arthur D. Healey from Boston was instrumental in helping her obtain an extension to remain in America while attempts continued to help her stay permanently so she could become a citizen and get a medical license to begin practice again. After she passed her examination in the United States, she said: "Women doctors were not numerous in the thirties. Women surgeons were rarer still. I was afraid I might not make a go of it."[62]

By the time World War II broke out, Sakin was an established plastic surgeon in the United States, but she decided she wanted to put her efforts elsewhere and she volunteered with the Army Medical Corps. She was commissioned a lieutenant 11 March 1944, and classified as a plastic surgeon, the only woman medial officer with that designation. Like many women medical officers she had a series of assignments, not always in her specialty. She started out at Lawson General Hospital in Plastic Surgery, but the Army decided to reassign her and put her in charge of a Blood Donor Mobile Unit with the American Red Cross where she remained for several months.[63] She believed this was a bad match with her skills.

In order to understand Sakin's perspective, we have to know something about what was going on with blood banks during WWII. In 1940, African-American surgeon, Charles Richard Drew, had developed a way to preserve and store blood so it could be ready for instant use. When Britain needed blood for its wounded, Drew helped establish blood banks in England and then in the United States.[64] These blood banks were invaluable because they were counted on to supply blood to local hospitals as well as to British ships and military bases.

When America declared war after Pearl Harbor, the US military also needed blood to transport to combat theaters, and the role of blood banks became even more crucial to the war effort. Across the country, patriotic citizens rushed to give blood and "the numbers of donors jumped to over 700 a week."[65] The American Red Cross conducted an extensive blood donor program during the entire war, but personnel shortages could not keep up with the demand, as qualified civilian doctors could not be found to head the centers. Worse, it was estimated that "the whole blood procurement program was being jeopardized because civilian physicians were leaving the centers to enter the Army or for other reasons," so it seemed feasible to consider whether it might "be possible to have a number of Army officers... assigned to the Red Cross Blood Donor Service." One estimate suggested that 56 bleeding teams would be necessary "each to procure 500 bleedings per week." It was recommended to the Surgeons General of both the Army and the Navy that they assign a small number of medical officers to temporary duty in the Red Cross bleeding centers, "on the ground that shortages of personnel were already jeopardizing the entire program… [and] that losses occurred when blood was collected by untrained and incompetent personnel."[66]

As staff shortages continued an attempt was made to utilize officers separated from service for physical disabilities, but this proved unsuccessful as they were often "unable to tolerate duty in the centers and entirely unable to withstand the hardships of work in mobile units." Also many officers had "to be relieved because of reactivation of their physical disabilities." It was felt that this solution would be poor public relations in view of the urgent appeals being made across the country for blood donors. The opinion of many of the volunteer physicians serving as local technical; supervisors was that a number of Army medical officers "of substandard quality had been assigned to the bleeding centers and that their handling of donors had sometimes created serious breaches in public relations." It was concluded that: "Essential as was the work of these blood donor centers, assignment to them was neither interesting nor desirable." Furthermore, attempts to rotate the officers were unsuccessful and many remained in blood donor centers for two years or more "without chance for promotion."[67]

In view of all these problems, one can only imagine how any highly qualified Army medical officer would have felt when hearing about assignment to a bleeding center. Yet it was in these circumstances that Dr, Genia Sakin, a leading plastic surgeon in civilian life, found herself as she packed up to work in a Red Cross Blood Donor Mobile Unit. From the Valley Forge General Hospital, a center for plastic surgery, she was sent to Pittsburgh to take the place of the blood bank's physician who was absent because of illness. "I was shocked when transferred to blood donor service for I had wanted to go abroad. Speaking many languages, I feel that is where I could do better work but in the Army one takes orders, not issues them."[68] Privately, Sakin was even more expansive in the remarks concerning her assignment. "While on Red Cross duty covering period of eight months I was obliged to furnish own living quarters and was requiring expenses of $7-$8 per diem in excess of amount which would have cost living at post."[69]

Finally by May of 1945, Sakin got another assignment at Northington General Hospital, Tuscaloosa Alabama, as a ward officer in the Plastic Section.[70] In October of the same year she was promoted to captain, and by 1947, having achieved the rank of major, she was one of only four women doctors who still remained in the Army. At that point she was stationed in Berlin at the 279th Station Hospital there.[71] To this day, one veteran recalls his meeting with the woman Army surgeon. Known only as Sebby, short for Sebastian, he had been stationed with the 298th Army Band in Berlin. He was only 18 years old in 1947 when learned that there was American Hospital nearby where he could have his nose fixed. "I had broken it playing football, in my younger days," he explained, "and the bone grew in crooked, plus I had a deviated ceptum [sic] in my left nostril. The operation was done by a Woman Russian surgeon named Captain Genia Sakin, because I needed plastic surgery and she was the only one available to who could do the operation."[72]

Around the same time, it looked like Sakin and the three other women medical officers would be relieved of their duties in 1947. General Raymond W. Bliss made every effort to have them transferred to the Women's Medical Specialist Corp because he was convinced that these officers were "practicing physicians and surgeons who have served the Medical Department with distinction during World War II. They possess special qualifications which render their retention on active duty greatly to be desired." He also believed that "the purpose of this exigency is solely to make it administratively possible to retain the services of these officers during the present crucial period when the Medical Department is confronted with an acute shortage of medical officers."[73] Regardless of the general's efforts, all four women were relieved of their duty.[74]

In many ways, the 1950s were the most rewarding years of Sakin's life, for it was only after she left the Army Medical Corps that she could devote herself completely to those who truly needed her special skills in plastic surgery. While donating her medical skills in Greece during 1950-51, she worked at four hospitals "assisted by the top surgeons of the country."[75] Her humanitarian efforts also took her to Turkey, Israel, Brazil, and Japan. In July of 1957 she came to the Philippines "to rest for three days after her ten-week stay in Japan where she worked among the indigent deformed people and the atom bomb victims in Hiroshima. The second day she was here she had to change her plans, for the lobby of the Manila Hotel where she had a modest room was crowded with disfigured people who begged her to help them."[76] Of course, she could not refuse and when she was not consulting or operating, she gave surgical demonstrations for the medical students at the Manila Central University Hospital. After six weeks, she had exhausted her funds and she had to go back to her office on Fifth Avenue in New York to resume her practice.

One of Sakin's many cherished memories was the Gimble Award which she was given in 1956 "as the most unselfish woman in America".[77] But she thought of herself as being more than a resident of New York City. Once, when asked about her citizenship, she replied: "I am an American citizen, and I love my country, but I am also a citizen of the world. I love humanity."[78] She succumbed to malignant lymphoma in the Massachusetts General Hospital, Boston, 11 September 1960 at the age of fifty-seven.[79]

In 1943, there were only a few other women physicians who had unique skills that the Army wanted, and they were classified in general surgery: Drs. Eleanor Hamilton, Isabella Harrison, and Anna M. Patton (Classified for General Duty and Surgery). Hamilton was the oldest at age 41, Harrison was 30, and Patton was the youngest at age 26. Hamilton was a medical graduate from Western Reserve University in Michigan, Harrison was from the prestigious Johns Hopkins, and Patton finished up at the WMCP which was known for graduating the most women physicians who went on to enter the Army Medical Corps or the Navy in WWII.[80] In view of her experience, Hamilton was given the rank of captain and the other two women, being much younger, were lieutenants when they volunteered.

In their personal remarks regarding their Army work, the women voiced different opinions. Hamilton observed: "I would not care for a permanent rank in the Army but I have been very glad for the experience I had had. In the 17 months of service I have been treated as an equal with the male officers. Have felt no discrimination either for or against me as a woman M.D. Have been allowed to pull equal duty with the men. A very satisfactory experience." Harrison reported: "I felt that, while I was not forging ahead in my profession, I was doing a needed job as far as the war effort was concerned. After my transfer to Ft. Des Moines, my special training was of no use and a great deal of my work was paper work and that which could be done by a [word unclear] administrative officer. The rest could have been handled easily by an intern with no special training." Patton's career was generally satisfying except for one assignment—that was when she was posted for three months to Ft. Oglethorpe, Georgia, to serve as an "instructor for WAC medical technicians."[81]

After the war ended, these three surgeons took various paths. Eleanor Hamilton was one of four women physicians who were retained in the Army. Classified in general surgery, she served as Chief of Obstetrics and Gynecology at Letterman General Hospital in California until 1947 when the last of the women medical officers were all released. One obituary notes that she passed away at the age of seventy-seven.[82]

Isabella Harrison was born on a dairy farm in New York State in 1914. She recalled that her mother, a homemaker, was "advanced for her time" in supporting her career. Her father was shocked by his daughter's plans, "but he went along with" his wife. Harrison volunteered in the Army Medical Corps 15 September 1944, and she maintained that the ready availability of antibiotics revolutionized the practice of medicine as "it broadened the scope of surgeries tremendously."[83] When her Army stint was over, she completed her residency at Church Home and Hospital and, in 1947 she became the first woman to serve as chief resident in surgery. She was also one of the first women to be certified by the American Board of Surgery.[84] Much of her later career was spent working for the Veterans Administration where she became a director of the residency program. She enjoyed the VA's emphasis on training and "was happy not to have to concern herself with the financial aspects of a medical practice. She never encountered gender-based problems from other doctors, though patients there could be more difficult."[85]

Harrison retired from medical practice when she was in her 70s, and she moved to Virginia Beach to be near her nieces since she never married and had no children of her own. In 1999, "she established the Isabella Harrison, M.D. Scholarship for Medical Education, providing scholarships for women medical students at Johns Hopkins who are interested surgical careers." She received the Distinguished Alumni Award from Johns Hopkins, which is an award that recognizes personal, professional, or humanitarian achievement.[86] Apart from macular degeneration that now prevents her from reading and from her lifetime hobby of bird watching; she has maintained generally good health. At age ninety-six, she elected to undergo hip replacement surgery in January of 2010 to relieve the pain from arthritis in her right hip. Although her own doctors advised against the surgery because of her advanced age, she was still determined to take on a new challenge—that is the kind of attitude that has served her well through her long life.[87]

After separation from Army service, Anna Patton married Jack Russell in postwar years although she continued to use her maiden name professionally. She and her husband continued to live near Pittsburgh, Pennsylvania, where she specialized in obstetrics and gynecology at both Magee and West Penn Hospitals. She died 12

November 2009 but was preceded in death by her husband. The couple had no children. In the "Guest Book" that many visitors signed following her death, one former patient noted that Dr. Patton had delivered seven of her mother's children as well as her sister's child and one of her own. She wrote: "I wasn't aware of her military service in WWII. I will especially remember her this Veterans' Day and always."[88]

Other Women Specialists

Although there were few women surgeons in the country in the 1940s, there were just as few specialists in ophthalmology. Bronislava Z. Reznick was the only woman ophthalmologist in the Army Medical Corps, and like Genia Sakin, she was assigned to the blood bank service during WWII although this was the case for a few other medical officers at various times. She was also among the first group of women doctors deployed to the ETO.[90] When it came to her medical training, Craighill's official list of women doctors noted only that Reznick graduated from "St. Valdimir".[91] While the facts about her background are sketchy, it is known that she was born 15 December 1899 and she was forty-five years of age when she volunteered. She listed her marital status as divorced, and noted that her home was located in Chicago, Illinois. Prior to the war, she was listed as an Assistant in Ophthalmology, in the College of Medicine, University of Illinois beginning 16 May, 1932, and continuing until 31 August of that year without salary.[92] Another source indicated that she "came from Chicago, trained in Otolaryngology, was assigned to her specialty" in the Army.[93]

Captain Reznick was appointed 25 August 1943. She had an assortment of duties starting with ten days in the dispensary at Ft Des Moines, Iowa, followed by an assignment as attending surgeon to WAC personnel and consultant in EENT at Camp Crowder, Missouri. Next she was sent to the Blood Donor Center in Louisville, Kentucky, which was where the Red Cross had established the regional blood donor center. After this, she worked in her specialty both in the States and lastly with the ETO where she was eventually placed in charge of the EENT section. Reznick stated that she treated "predominantly" male patients, and despite her numerous assignments, she felt that her Army experience was satisfactory. It is not known what happened to her in postwar years other than that she accepted a position with the Veterans Administration.[94] She relocated to Los Angeles, California, in 1983 and died there at the age of ninety-six on 21 September 1996.[95]

Although an occasional woman physician was classified in a highly specialized area of medicine, Celia Ekelson Ragus was the only woman urologist in the Army Medical Corps, and only a few scanty facts are known about her. Born in 1895, she graduated in 1923 from medical school at Long Island College Hospital in Brooklyn, New York, and completed one year of internship, rotating service, at the Metropolitan Hospital also in New York. In the mid to late 1930s she worked at Mt. Sinai Hospital in New York and was also in private practice until June 1943. She always used Ekelson professionally, although she was known by Ragus in the Army.[96] Among the oldest women medical officers, she was forty-nine years of age and married when she volunteered. She received her commission as a captain 16 August 1944 and was assigned as a ward surgeon with the Oteen VA Hospital in Asheville, North Carolina, the only VA facility in the southeast at the time devoted to the treatment of respiratory ailments. She wrote that she was "most unhappy" about this assignment. "My orders, read 'as there is no suitable vacancy for you in any army installation, you have been assigned to the Veterans Administration.'"[97]

In commenting on her Army assignments, Ragus declared they were "unsatisfactory". She noted: "Since I volunteered with this Army I was never assigned to perform duties commensurate with my training and ability." As to the value of her service both to the war effort and to her own experience, she noted both were also "unsatisfactory."[98] Following her discharge, she went back to New York City and worked at the Union Health Center. She expired at the age of 74 on 30 October 1969 of cerebral artery sclerosis. Her obituary referred to her as Celia Ekelson.[99]

Evelyn Meadows Bellaire was the only medical officer classified with a specialty in Tuberculosis. Prior to volunteering, she lived in Wallum Lake, Rhode Island, and she had completed her medical training at the Medical College of Virginia. She was commissioned a lieutenant 4 September 1943 at the age of thirty-one and reported that she was married with no children. She was assigned to Ft. Des Moines Station Hospital as a ward officer, and served as a dispensary medical officer where she conducted monthly physical inspections. Bellaire's impressions of her Army service were unsatisfactory as she believed she had been too long at one post.

Lt. Bellaire, it appears, was either asked to leave or quietly discharged because she was later listed as being "inactive" in service on Craighill's list of Army women doctors. Although no further information as to any discharge was noted, it appears that she had a serious drinking problem. Dr. Poe-Eng Yu, Army psychiatrist, confided to Craighill: "Lt. Bellaire is in one of her drinking episodes again" and confined to a closed neuropsychiatric ward at the Station Hospital. "It is too bad," Yu commented, "that such a nice girl as Lt. Bellaire would develop a bad habit that is not readily amendable to treatment. All of us women doctors who knew her at Ft. Des Moines agree that she was one of the finest doctors of the whole group. She was capable, conscientious, quiet and unassuming; between her drinking bouts (which is about every six months and only when she is on leave) she is a perfect lady. She is a hard worker and is well-liked by everyone who knows her."[100]

Pauline E. Garber, born 4 September 1908 in Strasburg Ohio, had an Army classification as a medical laboratory officer. She was a graduate of Wittenburg University, the University of Kansas (where she received a Master's degree in Chemistry), and the medical school at the University of Kansas in 1936. She interned at the Huron Road Hospital in East Cleveland, Ohio, 1939-41 and then accepted a position as an assistant professor of biochemistry back in Kansas until 1943.

Dr. Pauline Garber. Courtesy WIMSA.

At the age of thirty-six, Garber was commissioned a lieutenant 8 January 1944 and she listed Lawrence, Kansas, as her residence, also claiming her mother as a dependent. Pauline E. Garber was the only woman to be classified solely as a medical laboratory officer, and during her service she moved at least five times, and was stationed variously in the South at Lawson General Hospital and Ft. Benning, both in Georgia; the Huntsville Arsenal in Alabama, and with the 382*nd* Hospital at Camp Joseph T. Robinson, North Little Rock, Arkansas.[101] She worked with both male and female patients, and her duty assignments included being a pool laboratory officer, doing general duty and also surgery, and conducting duties as the assistant chief of Industrial Medicine.[102]

In 1945, Pauline Garber was one of three women doctors sent to the Far East, and she went overseas with the 382*nd* Hospital Unit to Okinawa, always being billeted with the nurses of her unit. Towards the end of the war, the 382*nd* moved to Pusan, Korea, and she became chief of Laboratory Services of the 71*st* Station Hospital in Pusan, having also achieved her captaincy in June of that year. Within eighteen months, however, she, along with the other two medical officers, was relieved from duty as part of the postwar drawdown of service women. She remained in the Army until September 1946.[103]

Her Army service also affected Garber's choices later on. In postwar years, she did a residency at the VA Hospital in Wadsworth, Kansas, 1949-52. She then worked as a pathologist at the VA Hospital in Alexandria, Louisiana, for a year, and then returned to work another year back at the VA Hospital in Wadsworth, Kansas. She married Harold F. Clark on 32 December 1956 in Tucumcari, New Mexico, and by the end of the 1950s she was employed at the Lancaster-Fairfield Hospital in Lancaster, Ohio. Garber was a member of the AMA and the College of American Pathologists (CAP), and in 1986 she was listed in the CAP under her professional name, Pauline E. Garber. She passed away 18 July 1991 at the Fort Hamilton Hughes Memorial Hospital in Ohio at the age of eighty-two.[104]

Women Doctors in Obstetrics and Gynecology

After receiving their commissions, four women were classified in Obstetrics and Gynecology: Margaret Craighill (discussed earlier), Jean Henderson, Ida Holzberg, and Jane Marshall Leibfried. (See Table 8). There was one major, two captains, and one lieutenant among them and their ages ranged from twenty-nine to forty-six. Thus, as was the case with other women specialists, they were highly qualified and experienced as all, but one woman, were out of their twenties. In terms of marital status, only Holzberg was married when she was commissioned.

Like Jean Henley, Margaret Janeway, and both Barbara Stimson and Eleanor Peck who had both served abroad in England, Jean Henderson was also a graduate of the College of Physicians and Surgeons at Columbia University. Single and age thirty-eight when she was commissioned a captain 23 September 1943, she listed her home in Samford, Conneticut.[105] She was stationed in the States and was on duty in the Pacific Area in Honolulu with the 318*th* General Hospital. She listed seven station assignments where she served variously as ward officer, attending surgeon, and instructor at the WAC technician training school.

When discussing her impressions of her Army experience, she felt that her assignments "could have been worse." She also admitted:

> My work, when I have been working, has been equivalent to an internship in a good hospital and I have seen a good many interesting cases and much of medical interest. I should say I have spent more time waiting than working. I do have the feeling that if I had stayed home I would have been of more value professionally...I'm not always happy in the Army. The usual gripes of not being promoted and of not being used to full capacity...but I am sure that when it is over I will be glad that I did join up and try, and that I would regret it if I had missed this whole experience.[106]

Ida R. Holzberg also hailed from the East coast as she was born 28 June 1898 in New York City, graduated from the Long Island College of Medicine in 1928, and interned at the New York Infirmary and then proceeded to undertake a residency at the same institution. She was in private practice in obstetrics and gynecology when she volunteered at the age of forty-six with the AMC, and stated that she was married with one dependent son. (Her problems with a dependency allowance are discussed in the following chapter). She was commissioned a captain 29 January 1944 and assigned first

to Ft. Knox and then to the WAC Technicians School at Camp Atterbury, Indiana, where she was posted as an instructor of surgery.[107]

In contrast to Ragus who disliked being assigned to a VA facility,
Holzberg was transferred to one January 1945 at her own request
as she was dissatisfied with working in a "pool" on gynecology and
surgical wards. In her remarks about the Army, Holzberg believed
that her experience was "difficult to appraise...I think, however, it
was worthwhile for both myself and the service." She indicated that
she had treated women patients predominantly, but she felt living
conditions were unsatisfactory, although she did not expand on her
statement in this regard.[108]

Following her discharge, Holzberg worked for the VA regional office in New York City until 1950 when she decided to switch out of
her specialty in obstetrics and gynecology. She undertook a two-year
residency in psychiatry at Bellevue Hospital and then returned to
work for the VA back in New York and then in Indianapolis, Indiana.
In the 1960s she assumed a full-time private practice in psychiatry,
mostly with adults, and then she became a supervising psychiatrist at
a state hospital in Poughkeepsie, New York, in 1965.

Holzberg was widowed sometime after the war and in 1973 she
remarried the socially prominent Chandler A. Chapman who died
only a few years later in 1980. As Chapman's third wife, it was joking-
ly reported that he wanted to have his own psychiatrist in the house.
She passed away at the age of ninety-five, 9 November 1991.[109]

Jane Marshall Leibfried was a native of Bethlehem, Pennsylvania,
and she received her medical degree from the WMCP in 1941. She
interned at Johns Hopkins University in obstetrics and gynecology
in 1942-43 and went on in 1943-44 to complete a residency back
where she had gone to medical school. Unmarried with no dependents, she listed her date of birth as 24 November 1915 making her
twenty-nine years old when she was commissioned a lieutenant 15
May 1944. She was stationed at the Red Cross Blood Donor Center in San Francisco, California, where she worked in a mobile unit

"taking histories and blood pressures, [and] checking donors." From there she went to a regional hospital at Oakland assigned as a ward officer in the obstetrics and gynecology section. Her work consisted of deliveries, ward care, and gynecological surgery.[110]

When it came to her impressions of her Army service, Leibfried noted that there were no quarters for women medical officers in either place she had been posted, although it was more difficult to find housing in San Francisco. Like other women doctors who had been assigned outside their specialty, she expressed great displeasure with this practice and much satisfaction when the reverse was true. In regard to the Blood Donor Center, she noted that "three to six hours work daily" there was "unsatisfactory". On the hand, she observed: "Since arriving at the Oakland Regional Hospital, I've been able to do obstetrics and gynecology exclusively. In spite of long hours, night work etc., I've gained excellent experience and training as well as being made to feel that in a very small way I've helped the war effort."[111]

After the Army, Leibfried continued her education and studied pathology in a VA hospital in 1946. From 1947 on, however, she devoted herself primarily to obstetrics and gynecology, and in 1950 she was Board certified in that area.[112] She maintained a private practice, worked for the Veteran's Administration Hospital in Philadelphia and the Riverview Home for the Aged, and was on the medical staff of the hospital of the WMCP serving as a clinical associate professor of obstetrics ad gynecology. She held membership in various medical groups including the Philadelphia Obstetrics Society and the Philadelphia College of Physicians.

Leibfried passed away 23 August 1982. At her memorial service, it was said that "she was a devoted physician and teacher who will be fondly remembered by her former patients, colleagues, students, friends, and family." In honor of her, the WMCP established the Jane Marshall Leibfried Memorial Fund.

—m—

On the whole, women doctors who specialized in narrow fields were satisfied with their Army assignments as they were usually in keeping with their background and unique qualifications. As was true for all the women medical officers, dissatisfaction was more likely to occur when postings occurred at different times outside their specialty area. Sakin, the only woman plastic surgeon, was very annoyed with being assigned so long to a blood bank center and Leibfreid had similar complaints about having to work at a bleeding center. Ragus, the only woman urologist, was miserable working at the VA where she was unable to secure a transfer, and Patton pointed out that her Army experiences were positive with the exception of being assigned as an instructor for WAC medical technicians. A few other women doctors like, Hamilton, Harrison, and Crandall, complained of the usual problems that plagued all doctors, male or female: administrative duties, too much paperwork, and conducting monthly physicals that ran into the hundreds.

After the war ended, their Army experiences were generally of little value as these were highly qualified and successful women physicians who returned to work in their specialty area. Genia Sakin for example, went back to her successful practice in plastic surgery; and as both Melson Barfield-Carter and Martha Howe were Board certified in radiology, they were needed and sought after in the medical community as well as in the academic setting in Carter's case. The exceptions occurred with a younger woman like Patton (twenty-six at the time she volunteered) who was assigned to General Duty in the AMC but later established herself in obstetrics and gynecology in civilian practice.

On the other hand, the Army did leave its mark on a few of these women. Woo was one of three reserve women physicians recalled to active duty in Korea—a good indication that women would choose an Army career if it were possible. Like half of the women psychiatrsits, Bronislava Z. Reznick, Isabella Harrison, Pauline E. Garber, Ida R. Holzberg, and Jane M. Leibfried were committed to VA issues at various times in postwar years.

~ NOTES ~

1. Quote and summary from Lemay Sheffield, Suzanne. *Women and Science: Social Impact and Interaction* (New Brunswick, NY: Rutgers University Press, 2005), 147. She describes how the plan of male radiographers backfired on them when they called for a college diploma as a requirement for certification as they thought this would exclude women. "However, obtaining this education did not prove to be a barrier for women even when the society increased educational requirements in 1936."

2. Notes from Redman, Helen C., "Women in American Radiology," *JAMA*. For a discussion of women in radiology, see Lewicki, Ann M., "American Association for Women Radiologists: Its Birth and 25 Years Later." *Radiology*, 237, October 2007, 19-25. For information on female radiologists and their intervention in women's health issues, see Siskin, Gary P. *Interventional Radiology in Women's Health* (New York and Stuttgart: Thieme Medical Publishers, 2009).

3. Davis, Wren, "The Changing Face of Women's Imaging," *Imaging Economics*, October 2005; available on line at http://www.imagingeconomics.com/issues/articles/MI_2005-10_02.asp.

4. Quotes from Redman. Also see Peter E. Palmquist, "Elizabeth Fleishmann: a Tribute" in Elizabeth *Fleischmann: Pioneer X-Ray Photographer* (Berkeley, California: Judah L. Magnes Museum, 1990). See also Yoshinaga, Shinji, et al, "Cancer Risks among Radiologists and Radiologic Technologists: Review of Epidemiologic Studies." *Radiology*, November 2004, No. 233, 313-321. Authors note one consistent finding among workers employed before 1950 was the "increased mortality due to leukemia."

5. Wren, "The Changing Face of Women's Imaging." Early on, radiology was referred to as roentgenology, named for Wilhelm Conrad Roentgen who discovered X-rays.

6. Heaton, Leonard D. Arnold L. Ahnfeldt, Kenneth D. Allen, Elizabeth M. McFetridge, Mindell W. Stein, *Medical Department, United States Army: Radiology in World War II* (Washington DC: Office of the Surgeon General (Army), 1966), 4,5,19.

7. Ibid, 19.

8. Miller, Amy, "The History of the X-ray." Created for Dr. Jeffrey McClurken's History of American Technology & Culture class, Mary Washington College. Also

see Kevles, Bettyann Holtzmann. *Naked to the Bone: Medical Imaging in the Twentieth Century* (New Brunswick, NY: Rutgers Univ. Press, 1997).

9. Since roenterology was a fairly new field then, Dr. Edna W. Brown, contract surgeon in WWI, had a longer Army contract than many other women doctors because the Army had a need for her skills. Dr. Ruth Ingraham was another radiologist at the first American Women's Hospital (AWH) in 1918. For more on the work of women doctors with the AWH, see Ellen S. More. "The American Women's Hospitals: Women Physicians in World War I," Library Publications and Presentations (1989).

10. Janeway Reponse (for Craighill) to Bell, 1943, letter, MDC Coll.

11. "Notes on Dr. Melson Barfield-Carter", provided by Dr. Perry Morgan, University of Alabama at Birmingham, Department of Radiology, 2009.

12. See "The Changing Face of Women's Imaging", and Pennycuff, Tim L. "From the Archives," *Alabama Alumni Bulletin*, Vol. 29, summer 2003. She entered UA in 1914 and received her BS in mathematics.

13. Nath, Hrudaya and Stanley, Robert J. "History of Diagnostic Radiology at the University of Alabama at Birmingham Hospital". *Alabama Journal of Radiology* 1994, 162: 713-717.

14. Summarized from Howe's alumnae records provided by DUCM.

15. Howe to Dr. Bell, 20 March 1969, letter, Howe's alumnae records from DUCM.

16. Marriage: *JAMA*, May 12. 1928, Vol. 90, #19, 1583.

17. Early on, the hospital ceased operation in 1861 when the entire student body and faculty joined the Confederate Army. For more on the history of the hospital, see *Alabama Alumni Bulletin* in preceding note.

18. A pin was also enclosed with the hope that she would wear it as a symbol of her "long dedication to medicine." However, she had stopped corresponding with the school after it became coeducational. See Director of Alumnae Relations to Martha E. Howe, 8 June 1979, letter, DUCM archives.

19. As many as 32,555 X-ray examinations were conducted in 1945 alone because Oliver G. H. served as a separation center. See *Radiology in WWII*, p. 145.

20. See Delehanty, Randolph, "Letterman Army Medical Center", California State Military Medical Museum, www.militarymuseum.org/LettermanAMC.html There is no Questionnaire for her and her Army assignments are from an untitled list which contains the appointments and assignments of women Army doctors, Histories of the Women's Health & Welfare Unit, Histories, Box 29, MDC Coll.;

hereafter referred to as "Histories". Also see *Women in Medicine*, 90, October 1945, 8.

21. Barfield-Carter to Craighill, 26 June 1945, letter, Histories, Box 29, MDC Coll.

22. Craighill to Barfield-Carter, 29 June 1945, letter, Histories, Box 29, MCD Coll.

23. Dr. Perry Morgan "Notes" from UAB indicate "the money was used for food delivered COD to the hospital."

24. "History of Diagnostic Radiology at UAB," 714.

25. Information in *Alabama Alumni Bulletin*, Vol. 29, summer 2003. Also see her obituary, JAMA. 3 Sept 1973, Vol. 225, No 10.

26. Fitzsimons became one of the Army's premier medical training centers. After its new main building (known as Building 500), was added in 1941, Fitzsimons was the largest structure in Colorado.

27. See "Section on War Service" regarding Martha E. Howe, M.D. in *MWJ*, February 1944, 27.

28. Howe alumnae records, DUCM.

29. Howe's quote from her 1960 WMCP Alumnae Questionnaire.

30. See Whayne, Tom F., "The History of Preventive Medicine in World War II". *Public Health Reports*, Vol. 74, No. 2, February 1959. All quotes from "Summary of World War II" United States Department of Veterans Affairs, Office of Public Health and Environmental Hazards. Website: http://www4.va.gov/oaa/pocketcard/worldwar.asp For more on preventive medicine, see Coates, J. B., ed. *Preventive Medicine in World War II, Vol. V: Communicable Disease* (Washington, D.C.: Office of the Surgeon General, Department of the Army, 1960). There are also two other volumes.

31. All statistics of the four women: Gertrude Cone, Martha L. Crandall, Elizabeth Garber Tate, and Theresa Ting Woo summarized from the Questionnaires, Box 30, MDC Coll.

32. Garber Tate quote in her Questionnaire and she is discussed briefly in "Women Physicians in the Army," *Women in Medicine*, Oct., 1945, 8.

33. Major Margaret D. Craighill to Dr. Martha L. Crandall, letter, Dated 13 April 1944, Official Correspondence, Box 5; "distinctive items" quote in "Women Medical Officers, AUS, Histories, Box 29; Crandall's comments in her PD Questionnaire, Box 30, all in MDC Coll.

34. Quotes in Crandall Questionnaire, Box 30, MDC Coll.

35. Biographical information supplied by Bentley Historical Library, Univ., of Michigan from their alumni files. Short Biography in "Chinese Woman Medical Officer", *The Atlanta Spotlight*, 14 December 1944, 145. Specialty training noted in Woo's Questionnaire, Box 30, MDC Coll.

36. The other two doctors recalled were Clara Raven and Alcinde de Aguiar, and both were sent to Japan. Dr. Ruth E. Church was also accepted, but she had not served in WWII. She was a graduate from the University of Wisconsin Medical School and received her Master's degree in Public Health at Columbia University, College of Physicians and Surgeons, New York City. See "First Women Physicians Report for Active Duty in the Army," *JAMA*, 6:5 (May 1951), 195; and also Raven, Clara, "Achievement of Women in Medicine, Past and Present—Women in the Medical Corps of the Army", *Military Medicine*, February 1960, 110. For quote on roles, see Witt Linda, *A Defense Weapon Known to Be of Value: Servicewomen of the Korean War era*, 133.

37. Harvard University Alumni Office had no other information about Woo' graduate work other than noting the degree, but she also did graduate study at Children's Medical Center in Boston. Also see "Dr. Woo Named to Head New School Health Program, 9 August 1957", unidentified newspaper clipping supplied by Bentley Historical Library.

38. She is listed in the Social Security Death Index, and National Cemetery Administration, U.S. Veterans Gravesites, 1775-2006. Brief article about her appears in *The New York Times*, 21, January 1951, 12.

39. Quote in Carter, Andrea Kaye, "Bushnell General Military Hospital and the Community of Brigham City Utah during World War II," thesis. Utah State University, December 2008. School data supplied by Tufts University Coll. and Archives. They indicated they had no further information.

40. See Cone's Questionnaire, Box 30, MDC Coll.

41. See "Bushnell Has Two Women Doctors", *Box Elder News-Journal*, 13 October 1943. Another WWII Army women officer, Margaret B. Ross, also graduated from Tufts in 1992. After she left the Medical Corps she practiced gynecology at Rumford, Rhode Island. Quote from her Questionnaire; she died 26 June 1960 at home in Rumford. Information supplied by Tufts University Coll. and Archives.

42. See Raven, Clara. "Tropical Medicine and World War II," *MWJ*, June 1948, Vol. 55, No. 6. She noted that there were actually about 450,000 hospital admissions among the Armed Forces of which number only 70,000 were hospitalized in the United States, and nearly all of the latter were relapses of infections acquired overseas.

43. Ibid, Raven, Clara.

44. Heaton, Lt. Gen. Leonard D., *Medical Department, United States Army: Personnel in World War II* (Office of The Surgeon General: Washington, D.C., 1963).

45. Biographical information, unless otherwise noted is from, Hoeger, August J. and Elizabeth, *The Story of Agnes* (The Evangelical Lutheran Good Samaritan Society, 1997). The Society provided the book to the author. Quotes from *The Story of Agnes*, 25, 29.

46. Ibid, 34.

47. Ibid, 45.

48. Ibid, 45-46.

49. Summary and quote from Hoeger's Questionnaire, Box 30, MDC Coll. Also see Cramer, Gisela and Prutsch, Ursula. "Nelson A. Rockefeller's Office of Inter-American Affairs (1940-1946) and Record Group 229", *Hispanic American Historical Review* 2006, 86 (4), 785-806. Authors noted he was charged with overseeing a program of US cooperation with the nations of Latin American to help raise the standard of living, to achieve better relations among the nations of the western hemisphere, and to counter rising Nazi influence in the region.

50. Quotes from *The Story of Agnes*, 51, 52. Tingo Maria was considered unreachable until 1936 when the Montana Road reached the settlement. It was not until 1942 that the US Government started to add more funding to the station. The nickname for the city is "the Door of the Amazonia".

51. Chimbote had less than a thousand inhabitants in 1835, but the opening of the Pan-American Highway created easy access to Lima in the 1930s. The population began to expand by 1943 with the establishment of a railroad and a nearby hydro-electric power station as well as an iron and steel plant.

52. *The Story of Agnes*, 53, both quotes.

53. Quotes if from Hoeger's Questionnaire, Box 30, MDC Coll.

54. *The Story of Agnes*, 59, 73.

55. See "Dr. Agnes Hoeger Memory Care Unit", *Village Times* (a publication of Good Samaritan Village at Kissimee, Florida), December 2005, Vol. 5, No. 12. The unit was designed to meet the needs of residents who not only suffered with Alzheimer's disease but "and/or other related dementias."

56. "Macho" quote in More, *Restoring the Balance*, 226; Residencies in Lopate, *Women in Medicine*, 126-127.

57. Morantz, Regina Markell, et. al. (eds). *In Her Own words: Oral Histories of Women Physicians*. New Haven and London: Yale University Press, 1982; 83. By the time Morani decided to become a plastic surgeon, she hunted around for some courses she could take and went to study under one of the leaders in plastic surgery, Dr. J. Barrett Brown, at Barnes Hospital in St. Louis, Missouri. She never found the time to marry.

58. Sakin: *Boston Traveler*, 21 March 1934.

59. Ibid. It was said that her mother and a sister were killed by the Nazis in Lithuania and a brother was killed in the Japanese bombing of Shanghai. See "Genia Sakin Dies: Plastic Surgeon," *New York Times*, 13 September 1960.

60. Quotes from, Finkler, Rita S. "A Committee for the Relief of Distressed Women Physicians," *MWJ*, May 1942, 135-136. By July 1942, this committee had assisted over eighty women physicians, out of which financial aid was given to twelve.

61. *Boston American*, 11 April 1934.

62. Hy Steirman, "Surgeon to the World." *Coronet*, April 1958, 64.

63. Assignments listed on her Questionnaire, Box 30, MDC Coll.

64. Drew discovered that plasma could be processed and preserved for a long time and transfused without regard to blood type or matching in place of whole blood.

65. "Blood Banks," *Woman's Auxiliary to the California Medical Association*, March 1956, Vol. 84, No. 3.

66. Kendrick, Brigadier General Douglas B., MC, USA. *Blood Program in World War II*. (Office of the Surgeon General, Department of the Army) Washington, DC: U.S. Government Printing Office, 1964, 109-110.

67. Ibid.

68. *The Morning Herald*, Uniontown, Pennsylvania, 15 November 1944.

69. Remarks from her Questionnaire, MDC Coll.

70. *The Birmingham News*, 21 *February* 1946.

71. Raven, "Achievements of Women in Medicine," *Military Medicine*, February 1960, 109. The other three women doctors were Major Eleanor Baldwin Hamilton, Major Poe-Eng-Yu, and Lt. Colonel Clara Raven.

72. "With the 298th Army Band in Berlin," by Sebastian (Sebby) PAPA. Online: www. Berlin-Brigade.de Sebby was also kind enough to send the authors a picture of Dr. Sakin which is also online. She served as chief of plastic surgery in the 97*th*

General Hospital, Frankfurt Germany and later as chief of surgery and chief of plastic surgery in the 279*th* Station Hospital in Berlin.

73. Raven, "Achievements of Women in Medicine," *Military Medicine*, February 1960, 109.

74. It would not be until 1950 that women doctors would be recalled and recruited for the Korean Conflict. Twenty-three women physicians served with the Army during the Korean War.

75. "Surgeon to the World", *Coronet*, 62. King Paul of Greece decorated her for serving in Greek Army hospitals and for her other work in plastic reconstruction. Some accounts note she was in Greece for about two years.

76. Araca, Emma, *"Angel with a Knife"*. Most likely, *Manila Times*, September 1957. In 1957, she received the Certificate of Honor of Manila Central University for operating on many Philippine people deformed by war accidents and for demonstrating her technique at the College of Medicine.

77. "Surgeon to the World", Coronet, 65.

78. Araca, Emma, *"Angel with a Knife"*.

79. "Genia Sakin Dies: Plastic Surgeon," *New York Times*, 13 September 1960. Also see "Obituary", JAMA 14 January 1961.

80. Eight women doctors from the WMCP went to the Army and seven went to the Navy, for a total of fifteen women.

81. Quotes in Hamilton, Harrison, and Patton Questionnaire, Box 30, MDC Coll.

82. "Obituary for Hamilton," JAMA, Vol. 248, Issue 4, 491-492, July 23, 1982.

83. Quotes for Harrison are from "96-year-old Pioneering Woman Surgeon Receives new 'Jiffy Hip'", *Newport News*, VA, 23 May, 2010. She was still alive at the time of this manuscript, although the author was unable to establish contact with her.

84. "Alumni Notes" for Harrison, February 2004, *Johns Hopkins Magazine*; and Harrison Questionnaire, MDC Coll.

85. Quote in "96-year-old Pioneering Woman." Biographical notes in the *American Medical Dictionary 1958*, 12th Edition.

86. "Alumni Notes" for Harrison, February 2004, *Johns Hopkins Magazine*.

87. Summary of her current interests and activities in "96-year-old Pioneering Woman."

88. See "Obituaries for November 12, 2009" for Patton, YourFoxChapel.com Also see biography provided by DUCM archives with pictures.

89. At one time or another, at least three other women besides Sakin and Reznick also worked in blood banks: Gertrude Cone, Clara L. Hughes, and Mae J. O'Donnell.

90. See JAMA 1945, 128: 292-295.

91. It seems most likely that this was a misspelling of Vladimir, but no country was named.

92. Board of Trustees Minutes—1932, University of Illinois, Urbana.

93. Raven, "Achievement of Women in Medicine, Past and Present—Women in the Medical Corps of the Army."

94. Reznick Questionnaire, Box 30, MDC Coll.

95. Birth and death dates for Reznick from the Social Security Death Index.

96. *American Medical Directory*, 19th Edition, Published by the American Medical Association, 1956. Long Island College Hospital was founded in 1858 as both a medical school and a hospital. It became the first U.S. medical school to make bedside teaching a standard part of its medical curriculum, an approach that was later adopted throughout the country.

97. See "Ragus to Major Margaret Janeway," letter, dated 13 January 1945. Oteen was derived from an American Indian word meaning "chief aim" as it was felt that the chief aim of every patient was to get well. In the 1920s and 1930s the hospital's focus was the treatment of tuberculosis and it was the only VA facility in the southeast at the time devoted to the treatment of respiratory ailments. Three other women, all captains were also assigned to a VA facility: Ida Holzberg, Catherine Gordon McGregor, and Grace Fern Thomas. Only Holzberg was happy about working at the VA as she had asked for a transfer. She was a specialist in obstetrics/gynecology who had been working in a "pool" on gynecology and surgical wards at two different stations.

98. See Ragus Questionnaire, Box 30, MDC Coll.

99. See *American Medical Directory*, Vol. 1, 1967, p. 212. Ragus Obituary in *JAMA*, Vol. 211, No. 6, 9 February 1970, p. 1022. It could not be determined if she was divorced or widowed in postwar years.

100. See Bellaire Questionnaire, Box 30, MDC Coll. Also see "Poe-Eng Yu to Major Craighill," letter, Dated 20 February 1945, Craighill's Personal Papers, Box 1, MDC Coll.

101. Between world War and World War II, Camp Robinson served as the Head-quarters of the Arkansas National Guard, but in early 1940 it was established as a temporary cantonment for the Thirty-fifth Division (a National Guard division) that was called to active duty for a year of training. It also served as a replacement training center for basic training and for medics, but in 1944 both were merged into the Infantry Replacement Training Center.

102. See Garber Questionnaire, Box 30, MDC Coll.

103. Notes were supplied from her WIMSA file; also see "U.S. Women at Nagoya," *New York Times*, 24 November 1945, 21.

104. Ohio Division of Vital Statistics, Death Certificate and Index, December 20, 1908-31 December 1953, State Archives Series 3094, Ohio Historical Society, Ohio. Biographical information for Garber, *Director of Medical Specialists Holding Certification by American Specialty Boards*, Vol. X (Chicago: *Marquis Who's Who*, 1961), 885. A death certificate indicates that Harold died 30 April 1965—which means the couple was not married that long. Her death certificate noted that she was widowed.

105. Henderson address in Samford, Connecticut, in "War Service," *MWJ*, February 1945, 40. Quotes from her Army Questionnaire.

106. Henderson service in Honolulu is described in "Women Physicians in the Army," *Women in Medicine*, 90, October 1945, 9; also see *JAMA* 19 February 1944, 514. She passed away 24 May 1980 in Fairlee, Vermont. Thanks to Jennifer McGillian, archivist, Archives & Sp. Coll., Augustus C. Long Heath Sciences Library, Columbia University Medical Center.

107. The training school opened 14 July 1944, and only women between the ages of 20 and 49, with no dependents under 14, could be accepted for training there. "School Established for Training WAC Technicians: to Be Located at Camp Atterbury", *Indiana Evening Gazette*, 14 July 1944.

108. Quote and assignment in Holzberg Army Questionnaire.

109. Marriage and psychiatrist joke noted by Robert H. Boyle, *At the Top of their Game*, Winchester Press, 1983, 10. He also noted that Holzberg was a "petite" woman and Jewish like Chandler's second wife. Death reported "In Memoriam", *Psychiatric News Bulletin of the APA*, 21 March 2008, Vol., 43, No. 6.; Social Security Death Index Master File. Also see *Bio. Dir. Of the APA* 1968 for her professional experiences.

110. Information in "Questionnaire to Alumnae: the WMCP" supplied by the DUCM Sp. Coll. and Archives. Also see "Dr. Leibfried, MCP Professor," *Germantown*

Courier, Philadelphia, Pa 1 September 1982; supplied by the DUCM SP.Coll. and Archives. DUCM also supplied picture of her from 1940.

111. Quotes in Leibfried's Army Questionnaire.

112. Pathology at unnamed VA hospital noted in "The WMCP Alumni/Alumna Census" form dated 14 December 1975.

Table 6.
Women Army Medical Officers:
Roles in Preventive Medicine

Tropical Medicine:

Agnes Hoeger (only one with this Army specialty)

Sent to the School of Tropical Medicine, Washington, D.C.

Clara Raven (Pathologist)

Aurelia Rozov (Internist)

Theresa T. Woo (Pediatrics and Communicable Diseases)

Instructor, Tropical Diseases Section:

Anna M. Patton (General Duty)

Martha Crandall (Communicable Diseases)

Chief of Contagious Diseases Section:

Angie Connor (Internist)

Martha Crandall (Communicable Diseases)

Table 7.
Women Doctors' Classifications:

In Preventive Medicine, Communicable Diseases after Commissioning:

Name	Rank at Assignment	Age/Status	Dependents	Ward Duties
Gertrude Cone	Lieutenant	33/Single	Mother	Yes
Martha Crandall	Lieutenant	28/Married	No	Yes
Elizabeth Garber Tate*	Lieutenant	26/Married	No	Yes
Theresa T. Woo	Lieutenant	33/Single	No	Yes

Garber Tate was also classified as a General Duty Officer.

Table 8.
Women Doctors in
Obstetrics and Gynecology

Name	Rank at Assignment	Age	School
Margaret Craighill	Major	45	Johns Hopkins
Jane M. Leibfried	Lieutenant	29	WMCP
Jean Henderson	Captain	38	Columbia
Ida Holzberg	Captain	46	Long Island

CHAPTER SIX:

More than They Expected: Nonspecialists and Other Problems in Service

The classification system for Medical Corps officers had its flaws. Because evidence of their training was more readily ascertained, specialists who were diplomats of specialty boards could be more easily placed in their specialty. At the same time, there were doctors well-trained in some branch of medicine for which no specialty board yet existed, and, therefore, they were classified as nonspecialists although some of them had been generalist physicians in civilian life. "There was also the case of doctors who had simply not acquired membership in a specialty board even though they were as competent in the specialty as those who had."[1] This was the situation for the women nonspecialists who were classified or served as General Duty Officers.

Women Medical Officers, General Duty

At least twelve women physicians were classified as Medical Officers, General Duty, although the count rises somewhat if we include other doctors who did not return their Army Questionnaires or, in the case of Anna C. Besnick, left their classification blank. Even counting only the twelve the women with returned forms, they constituted the second largest group after neuropsychiatry. (See Table

9). The women ranged from twenty-five to fifty-three years old, with the mean age being thirty-five. Eight of them were lieutenants and four were captains. In looking at their classifications, however, four of them were classified in dual areas. Many of them were discussed earlier, so the focus of this chapter is to expand on the various roles they held during their military service, some of the problems they encountered, and what they did after discharge.

When we think about the career paths of physicians, we generally presume that the young college graduates went directly to medical school or, at the very least, worked one or two years to save money before embarking on a four-year commitment—or five years if we count an internship. This was not the case for Elvira Clara Seno. She was born 3 May 1909 in Slade Corners, Wisconsin, went to high school there, and received her Bachelor's Degree from the University of Wisconsin in Madison in 1930 having majored in zoology. She worked for the next ten years as a bacteriologist in Woodworth, Wisconsin, before deciding to return to her alma mater in 1939. She received a Master of Science Degree in Bacteriology in 1941 and then continued on to medical school at the same university. (Her Master's thesis shows the influence her undergraduate training had on her, as she wrote on the "Antigenic value of rabies vaccine as tested in white rats"). After receiving her MD she accepted an internship at St. Joseph's Hospital in Marshfield, Wisconsin, and from there volunteered for the AMC and was commissioned a lieutenant 11 December 1943.[2]

Following her four-week orientation course at Lawson General Hospital, Seno was sent to three hospitals located in Georgia and Texas where she was assigned many varied duties. She served as a ward officer for females and males as well as enlisted WACs, and at one time worked in a contagion ward with enlisted males only. Her last two assignments were overseas in the ETO in the 239th General Hospital and the 195th General Hospital. While she was overseas, she served in neuropsychiatric wards, which was her first real exposure to a new specialty—and this experience would make her reconsider her path in medicine a few years later. When reflecting on her Army experiences, however, she observed: "My service in the Army to date has been one of the most worthwhile experiences of my adult life. At no time have I been discriminated against professionally because of sex."[3]

Seno apparently meant what she said about meaningful experiences because following her discharge, and until her retirement, she committed herself to the medical problems of veterans. She began by working as a ward physician in various VA hospitals in Wisconsin, Washington, and Colorado from 1947 to 1956. Like Margaret D. Craighill, however, she had witnessed first-hand the impact of psychiatry in military medicine, and she undertook a psychiatric residency at a VA hospital in Downey, Illinois. Afterwards she worked as a psychiatrist at Chicago Wesley Memorial Hospital for a year, and from the end of 1957 to 1963 she was a staff psychiatrist in VA hospitals in Iowa, Wisconsin, and Illinois. But Seno always seemed to be drawn back to her home state, so by 1963 she returned to Wisconsin to stay and she went on to be a psychiatrist at the Mendota State hospital until 1965. During the same period, she was a Clinical Instructor of Psychiatry at her alma mater where she had received three degrees. By 1965 she was even more inclined to settle down and she returned to work as a staff psychiatrist at the VA hospital in Wood, Wisconsin, where she had served on the staff back in 1947.[4]

When Seno retired from medical practice in 1974, she bought a farm near Slade Corners where she had grown up. She restored the fields and pastures and she even built a pond and purchased a 26-acre marsh to protect the area. One of her dearest wishes was to show others, especially children, the value and importance of nature and forests. In 1994, a non-profit educational foundation was created to accept the gift of the land and manage the property in keeping with Seno's wishes. Today, "new school classes and groups come to enjoy, learn, and appreciate this wonderful gift" at the Seno Woodland Education Center. She died 31 October 1996 in Burlington, Wisconsin.[5]

Some women doctors who were classified as Medical Officers, General Duty, had experiences they might never have had if it weren't for the Army Medical Corps. Dr. Miriam Mills, born 11 November 1918, was one of the youngest doctors at age twenty-five, and she was fluent in French and German. She had started out at the medical school in Mississippi and transferred in her third year to Vanderbilt where she completed her internship and started a residency. While her reasons for leaving Mississippi are unknown, Vanderbilt had a patriotic staff and student body as it was one of several medical schools across the United States in 1940 to form reserve units in the event the United States entered the Second World War. In 1943, the medical unit, the 300th General Hospital Unit, served in Naples, Italy, where it established a 200-bed hospital with the physicians and nurses who were Vanderbilt graduates and staff although it did not have any women physicians in the Unit.[6] It seems reasonable to conjecture that Mills may have identified with the staff and students at Vanderbilt as she, too, decided to become part of the war effort.

Lt. Miriam Mills accepted her appointment 26 October 1943, was classified as a Medical Officer, General Duty, and was given as many as seven different assignments. For a brief time she worked as a ward surgeon in communicable diseases and in three different psychiatry wards. She was also sent for training in neuropsychiatry, but did not complete the course because she was reassigned to a special team for the "Study of Fatigue Influencing the Effectiveness of WAC Personnel" in June 1945. As part of her duties she traveled to more than 30 WAC installations from as far east as Washington D.C., and as far west as California.[7] Mills was promoted to captain August 1945.

In her remarks on her Army Questionnaire, Mills pointed out that she had requested overseas duty. She also noted: "As this officer entered the Army directly from an internship, her value to the service has been limited to some extent [due] to her lack of experience."[8]

In looking at what Mills did immediately after the war, it appears that the Army rekindled her interest in psychiatry as she returned to Vanderbilt and completed her residency in the specialty. Sometime before 1953 she married Andrew W. Lockton and they moved to Marina del Rey, California. She passed away 25 April 1985 in Los Angeles, California.[9]

Marjorie Hayes was just two years older than Mills, having been born 25 September 1916, and she indicated that her home address was Brunswick, New Jersey. As the second daughter of a geologist, she traveled around the world with her parents on geologic expeditions when she was growing up. She received her undergraduate degree in music from Vassar College in 1937; and before she entered medical school, she spent a year in Europe and was in Vienna when Hitler invaded. "She was asked to register her race and listed it as Eskimo. The Nazis had limited experience with Eskimos and sent a 'scientist' to measure her head for proper classification."

Hayes proved to be not only a good student but a good sport over the next few years. As soon as she returned to the States, she entered medical school and received her degree from the Johns Hopkins Medical School in 1942. At that time, the medical school curriculum was compressed to prepare physicians for service in WWII, but she "never noticed any harassment or hostility from the male medical students or faculty, although during the first day of anatomy class, the male students did pay catch and keep away with a set of male genitalia" which she thought was done in good fun rather than with any spitefulness because she was a woman. Like many students, she was short on funds so she took part in some scientific experiments to earn money for tuition, but she was able to finish on time and she proceeded to intern at the hospital associated with the school. She completed her internship during the war, and while other women stated they had patriotic motives for volunteering, "she enlisted to follow" her British boyfriend to London.[10]

The Army had other plans, however, and after Hayes was commissioned a lieutenant 28 August 1943 she was stationed in the States for the next two years. During her service, Hayes described her military career as being filled with a "great variety" of assignments as she was stationed at nine different places in the United States and abroad. Of all the women medical officers, however, she seemed to have some of the most interesting jobs. At her first posting in the SGO, Division of Occupational Hygiene, she was "in charge of the testing of protective clothing (gas proof) for women." At another time she was sent to the Signal Corps Photographic Center in Los Angeles, California. Here her duties included being the technical adviser for a training film on personal hygiene entitled, "Strictly Personal". She also conducted an orientation course for women medical officers, had Colored WAC sick call, and served as a ward officer in two communicable disease sections as well as malaria and acute rheumatic fever wards, and was an instructor at the WAC Technician Training School at Wakeman General hospital, Camp Atterbury, Indiana.

Once shipped overseas, she served in two different hospitals in the Pacific area; but it was her ninth assignment beginning 16 July 1945 that gave her the greatest feeling of pride. She was sent to the Philippines and landed first in Manila and then at the 118th General Hospital in Leyte where Unit 118 was stationed. This unit was one of several university-affiliated hospital units to serve during wartime, and it was composed of Johns Hopkins doctors and nurses who had volunteered and served together for more than three years. One can only image what a pleasure it was for her to serve side by side with the members of this unit, being a graduate of the same medical school herself. In fact, she later mentioned proudly that she had served as a ward officer with the "Johns Hopkins Unit, *my* civilian hospital."

In considering her overall satisfaction with the service, Hayes noted:

On the whole, my Army experience has been satisfying and pleasant—my only complaint would be that it took me a year and a half to persuade anyone to send me overseas. I have been treated everywhere primarily as a physician, secondarily as a woman, and have had assignments involving, for the most part, greater responsibility than that accorded my male colleagues with equivalent training. I have even had a great deal of valuable medical experience per se, and I feel that I have been given the opportunity to contribute about as much to the war effort as anyone with my type of training could be expected to, within the Army organization.

But the Army had opened up her eyes to other possibilities, specialization, being the main one—and like a few other women doctors, she decided to become a psychiatrist in civilian life. After she left the service, Hayes got a psychiatric residency at Peter Bent Brigham Hospital, Boston, Massachusetts 1946-47 which she followed up immediately with a position as psychiatrist at a VA hospital in Framingham, Massachusetts in 1948. The next year she did postgraduate training at the Judge Baker Guidance Center in Boston (1949-51) while she was a Fellow in psychiatry at Putnam Children's Center at the same time. She remained at the Putnam's Children's Center as a staff psychiatrist from 1951-57 and then she went to Chicago and worked at Michael Reese Hospital as the director of Child Psychiatry 1957-58. After this, Hayes moved to California where she became the Director of Children's Services, Berkeley Psychiatric Clinic, Herrick Hospital. All in all, she was licensed in four states: Maryland, Massachusetts, Illinois, and California.[11] She finally settled in San Francisco where she taught at the Langley Porter Psychiatric Institute there and established a private practice before moving to Orinda, California. She also served as the first president of the Northern California Child Psychiatry Society.

By 1971, she had discovered the love of her life and she married Roger Wayne Wallace, a physicist and nuclear engineer at the University of California, Berkeley. They remained married until her death. She succumbed to Alzheimer's disease at the age of ninety-four on 22 January 2011.[12]

As Craighill had reiterated time and again, the majority of women medical officers were assigned to work with WACs as one time or another. This proved to be true as well for Mary Mulloy who was in her twenties when she volunteered. A graduate of the University of Texas Medical School, she was commissioned a lieutenant November 1943 and assigned as an assistant surgeon to the Medical Activities School, Ft. Myer, Virginia. Once assigned as a Medial Officer, General Duty, she spent the greatest part of her time with female patients, most of them WAC enlisted personnel. She related that she had daily sick calls where she saw 40-80 WACs, conducted monthly physicals for about 2000 WACs, and was responsible for pregnancy discharges. In addition, she was medical officer of the day (O.D.) every third night and every third weekend, and she was responsible for monthly physicals and pregnancy discharges. Her overall impression: "Over a year in a dispensary is medically unsatisfactory." She was later promoted to captain.[13]

If women medical officers did not like having O.D. duties, they took them as a matter of course. Capt. Poe-Eng Yu, a psychiatrist for instance, said that when she assumed that duty, she slept in the regular O.D. room, where, as a rule, only men O.D.s slept. Capt. Jean Henderson, specialist in obstetrics/gynecology, claimed that she had never rebelled at taking hospital O.D. but she did "resent being made a WAC line officer." She wondered if there was an Army regulation governing this or if it was up to the whim of the commanding officer of the WAC. The men officers claimed exemption on the ground that "they are male and have to have a female escort when entering barracks and it is awkward at night."[14]

Because a woman doctor ended up being classified in General Duty, this did not necessarily mean that she had less experience than some other specialists although this was sometimes the case. For instance, Catherine Gordon McGregor, a highly experienced physician at age 53 and a graduate of the University of Minnesota Medical School, was commissioned 30 June 1944 and classified in General Duty. Straight away, she was stationed at the VA Facility in Minnesota where she remained for her entire Army career treating predominately male patients. Unhappy with this arrangement, she asked for specialized training in neuropsychiatry so she could be re-assigned, but she never got what she wanted.

She reported: "I have asked repeatedly for the course in Military Psychiatry but so far have been refused." She made it clear, however, that this was only one of her concerns.

> My whole experience in the Army is one of keen dis-appointment. I am assigned to a position which can be satisfactorily filled by any intelligent, educated person without medical training. I am willing to ac-cept any assignment, to an administrative position or any other post in the Army, if it were of such a na-ture as to require a doctor to discharge its duties.
>
> Although there is a definite need for a woman physi-cian in this set-up, there is a deliberate effort to prevent me from using my medical skill and training. As to be-ing any Army officer, the Veterans Administration dis-regards this status completely and considers us merely employees. However, when it is advantageous for them to impose additional work without any cost to themselves they tell us we are in the Army. Then they deprive us of the usual rights and prerogatives of Army officers by tell-ing us we are working for the Veterans Administration.
>
> I entered the Army expecting to be very proud of being

an Army officer. I am sorry to say it has only been to my disadvantage.

She continued to practice medicine after the war, and she expired 6 January 1972 at the age of 80 of arteriosclerotic heart disease and ventricular fibrillation.[15]

Although not as old as McGregor, Gladys Osborne was another mature and experienced physician who encountered a different kind of problem related to dependency issues. She was born 20 December, received her undergraduate degree from Duke University in 1925, finished medical school at Vanderbilt in 1929, and married Dr. Dudley Smith in 1935 although she did not assume his name professionally. From 1932-1935, Osborne did her internship and residency at Women's and Children's Hospital in San Francisco, California, and went into private practice in Waynesville, North Carolina.

It was while Osborne was in North Caroling that she developed an interest in nutrition. As part of her work, Osborne visited nutrition clinics around the country. In 1942 she became an instructor of medicine at Vanderbilt University School of Medicine and she taught there in the nutrition clinic as part of her responsibilities. The next year, at the age of thirty-nine, she opted for an Army commission with her husband's encouragement as he was now a Major in the Army Medical Corps. She had several different assignments at various stations including Lawson General Hospital, Atlanta, Georgia, where she served as a ward officer for eight months; Chief of the Out-Patient Clinic at Foster General Hospital in Jackson Mississippi, for nine months; and then at the Office of the Surgeon General for one month as duty officer in the Nutrition Division.[17]

It was at her last assignment, however, that her specialization in nutrition proved to be an invaluable asset. After hostilities ended in the European Theater in May 1945, occupying forces in Austria had to assume a major responsibility One of the most serious and urgent problems was the immediate need to safeguard public health and prevent the spread of epidemics. In the first days of the occupation, the major task facing the U.S. Army "was that of halting, under conditions of extreme filth, malnutrition, and starvation, the spread of serious communicable diseases by disease-infested victims of Nazi oppression among a civilian population that was both demoralized and confused." In addition to the indigenous population which was estimated at somewhat more than 1 million inhabitants, "there were an estimated 700,000 displaced persons and refugees, including about 80,000 concentration camp inmates of five large camps, 200,000 displaced Austrian refugees, and 250,000 disarmed enemy forces (prisoners of war)." The control of communicable diseases was imperative as well as the treatment problems of the total civil population.

Thus, in April 1945 Osborne found herself organizing a team for a nutrition survey for the ETO, and by May she was in Versailles, France, with SHAEF as the Chief of that nutrition team studying the effects of war-time nutrition in Europe among civil populations. From the end of May to April of 1946 she continued to head up the survey team with German Occupation Forces, and that team covered over 20,000 miles and examined 25,000 Germans in many large Bavarian towns.[18]

Problems related to Dependency Allowances

While in service, Osborne and her husband, Major Smith, encountered a problem with dependency allowances since they were both medical officers in the United States Army. Long-standing issues related to dependents had also occurred in the Spanish-American War with the nurses who served on contract and, therefore, had no rights and privileges because they were not part of the regular Army. Although Irene Toland was a physician, for example, she served as a nurse on contract during the Spanish American War since women doctors were not accepted in the military. When she died in service of typhoid fever, her young son was left an orphan. Dr. Anita Newcomb McGee wrote to the family attorney on 19 January, 1899: "I take the liberty… to inquire whether Dr. Toland had any relatives who would, under the Pension Laws, be considered dependents. It is desirable that a test case should be made at the Pension Office so that if it is found that existing laws do not cover the case, Congress may be appealed to."[19] Nearly fifty years later, women doctors were still fighting for equality in the Army when it came to allowances for dependent husbands, children, and parents in WWII.

With regard to Major Smith, however, his claim was based on the fact that he had received a dependency allowance for his wife until her entrance into the service on 1 November 1943. At this juncture, his dependency allowance was stopped because of the decision of the Comptroller General. At the same time Osborne started active service at Lawson General Hospital, she learned that she was not entitled to dependency allowances because she was a woman. Craighill explained: "It is obviously an unfair decision but one that has been made. It ties in with the whole problem of not giving dependency allowances to women on the same basis as to men—only this in reverse. My whole point is," she said, "that men are not questioned as to whether their wives are actually dependent on them financially and they are penalized only if the wife happens to be in the service. Otherwise, they are given dependency allowances without question." At the same time, women could have dependent husbands, by reason of mental or physical capacity, and they were not given allowances for them in any eventuality, although legally they would be responsible for their husband's debts. Craighill suggested that Osborne write a letter and send it through official channels protesting the situation, although the matter of dependency allowance was being formally taken up by the Legal Department at that time.[20]

Not only did Osborne write letter, but her husband, Major Dudley W. Smith, wrote to the Dependency Bureau the next month. He made it very clear that he was not interested in obtaining two dependency allowances for himself and his wife, but he felt it had been unjust to remove his dependency allowance for his wife in the first place. He wanted it restored—and he felt this was a serious issues for other married officers in the Army, as the basis of payment of dependency allowances was "conditioned by the presence of a wife and not in the slightest whether she is truly a dependent as related to financial support."[21] Some officers claimed wives as dependents even though they were employed overseas by the Red Cross and there were also many so called dependent wives whose incomes far exceeded their officer husband's income. Major Smith summed up his thoughts on the matter this way:

> As to the matter of gross income, the loss of dependency allowance under the above conditions seems even more reprehensible... Prior to my wife's entrance into the service, my total income with all allowances was approximately $427.00 per month. Now our combined income amounts to $492.00 per month. The Army obtains the service of two medical doctors for the price of one, plus $65.00, a very neat bargain indeed.[22]

On 16 February 1944, Major General Jay L. Benedict, president of the War Department Dependency Board, wrote back to Major Smith informing him that the term "dependency allowance" had no specific meaning. It might refer to the rental allowance or subsistence allowance, or both, of an officer with dependents. Whatever the case, however, he wanted to make it clear that if public quarters were assigned, rental allowance was not payable. "In any event," he concluded, "it is presumed you are aware of the fact that opinions of the Comptroller General are not subject to reversal or review by any administrative officer of the Government." The only recourse for an individual was to apply to the Court of Claims.[23]

Even as Captain Gladys Osborne and her husband carried on their fight, other women officers, including Major Craighill, were also calling attention to the problems with dependency allowances.

Craighill wrote to Judge Dorothy Kenyon, who had been active in promoting the bill to commission women medical officers, about the Assistant Comptroller General's decision to deny dependency allowances for women medical officers, especially when it came to dependent mothers and fathers. This decision was made on the ground there was "no language" warranting that Congress intended to grant the increased rental and subsistence allowances as for officers with dependents under the Pay Readjustment Act of 1942, with respect to dependents of male officers, nor was "there any evidence found in the legislative history of the Act which would support such a determination." Craighill hoped Kenyon could get an answer to this question: "Have you any information on the subject which might be helpful in convincing the Comptroller General that Congress did not mean to exclude women medical officers from such allowances."

While Craighill also supported the cause of women in their fight regarding dependent husbands, she was loath to take a stand in 1943 as she knew "Congress would not consider a husband as a dependent, even though wives must not show any real financial dependency." She based this on the fact that there were only a "few number of women physicians" in service to whom this applied at the time. This was an issue that did not go away, however, as servicewomen continued to battle for equal rights through the 1960s. It was not until Sharon Frontiero, a married lieutenant in the Air Force, applied for increased housing and medical benefits for her husband that a case was brought to the District Court in Alabama.[24]

Meanwhile, as the number of women medical officers increased in WWII, it became clear that more of them were supporting one or both parents. One female officer confided that she even knew of a colleague who was skipping meals as she was "sending practically her whole check home to her mother."[25] Capt. Machteld Sano wanted to be shipped overseas so she could be near her aging and sick parents in Belgium, and Maj. Margaret Janeway also claimed a dependent mother for whom she eventually received an allowance, and she cited "dependency" as the reason for relief from active duty as of 6 November 1945

By 23 August 1944, the Chief Consultant in Surgery in the ETO decided to champion the cause of women medical officers as he felt that after they were admitted to the Army Medical Corps they were "discriminated against in that they are not allowed allowances for dependents." He cited two specific instances known to him personally where the women doctors were told there was no sex discrimination and that they would be paid according to men officers and, as they were supporting their mothers, they rightfully claimed this dependency. Four months later the Comptroller of the Treasury ruled against this and, therefore, they had to pay back some $400 or $500, on top of having given up a valuable practice to serve their country. "It is hard enough to go and serve one's country in a foreign land… [but] to have to pay this sum to the Government when one only receives the pay of a Captain seems a great injustice," he said.[26]

Dependency allowances were also a grave concern for a handful of officers with children. Both Capt. Zdenka Hurianek (later Moore), a neuropsychiatrist, and Capt. Ida R. Holzberg, who specialized in obstetrics/gynecology, had young sons, and they maintained that not receiving a dependency allowance was a hardship for them. Holzberg, in particular, claimed that when she applied for a commission in New York City and was asked if she had any dependents under 18, she replied that she had a son who was eleven years of age. She was reassured that "he would be considered a dependent." She was not only dismayed but shocked when her first check arrived and there was no such provision. After making inquiries she learned that because she "was a woman" her child could not considered a dependent. Holzberg had also counted on having her son live with her while she was in the United States as she did not think a child should be separated from his mother permanently. However, she could not live with him if she were assigned quarters in the barracks. Should he become ill, she worried, not only was he not considered her dependent, he could not be treated in any Army Hospital, but would have to be "treated elsewhere." In appraising her Army experiences later, she maintained: "I do think the attitude towards women and their dependents has been very unfair. Women with large incomes are being supported by the Army as wives but children of mothers are not."[27]

Women medical officers had valid complaints when it came to dependency allowances, but a change finally came on 7 September 1944 when the Pay Readjustment Act of 1942 was further amended. In substance, it stated that any female member of any of the services mentioned in the title of the Act, or the reserve components, "shall be entitled to all allowances, and benefits authorized in this Act on account of dependents but only in the case of a husband, a child or children, or a parent or parents in fact dependent upon her for their chief support." There were to be no back pay or allowances as the amendment would not become effective until the first day of the first calendar month after enactment of the Act—which would mean October of 1944. Women would still have to prove, however, that their dependents were, in fact, dependent on them for support.[28]

Other Women Medical Officers with Various Designations

Some confusion existed in the classification system as we have noted. While the following women did not return their Questionnaires, thereby verifying their status, they were mentioned in other records as having a designation. Thus, Eleanor B. Gutman was not listed with a specialty, but elsewhere Craghill referred to her as a Medical Officer with General Duty.

Gutman was a highly experienced and successful physician in civilian life. Born in 1904, she lived in Salem, Oregon, received her BA degree from Smith College (1926), and was the only woman Army doctor in WWII who graduated from the Yale University School of Medicine (1930). In the 1940s she maintained a private practice in both internal medicine and gynecology in New York City when she decided to put her career on hold and sign on as a contract surgeon in September of 1942.

With her expertise in two vital areas, it can be seen why the WACs would have wanted Gutman. In fact, she was immediately sent to the post hospital at the first WAAC/WAC training center in Ft. Des Moines, Iowa. As soon as commissions were available, she received her captaincy on 19 June 1943, but continued to serve with the WACs for the rest of the year. (Had she been classified, it would have been as an internist). In December 1944, she was shipped overseas with them to the Mediterranean Theater (MTOUSA), first to Africa and then on to Italy.[29]

In postwar years her career continued to grow and expand, but the Army had left an indelible mark on her in terms of veterans' care and preventive medicine. Gutman accepted one of the first appointments of women doctors with the VA in 1946 and served at the branch office in Seattle. Eventually, however, she returned to her home state of Oregon, and she was a health officer in Coos County, Oregon by 1949 and in 1956-57 she became the director of the Vision Conservation Section of the State Board of Health in Portland. One of the primary dictates of this program was to determine the role of public health in the conservation of vision, especially in regard to the detection and prevention of glaucoma and aging. She continued to devote herself to issues of the elderly among her many interests, and in 1962 she was called on as an expert witness by the United States Congress, Senate Special Committee on Aging. Like many of the other former women medical officers, Gutman was also drawn to institutional work in the state, and in 1962 she engaged in the practice of psychiatry and public health in the Oregon State Hospital at Salem, Oregon.

Gutman succumbed to adenocarcinoma of the colon at the age of fifty-eight on 2 March 1963, and she was buried in the Willamette National Cemetery in Portland, Oregon. The Eleanor B. Gutman

Rehabilitation House (for ex-mental hospital patients) in Portland was named in her honor.[30]

Although Anna C. Besick did not provide her classification, she performed the same duties as a Medical Officer, General Duty, so this appears to be her primary designation. At forty-five years of age when she was commissioned a lieutenant 27 March 1944, she was one of the most senior of the women doctors; and she indicated that she was divorced and had two parents as dependents. A graduate of the Chicago Medical School in 1929, she had been living in Cicero, Illinois, before she volunteered.

Assigned as a ward officer, Besick spent all her time in the South, something she did not like as she came from a colder climate in the mid-west. She was posted first to Lawson General Hospital, Atlanta, Georgia, and then to the Atlanta Ordnance Depot. At her third posting, she was a dispensary medical officer at Fort Oglethorpe, also in Georgia. She worked mostly with male patients, but she felt that there was "too much paper work—not enough medical work." Overall, she concluded: "I feel that I wasted my time." In personal correspondence to Craighill, while she was in the Dispensary at Fort Oglethorpe, however, she wrote:

> Please consider this letter as unofficial. I would, however, like to state my problem to you and will adhere strictly to what you may be able and willing to advise.
>
> I feel that I am wasting time and the government's money and while I am still willing to serve my country, would prefer to be in a more healthful climate. I cannot seem to adjust myself to all these insects, especially ants and roaches, in the south and together with too many months of hot weather, have been very uncomfortable. Have tried to do my duty and believe that my work has been satisfactory thus far.
>
> Inasmuch as I am not getting younger, (being 45 years old) am wondering if there may be a possibility of getting

a discharge, as I feel that I can be of more use in civilian practice. If a discharge is out of the question at this time, would it be at all possible to be transferred…

On 25 June 1945, Besick was relived from active duty because of "undue hardship on aged, ailing parents." She died in 1974 of coronary artery disease.[31]

At age forty-four, Margaret B. Ross was a year younger than Besick, and she reported that she was living in Rumford, Rhode Island at the point she volunteered in WWII. She was, from all accounts, an excellent student. In retelling something of her school years, she wrote: "At the fond age of 17 years, I proceeded to Tufts Pre-Medical School in search of knowledge—plus all the enthusiasm of youth. After a hectic two years Pre-Medical I entered medical school in the accelerated program during World War I—with much studying and two summers spent at Tufts, the necessary medical degree was produced in June, 1922."

Ross did not have a classification either, but elsewhere Craighill's records referred to her as a surgeon. Unlike some women medical officers who were shifted around to numerous duty stations, Ross was posted to only three locations following her commissioning as a captain 21 September 1943: Ft. Des Moines, Iowa, Ft. Oglethorpe in Georgia, and Mason General Hospital in Long Island, New York. A large facility, Mason consisted of Edgewood State Hospital, three buildings from Pilgrim Hospital, and several other temporary buildings that were constructed during the war. It was also the hospital where some Army doctors received specialized training in neuropsychiatry. Since Ross did not submit an Army Questionnaire, it is not known how she viewed her military career. When it came to her own civilian practice in postwar years, however, she noted: "I have had a very enjoyable successful career. City Physician, Holyoke Massachusetts, at age 25…Now practicing Gyn. at Rumford." She expired 26 June 1960 unexpectedly of a heart attack at home in Rumford,

Rhode Island. Apparently she had married in postwar years as her obituary listed her as the wife of Edward W. Roath.[32]

Only some scanty facts are known about Dorothy Vohr who came from Lee, Massachusetts. She was a 1932 graduate of Middlesex University School of Medicine in Waltham, Massachusetts. At thirty-seven years of age, she was commissioned a lieutenant and later promoted to captain. She had no designation, but she, like Ross, was referred to on one of Craighill's lists as a surgeon. She served at Ft. Des Moines, Iowa, and Ft. Meade, Maryland; lastly at Wakeman General and Convalescent Hospital, Camp Atterbury, Indiana, which was the largest hospital of its kind during the war. At Wakeman, Vohr was assigned to the WAC Medical Department Enlisted Technicians (MET) School. Camp Atterbury was also the site where on 22 May 1943, the first black unit of WAACS was assigned to the Fifth Service Command.[33]

At one time, Vohr must have confided in Janeway about concerns at one of her assignments; and given the date of the response, it coincided with her time at Wakeman where she probably served as an instructor and, like quite a few other women doctors, felt such work was not what they had signed up for when they volunteered. "One of the disadvantages we have in the Army," Janeway wrote back, "is that we have to 'sell' ourselves each time we move and no matter how good our recommendations may be, we have to prove ourselves before we are accepted. You have got to feel your way along," she continued, "take what opportunities are offered to you, find others that are not, and generally make yourself indispensable, in spite of the reactions of those with whom you may be associated. It is a tough, uphill proposition…" We will never know what troubled Vohr, but she was finally relieved from active duty May 1945, which coincided with the discharge dates for other women medical officers. She died 14 December 1956 at the age of forty-nine.[34]

Eleanor Hayden came from a socially prominent and well-to-do family in New York. Born 20 May 1907, she claimed New Rochelle,

Westchester County, as her home before the war. She graduated from Mount Vernon Seminary in Washington D.C. in 1926 and had an interesting life as she was a Broadway actress until the depression struck in 1931 and she decided on a career in medicine, graduating from New York University (NYU) in 1936, and then obtaining her medical degree from NYU's College of Medicine in 1939. Shortly after that, she helped to organize the Brooklyn Red Cross Blood Bank and was in charge of its Mobile Unit.

Hayden remained with the Blood Bank until she volunteered as a contract surgeon in 1942 and was sent to Ft. Des Moines where she served with the WAACS—and she remained with them after she was commissioned a lieutenant 10 August 1943.[35] In September of that year she was posted to Ft. Oglethorpe and then in July of 1944 she was stationed at Camp Butner in North Carolina, an Army infantry training center which also housed Axis prisoners of war. In November of 1944 she was sent on to serve at the Army Rest Center at Lake Placid, New York. Her last assignment was in an Army dispensary in New York City in March 1945, after which she was released from active duty the following month.

She was engaged to Fernand M. d'Orbessan in August of 1944 and they were married while she was still in the Army, but they were divorced after a short-lived marriage. Her married name appeared on some Army records, but she reverted to her maiden name professionally after the war when she maintained a medical practice in Whitestone, New York. In 1953 she was a Health Officer in Training with the New York City Department of Health. In 1956, one newspaper pictured her on the front page giving an inoculation to Santa Claus as a publicity stunt to encourage people to get their shots for polio.[36] She passed away on 27 April 1993.

Christine Amanda Wood Martin is another doctor who was difficult to track, probably because she died when she was in her early forties. She was born 15 April 1916 in Marshfield, Wisconsin, and she attended high school in her hometown and graduated from La-

Crosse State Teachers College (Wisconsin) in 1936 with a degree in Physical Education. The next year she entered Stanford University in California, but transferred to the University of Wisconsin her second year and received her medical degree from there in 1942.[37]

She was commissioned a lieutenant 9 August 1943 at the age of twenty-seven under the name of Martin, which means she married sometime around the time she volunteered. She had varied assignments at the Air Corps at Fort Sam Houston, Texas, and "had her residency at Randolph Field" also in Texas.[38] Her last assignment was at the METS School at Ft. Oglethorpe, Georgia, and she achieved her captaincy May of 1944. She died during 1957-58 in San Antonio, Texas.[39]

—ⷱ—

Women doctors, who were classified as General Duty Officers or for whom no designation was listed by them, were just as well-qualified as any of the Army doctors, male or female. Out of the eighteen women listed in both groups, four of them had dual classifications. Six women held the rank of captain, and if age can be related to experience, only one-third of them were in their twenties when they volunteered. Eleanor K. Peck and Josephine M. Stephens had also been among the first to volunteer in Great Britain, while Peck, Stephens, Garber Tate, and Hayden had been contract surgeons before they were commissioned.

Drs. Elizabeth Garber (left) and Mary Moore.
Courtesy private collection.

Regardless of whatever classification they were given, women doctors continued to meet with the same disappointments and problems related to being in the military. They had too much paperwork, they had O.D. duties, dispensary duties, conducted monthly physicals, were unable to get overseas assignments, and they were sometimes prevented from using their medical skills and training to the fullest. Worst of all, they could not get specialized training when they requested it; and they continued to face inequities related to dependency allowances because they were women.

Conversely, the women were the first to admit that there were many satisfactions in being an Army doctor and the military opened up their eyes to other possibilities, such as specialization in postwar years. Four of the doctors (Gutman, Seno, Mills, and Hayes) switched their career paths because of their Army experiences. Like Craighill, all of them went on to practice psychiatry. While it was not possible to discover what all the women did in postwar years, we do know that Gutman and Seno also worked in VA facilities.

~ NOTES ~

1. *Personnel in WWII*, 279. With the increase in specialization after WWII, the generalist was a casualty until Family Practice was recognized as its own specialty in 1969 by the AMA.

2. Biographical information in Seno's questionnaire, "Wisconsin Medical Alumni Association" folder provided by the University of Wisconsin Archives.

3. Assignments and quote from Seno's Army Questionnaire.

4. She was certified by the American Board of Psychiatry and Neurology in 1962. Career locations in *Bio. Dir. Of the Amer. Psychiatric Assoc.*, 1968 ed.

5. Information on Mendota State Hospital from her Alumni Questionnaire, Univ. of Wis. Archives. For information on Seno's farm, see the Woodland Education Center on line: www.wisconsinwoodlands.org.

6. See Mills' "Officer's and Warrant Officer's Qualifications Card," in Histories, Box 29, MDC Coll. Rosenfeld, Louis. The Fighting 300th: A History of the Vanderbilt University Medical Unit During World War II. Nashville: Vanderbilt University, 1985, 101.

7. Biographical information for Mills provided by Special Collections., Vanderbilt University. Med. Center, Nashville, Tenn. Also see Mills Questionnaire, MDC Coll.

8. Quotes, Questionnaire, Box 30, MDC Coll.

9. See Social Security Death Index for Mills. Thanks to Christopher Ryland, assistant director for special Coll. at Vanderbilt, for supplying information regarding Mills and another Army doctor, Gladys Osborne. She had started a residency in psychiatry before the war.

10. All Hayes quotes from Tribute to "Marjorie Winchester Hayes Wallace, M.D.," on line: www.plumsite.com/memorials.html The tribute was written by a longtime friend.

11. Biographical information for Hayes supplied by Johns Hopkins Medical School (JHMS), Alan Chesney Mason Archives; and see *New England Journal of Medicine*, Vol. 235, 1946, p. 771; *Bio. Directory, APA*, 1968 ed, p. 304. Quotes from her Questionnaire, Box 30, MDC Coll. Also see "Women Physicians in the Army of the United States," *Women in Medicine*, 9. For more on the Hopkins Unit overseas,

see Joanne P. Cavanaugh, "Women of War," *Johns Hopkins Magazine,* November 1998.

12. Marriage noted in "Tribute". Also see Social Security Death Index.

13. See Mulloy's Questionnaire, Box 30, MDC Coll. 12.

14. O.D. duties: "Poe-Eng Yu to Major Craighill," letter, Dated 20 February 1945, Craighill's Personal Papers, Box 1, MDC Coll.; "Capt. Jean Henderson to Major Janeway," letter Dated 12 September 1944, Official Corres., Box 5, MDC Coll.

15. See McGregor Questionnaire, MDC Coll.; quotes are also from there. Obituary in "Deaths", *JAMA* 24 July, 1972, Vol. 221, No. 4, 421.

16. Information on Osborne, provided by Duke University Medical Center Archives; also see "Duke University Commencement Program for 1925" which they provided.

17. Duty stations listed on Questionnaire, Box 30, MDC Coll.; and also noted on her "Biographical Sketch" courtesy of Special Coll., Vanderbilt University Medical Center.

18. Quotes from Medical Department, United States Army: Preventive Medicine in World War II, Volume VIII, Chapter XIV, 512-513. German survey noted on her Questionnaire, Box 30, MDC Coll.

19. McGee to Toland Family Attorney, Dated 12 January, 1899, letter, Case Files of Applicants Seeking Appointments as Army Nurses, 1898-1917," in Records of the Office of the Surgeon General (Army) 1898-1917, RG 112, Entry 104, box 509, NARA.

20. Craighill to Capt. Gladys Osborne, Dated 10 January 1944, letter, Official Correspondence, Box 5, MDC Coll.

21. Major Dudley Smith to Maj. General J. L. Benedict, Dependency Bureau, Dated 6 February 1944, letter, Histories, Box 29, MDC Coll.

22. Smith's letter, Ibid.

23. Major General Jay L. Benedict to Major Dudley W. Smith, Dated 16 February 1944, letter, Histories, Box 29, MDC Coll.

24. Major Margaret D. Craighill to Judge Dorothy Kenyon, Dated 23 December 1943, letter, Histories, Box 29, MDC Coll. Frontiero's suit was rejected initially as under laws enacted by Congress, wives of male members of the Armed Forces were automatically defined as dependents while husbands could not be qualified as such unless they received over half of their support from their wives' earnings. This amounted to different treatment for female and male members of the uniformed

services, and as such, violated the due process clause of the Fifth Amendment of the United States Constitution. After the District Court affirmed the constitutionality of the existing policy, she immediately filed a direct appeal to the U. S. Supreme Court which later overturned the ruling of the lower court. See Frontiero v. Richardson (1973) 411 U.S.677; and Klebanow, Diana and Jonas, Franklin L., *People's Lawyers: Crusaders for Justice in American History* (New York: M.E. Sharpe Inc.), 367, 397.

25. Quotes about meals, Capt. Adele C. Kempker's Statement, Dated 16 August 1944, Extract, Histories, Box 29.

26. Champions cause: Elliott C. Cutler, Chief Consultant in Surgery, ETO, to The Honorable David Walsh, United States Senate, Dated 23 August 1944, letter, Histories, Box 29, MDC Coll.

27. Capt. Ida R. Holzberg to Craighill, Dated 15 March 1944, letter, Histories, Box 29, MDC Coll.; Questionnaire, Box 30, MDC Coll.

28. Extract from Public Law 421—78th Congress (Chapter 407, 2D Session) (H.R. 1506), Amend the Pay Readjustment Act of 1942, Approved 7 September 1944.

29. Gutman gave her height as five feet, one inch; weight of 125 pounds, in U.S. World War II Army Enlistment Records, 1938-1946, NARA, College Park, MD. Also see "Two WAAC Surgeons Become Army Medical Corps Officers," the *Journal of the American Hospital Assoc.*, Vol. 17, 104; "Medicine and the War", *JAMA* 1943, Vol. 122, No. 13, 877; *World Who's Who of Women* (United Kingdom: Melrose Press, 1973), 442. Thanks to Cushing/Whitney Medical Library at Yale University for help in locating biographical and related materials.

30. See *JAMA*, 1963, Vol. 184, No. 10, 847; National Cemetery Administration, U.S. Veterans Gravesites 1775-2006; Oregon Death Index, 1903-98.

31. See Besick Death: JAMA, 1974, Vol. 228, No. 4, 517-518; Texas Death Index; her Questionnaire, Box 30 MDC Coll. Also see Besick to Craighill 16 December 1944, letter, Official Correspondence, Box 5, Ibid.

32. Information on Ross supplied by Tufts University Archives: "Ross' Own Account," probably intended for the alumni news, one typewritten page, undated; and Alumni Card returned from the Ross family noting the date of her death. Information supplied by the Providence Public Library which also supplied an obituary from the *Evening Bulletin* 17 June 1960, 29. Her birthdate is given at 1900 in the Rhode Island Historical Cemeteries Transcription Project, on-line.

33. Information on Vohr supplied by Brandeis University Archives, formerly Middlesex. Also see JAMA, 1956, Vol. 160, Issues 9-13, "Death" of Dorothy Vohr.

34. Janeway to Capt. Dorothy L. Vohr, letter, Dated 13 January 1945, Official Correspondence, Box 5, MDC Coll.

35. Actress noted in *Medical Woman's Journal* 50:7 (July 1943) 179. Biographical materials For Hayden supplied by Mark A. Miner as part of his family genealogy, see Minerd.com.

36. Army records misspelled her married name as D'Orbisonn. Her picture in, "The Girl Who shot Santa Claus," *Stars and Stripes Newspaper*, Pacific Editions, 1945-1963, Provo, UTR, USA on-line.

37. Information supplied by the University of Wisconsin Archives from their deceased alumni files for Christine Wood Martin.

38. Quote regarding residency from "Women Physicians in the Army of the United States," *Women in Medicine*, 7.

39. Obituary in "Necrology" Section from *Wisconsin State College, LaCrosse, Wisconsin, Alumnus News, 1958*. Statement notes she died during the year, so it is unclear if that was 1958 or 1957.

Table 9.
Twelve Women Army Medical Officers Classified as General Duty Officers*

Name	Rank and Age at Commission
Garber, (Tate) Elizabeth (and comm. diseases)**	Lt., 28. (See Chapter 5)
Hayes, Marjorie	Lt., 27
Kotrnetz, Margarete E. (also anesthetist)**	Lt., 37 (See Chapter 4)
McGregor, Catherine Gordon	Capt., 53
Mills, Miriam	Lt., 25
Mulloy, Mary E.	Lt., 26
Osborne, Gladys, H.	Capt., 39
Patton Anna M. (and surgery)**	Lt., 26 (See Chapter 5)
Peck, Eleanor, K.	Lt., 36 (See Chapter 1)
Seno, Elvira C.	Lt., 34
Shirlock, Margaret E. (and psychiatry)**	Capt., 44 (See Chapter 3)
Stephens, Josephine M.	Capt., 41 (See Chapter 1)

*This comprised the second largest group of women doctors (following the psychiatrists/neuropsychiatrists) assigned in one area

**Note some women had two classifications and were discussed in earlier chapters.

Table 10.
Women Army Medical Officers
for Whom There Were No Questionnaires

Name	Rank and Age at Commission:
Besick, Anna C.*	Lt., 45
D'Orbison, Eleanor Hayden**	Lt., 36
Gutman, Eleanor B.	Capt., 39
Ross, Margaret	Capt., 44
Vohr, Dorothy	Lt., 37
Martin, Christine Wood	Lt., 27

Note: These women had classifications as they were mentioned elsewhere in different specialties, i.e. Gutman, medical officer.

*She was the only one here who submitted an Army Questionnaire, leaving the classification blank although she appears to have been assigned to General Duty.

**Army misspelled her married name which should have been d'Orbessan.

MERCEDES GRAF

CHAPTER SEVEN:

"I Do Not Regret Having Had the Opportunity to Serve My Country":
A Look Back at Women's Experiences as Medical Officers in the United States Army

In their book, *They Fought Like Demons: Women Soldiers in the Civil War*, the authors concluded that women were effective in combat and performed their full share of military duties. "Women soldiers bore all of the same hardships and dire consequences of soldiering as their male comrades. They suffered wounds, disease, and internment as prisoners of war, and they died for their country, too."[1] If we make similar comparisons between women and men Army medical officers in WWII, the conclusions are not as dramatic. We know with certainty that regardless of gender, Army doctors performed their share of military duties, but none of the women died in combat because of regulations that prevented them from being on the battle lines. Considering the number of women doctors who requested overseas duty, however, they were willing to put themselves in harm's way.

In her article on soldiers as citizens, Kerber points out that there are "hierarchies of military sacrifice, just as there are hierarchies of citizenship." One cogent example she provides relates to the experiences of black American soldiers who were inducted and given the task of loading and unloading ammunition. "But when the ammunition exploded and they died, they were not awarded the Purple Heart because they hadn't been killed in combat (combat being narrowly defined as fighting the enemy on the battlefield)."[2] Thus, Dr. Mary Edwards Walker, the only woman up to the present time to be awarded the Medal of Honor, had her medal revoked on the same grounds—her wartime sacrifices were not in combat. And if we look beyond combat service in Walker's case, she was the first woman Army doctor who displayed signs of Post-Traumatic Stress Disorder (PTSD) from her captivity as a POW during the Civil War.[3]

Turning to women physicians for another example in the hierarchies of military sacrifice, Dr. Irene Toland volunteered as a contract nurse in the Spanish-American War, and was immediately sent to the General Hospital in Santiago, Cuba. One month later she was stricken with typhoid fever, and she died aboard a hospital ship in the harbor on 25 September 1898. Although her death was in the line of service, as was the case with the black soldiers, she was not awarded a medal either. Instead, a handwritten note appended to her Personal Data Card (service record) stated: "Not a graduate [nurse]."[4]

All the women Army doctors in WWII were volunteers, who were willing to take the same risks as their male colleagues, especially if we judge by how many wanted to serve overseas. At peck strength, the medical corps consisted of 48,837 doctors, including the women who numbered 76, by November of 1944.[5] Of the male doctors until 1946, there were 203 battle deaths with 129 more being killed in action.[6] In regard to the men, those who were attached to National Guard Organizations came in automatically when the guard was mobilized before hostilities began. As the Army grew, the Reserve Corps was called into active service. But by and large, the vast majority of male doctors came through the local recruiting boards where they were permitted to apply for commissions directly to The

Surgeon General or to the Procurement and Assignment Service, which would send the papers to The Surgeon General. (Originally an unofficial voluntary organization to assist in the selection of doctors, the Procurement and Assignment Service was eventually made official as a component of the War Manpower Commission). The rare exception occurred when an eligible doctor declined a commission. He was then certified to his local draft board and drafted as a private in the Army. Some of these men were subsequently commissioned while a few served through the war as enlisted men.[7] By 1944, however, there was great concern that the draining off of doctors for the war effort would drastically affect communities and civilian hospitals. In October of that year, The Surgeon General asked that the General Staff stop procurement in all but cases involving individuals commissioned for specific reasons.[8]

The Surgeon General classified all applicants as to specialty, made an assignment, and requested the Adjutant General to issue orders placing then on duty. Later there developed many discussions over a special draft of doctors under the Selective Service Act when the Procurement and Assignment Service "could not induce a high percentage of available physicians to accept commissions by May of 1943" after the Medical Officer Recruiting Boards ceased to function across the country.[9] The Surgeon General also considered that it was necessary to recommend stronger means of compulsion and by October of 1943, the Secretaries of War sent a letter to Paul V. McNutt, Chairman of the War Manpower Commission, stating that the shortage of doctors was "so critical as to endanger the health of our forces." They requested a special call on the Selective Service System for 12,000 physicians, 5,000 for the Army and 7,000 for the Navy. McNutt replied that the Army and Navy "would get such a special call only over his dead body."[10] While there were further discussion of a draft of doctors during the following year, the efforts of the Secretaries of War and The Surgeon General came to nothing for the remainder of the war.

Special incentives existed for male doctors that were not extended to the women. Shortages for doctors had become acute in 1943 when Medical Officer Recruiting Boards were abolished by the Army Service Forces. Following this, medical officers had to be recruited chiefly from graduates of medical schools as they completed shortened internships. The Army Specialized Training Program and the Navy College Training Program (V-12) were both established in December 1942. The first program applied to student of medicine, dentistry, and veterinary medicine as well as to all students of specialized or professional subjects who might be considered officer material for the Army at large. As such, enlisted men selected for the Army program were placed in training units at colleges and universities around the country where they continued, if already students, or entered the regular course of instruction. To enter the Army program, medical students "who were members of the Medical Administration Corps might resign their commissions and enlist in the Enlisted Reserve Corps, after which, they, together with other medical student who were already members of the Enlisted Reserve Corps, were called to active duty with the program without interrupting their studies."[11]

Members of the Army Specialized Training Program were granted the status of privates, or privates first class, in the Army, and the Army defrayed all their expenses including food, clothing, lodging, and the cost of the schooling. Upon graduation, students were commissioned in the Army of the United States. At the point the program was set up, The Surgeon General estimated that Army needs would be met until 1947. To meet the requirements for doctors and dentists after that year, students were to be selected from among those who had successfully completed two or three terms of the "Basic Curricula" of the program, which was the introductory course which all new students had to enter. The Army program ended a year later than that of the veterinary or dental phases. As a result, "proportionately more medical graduates" became available for commissions which permitted the Medical Corps to solve its postwar personnel problems.[12]

One author pointed out that "nearly 80 percent of the students in American medical schools were involved with the specialized training programs (55 percent in the Army and 25 percent in the Navy).[13] Thus, while up to 80 percent of the male medical students in some war years had their expenses entirely financed by the government through such plans, women received no such incentives.[14] One father, whose daughter was finishing medical school, wrote to Dr. Margaret D. Craighill and observed: "The Government is paying male students in colleges of the United States $50.00 a month, tuition, uniforms and everything else, while the girls have to pay their own way, including tuition." He wondered why women students weren't being treated on the same basis as the men. And while he made no mention of it, service in the Army for students graduating from medical school had been deferred for at least the 1-year internship, with some further deferment of service for a junior residency and then a senior residency. As there was no assurance that such deferments would be given, the result was that civilian hospitals had to count on "an inadequate number of women and of men who were physically disqualified for military service." In what was proposed as the "9-9-9 Plan" beginning on 1 January 1944, internships and each class of residency were to run for only 9 months apiece, so that the greatest possible postgraduate deferment for military personnel became 27 months instead of the previous 36. The Association of American Medical College as well as numerous individuals criticized the plan as they felt in shortening the internship it lowered the standards of medical education.[15]

Dr. Craighill wasted no time in drafting a reply to the concerned father. "[U]ntil women doctors prove their merit in the Army, the Army is not too interested in broadening the opportunities." She went on to say that there were some benefits, however, to the present discrimination. "In order to receive this Government aid, men must cut short their premedical education and their post-graduate training. Both of these things are open to women, by virtue of their independent position...At present women are the only ones who can maintain the old standards of medical education which have been proved of merit and I believe they will benefit in the future by this advantage" for postwar medical practice. In a memorandum she sent out the same day, she recommended that women students who had completed the first two years of medicine satisfactorily be eligible for enlistment in the WAC for completion of their medical training; that they agree when obtaining their medical degree to serve in whatever capacity the government required during the duration and for six months thereafter; and that they be discharged from the WAC upon attaining the medical degree, but be commissioned in the Army, Navy, or Public Health Service, or retained in civil practice, at the convenience of the government.[16]

Craighill's recommendations did not see the light of day. Women medical students never had the advantages available to their male colleagues although more internships and residencies became available because of the dwindling supply of male doctors as they entered the war. In one year, the number of hospitals accepting women doctors increased by a whopping 400 percent, from 105 in 1941 to 463 at the end of 1942.[17] Hospitals were forced to bow to the inevitable as applications dropped and "the quality of those applying left much to be desired." In 1943, Massachusetts General Hospital opened its first internships to women, and Harvard Medical School broke with tradition and replaced the available pool of "mediocre men" with a groups of "very superior women.[18] Unfortunately all these gains were lost in postwar years because many women doctors were removed from their hospital staff and clinical positions in order to make room for returning male doctors.

Many male veterans, who returned to civilian medicine in 1946, had another advantage which women did not share. Those who served as combat doctors had accumulated a wealth of experience related to surgery and improvisations on the field of battle in the treatment of shock or the management of various types of wounds. Men who had worked in the large hospitals, and particularly in the specialty centers, had been exposed to the latest advances in medical treatment. There were many who believed "that the pressures of World War II had advanced medical science out of all proportion to the duration of the conflict." While it would be surmised, therefore, that the women psychiatrists/neuropsychiatrists advanced in their specialty since they tended to treat exclusively or predominantly male patients who had been exposed to the psychological effects and trauma of war, this was not borne out by the comments made by the women themselves. Capt. Clyde Adams felt she was better trained to treat psychotic patients rather than male "psychoneurotics", and Lt. Elizabeth Bremner maintained that she had been trained as a child psychiatrist and the sooner she got back to it, the better. Capt. Elizabeth Bryan stated that the men "over her" rarely had as long or as good psychiatric experience as she, and Capt. Margaret Shirlock believed that she had not learned much in the way of medicine as a psychiatrist, but rather in how to deal with people. Finally, Capt. Mary J. Walters contended she did not get much in the way of training in neurology and that "she could arrange for neurology better in civilian hospitals."[19]

It must not be assumed that male physicians necessarily received preferential treatment when it came to assignments as they also held posts in the States which were not professionally challenging and consisted of routine duties. Army medical historian McMinn noted that male gynecologists also attended female members of the Medical Department, WACs, and the dependents of Army Personnel; and like the women doctors, these specialists were not able to devote full-time to their specialty as "administrative duties took a higher proportion of their time than it had done in civilian practice." In the Air Corps, doctors were sent to the school of aviation medicine and then assigned to squadrons as flight surgeons. Because the instances of illness were low and all the serious cases were immediately sent to a hospital, the doctor frequently spent long periods with very little to do including any real medicine or surgery; and instead was faced with a great deal of dull paper work. "He was often unhappy…[and] young men lost rather than gained in professional skill."[20] Thus, men who were assigned to the same specialties in the Armed Forces that they had in civilian life did not necessarily gain any more new experiences than many women doctors.

Proper assignments proved to be a problem for medical officers, regardless of gender. While we have seen that many women doctors were dissatisfied at one time or another, especially if they were assigned exclusively or predominantly with the WAC, a survey of 427 male officers showed that while 366 had good assignments, 44 had fair assignments, and 17 had misassignments.[21] The biggest problem occurred when a male medical officers might have substantially more skill and experience or substantially more rank than was required for the assignment—the same situation that existed for the women medical officers. In this regard, Lt. Genia Sakin (later Capt.), plastic surgeon, complained of working long months in a blood bank center, and Capt. Grace Fern Thomas asked to be transferred from a VA facility because her specialty in insulin and electroshock therapy was ignored and she was placed in charge of a small group of female patients. Meanwhile a male medical officer with less rank and no adequate previous experience was assigned to be in charge of shock therapy. As for Lt. Elizabeth Khayat (later Capt.), she felt that one's accomplishments should be taken into consideration when making assignments. A pathologist, she was referred to as a WAC laboratory technician. And Capt. Margaret E. Shirlock, a psychiatrist, pointed a problem common to all doctors, dealing with red tape: "I consider that I put forth my very best effort in the various assignments, however, many times the results were unsatisfactory and discouraging due to the maze of channels."[22]

There were also two other causes of dissatisfaction with assignments according to this survey of male doctors. An officer might be assigned to the wrong occupational field when his skill was needed elsewhere. Certainly this was true for women doctors like Lt. Bernice Joan Harte (later Capt.) who had special training in the Army as a neuropsychiatrist and was transferred to Ft. Des Moines, Iowa, where she felt her "special training was of no use." Lt. Jean Henley (later Capt.), an internist serving as a general ward officer, observed that she not been used "in the most effective way" for which her training had prepared her, and Lt. Mary E. Mulloy (later Capt.) commented that "Over a year in a dispensary is medically unsatisfactory." Capt. Machteld Sano, pathologist, believed that the Army has not made use of her qualifications which were related to research in the fields of surgery and medicine. She concluded: "It is only hoped that at one future date the Army may make some better use of its medical staff considering their special qualifications and past work."[23]

A male medical officer might also have substantially less skill and experience than were required for the assignment. An amendment to the Selective Service Act on 20 December 1941, sanctioned military service for those between 20 and 45 but was lowered the next year to 37 years. This had "certain adverse effects on the procurement of Medical Department officers." An expected outcome was that many younger doctors were commissioned, but the Army "found it more difficult to procure qualified specialists than general practitioners." In order to deal with the problem, the Army commissioned general practitioners and then trained them at military installations or in civilian schools in the various specialties. Approximately 8,000 male doctors completed some specialty training during the war but it is unknown how many were actually classified as specialists or even served in that capacity.[24]

Obviously, the Selective Service Act did not affect women doctors whose ages ranged from twenty-four to fifty-three with the majority of the women being in their thirties and forties. Given that the women were older, they were experienced, and there were many specialists among them. Like the men, a few did get specialty training in the Army, and this happened in anesthesia, neuropsychiatry, and tropical medicine. Sometimes, however, specialty training was denied them. Capt. Catherine Gordon McGregor, assigned as a medical officer, general duty, reported: "I have asked repeatedly for the course in Military Psychiatry but so far have been refused." Miriam Mills noted that she had started the course in neuropsychiatry which she wanted, but she could not finish because of Army orders. While at Foster General Hospital in Jackson, Mississippi, Lt. Cornelia Wyckoff, classified as a pathologist, was assigned to X-Ray for six months. Since she liked it so much she asked to be sent to the X-Ray school in Memphis, Tennessee, but the request was disapproved because of her classification. Major Margaret Janeway, explained: "First, because you have had excellent raining as a pathologist in a first rate hospital and second, because the Army needs good pathologists and when they have one, are not willing to train her in some other specialty. The Classification Division went into an uproar when I told them what you were doing, said they were tearing their hair for well trained pathologists and they certainly would not let you take a course in X-Ray."[25] Wyckoff, at least, enjoyed working in X-Ray, whereas McGregor noted that at the VA Facility where she was assigned in Minneapolis, Minnesota, her work was "primarily administrative."

Inequities in the system of promotion and in the distribution of rank among male Medical Department officers caused concern and criticism dating back to the early war years. In March of 1943, The Surgeon General proposed that all first lieutenants of the Medical and Dental Corps be promoted to the rank of captain upon the completion of 6 months' satisfactory service. The new policy gave members of the Medical, Dental, and Veterinary Corps a better chance of promotion to the grade of captain than that possessed by officers of other corps. In the Nurse Corps, the percentage of personnel in the grade of second lieutenant was far higher than in either of the male officer corps having members in that grade.[26] As far as data were concerned for 75 women medical officers at the date of their appointment, there were three majors, thirty-two captains, and 40 lieutenants. By September of 1945, there was one lieutenant colonel (Craighill who had been promoted from major), two who were promoted from captain to major (Loizeaux and Bowditch), and 17 promoted from lieutenant to captain although more than half the women saw at least twenty months' service. More lieutenants received a promotion than any other grade while those women with the initial rank of captain seemed to maintain that rank with the two exceptions noted above; and by September 1945, there were only four majors among the women doctors. On 28 February 1945, 17 were serving overseas.[27]

"The Surgeon General was keenly aware of the morale factors involved in problems of rank, promotion, and pay." Furthermore, policies in regard to these issues varied from corps to corps and the way in such policies were applied might also vary somewhat from one command to another. There were also differences for personnel if they were serving overseas of in the Zone of Interior. In February 1946, The Surgeon General was able to recommend a one-grade promotion for many of the medical officers who were serving as chiefs of services and sections in Zone of Interior hospitals, but unfortunately hostilities had ended by this time and many of the officers who would have profited from this promotion, had returned to civilian life.[28] In 1947, all but four women officers had been released, and even though Surgeon General Raymond W. Bliss fought hard to keep these few, he was unsuccessful. When the Korean War started, there were no women Army doctors in service although there were three women doctors in the regular Navy and twenty in the Naval Reserve. It was August of 1950 before Congress consented to a draft for male physicians and the services began special residency programs to aid the recruitment and retention of physicians. Again, none of these advantages applied to the women doctors in the country, but when the enabling legislation was passed, the Army recalled three reserve women physicians to active duty—Drs. Clara Raven, Alcinde de Aguiar, and Theresa T. Woo.

The War Department conducted a study in November 1946 in which it polled Medical Corps officers, former members of the Army Specialized Training Program, to discover their opinions about volunteering for the Regular Army Medical Corps. "All but 1 of the 385 who answered the questionnaire stated that they were not planning to apply for commissions in the Regular Army...Also, 267 of the 385 said they would like to get out of the Army at once, if possible."[29] While many reasons were enumerated for not wanting to stay on, two of the top concerns were insufficient financial compensation, which was related to rank, and dissatisfaction with assignments.

Sixty-three women medical officers responded to the questionnaire that was sent to them from Criaghill's Office in September of 1945 regarding their Army experiences. The first question called for the officer to state "impressions of your experiences in the Army in regard to assignment." The women were asked to circle satisfactory or unsatisfactory, and if the latter, explain. The majority, or 47 women, gave written responses ranging from very satisfied and completely satisfied to reasonably satisfied, somewhat satisfied, personally satisfied, and satisfied except for present assignment. Eight women replied they were dissatisfied, five had uncertain or mixed feelings, and three questionnaires were left blank. The next question asked the women officers to state their satisfaction in relation to being assigned in their specialty. Twenty-seven were satisfied with six more being partially satisfied; fifteen replied they were not satisfied, and there were fifteen with no responses. Thus, the majority of women doctors were satisfied with their Army assignments. Specialists, however, were satisfied when they were assigned in keeping with their specialty and they expressed considerably more dissatisfaction when they were not. Thus, few of the specialists were assigned for the duration to their field of expertise. At different times, they were more likely to have assignments not related to their specialty, which created dissatisfaction. At the same time, a few of the women were not assigned to their specialty at all, like Lt. Pauline Garber Clark (later captain) who had been a pediatrician in civilian life and was assigned as a Medical Officer, General Duty, or Capt. Celia Ragus, a urologist, who was never assigned in keeping with her abilities and training as she served as a ward officer or an assistant pathologist.[30]

The questionnaire did not survey satisfaction in regard to overseas duty, an experience that many women doctors clamored for before more than two dozen women eventually served abroad. The feasibility of utilizing female personnel in certain oversea areas was seriously questioned at times throughout the war. In the European and North African Theaters, nurses habitually moved with their units into forward areas and a few women doctors accompanied them. In certain other theaters, commanders were reluctant to allow women either in combat areas or in those places where material comforts were few.[31] Nevertheless, Capt. Marjorie Hayes reported that her only complaint was that "it took me a year and a half to persuade anyone to send me overseas." Similar concerns were reflected in the personal correspondence of some of the medical officers. Lt. Delores Amar (later capt.) wrote that she had "three near opportunities" to go overseas but each time she was told she couldn't go because she was a woman. Capt. Machteld Sano, however, had a special reason why she kept applying, as she wished to be near her aging and sick parents in Antwerp, Belgium. Finally, for the women who counted themselves lucky to have served abroad, they received the overseas ribbon which they considered a badge of honor. Although their experiences are detailed in an earlier chapter, perhaps the comments of Capt. Poe-Eng Yu, who served in North Africa, sum up the feeling of many of these women doctors: They were "flattered to be recognized that way " even if they had been nowhere near the front lines.[32]

As we have seen, women doctors were concerned with the same problems during their wartime service as the men. Capt. Josehine

M. Stephens maintained that "insufficient rank was the source of my difficulties or unpleasantness that I met in the Army." Capt. Eleanor B. Hamilton, whose specialty was obstetrics/gynecology, also agreed with the men when she said, "I would not care for a permanent rank in the Army but I have been very glad for the experience I have had." Lt. Alcinda de Aguiar noted that "Regarding my willingness to stay in the Army: I wish to be separated as soon as the emergency in NP Service will permit." Her comment is interesting as she one of the three women to be recalled in the Korean War, although the inducement may have been that she got an overseas assignment to Tokyo, Japan.[33] Related to the problem of insufficient financial compensation that the male doctors cited, was the issue of allowances for dependents for some WWII women doctors. A few of them had left better paying practices in civilian life where supporting dependent parents or children was not the financial burden it proved to be in the Army until an allowance for dependents was granted to women doctors on the same basis as men.

Lt. Anna C. Besick summed up the feelings that quite a few doctors shared at one time or another as they carried out routine and boring administrative tasks: "I feel that I wasted my time."[34] While the ups and downs of the flight surgeons have been touched on, especially in regard to their paper work, no one needed to point out that such feelings might be expected when about 2,000 male Army doctors had to be stationed in separation centers to perform the final physical examinations in November 1945 so that thousands of troops could be promptly released. This was akin to the frustration that both male and female doctors encountered as they conducted the monthly physicals for the WACs after they were inducted. Lt., later Capt., Mary E. Mulloy was on sick call where she said 40-80 WACs daily, and conducted roughly 2000 physicals a month. She felt: "Over a year in a dispensary is medically unsatisfactory."[35]

In considering the postwar careers of women doctors, we know that, like their male colleagues, they returned home to pick up where they had left off. Of the more than 45,000 eligible male medical officers who had served in WWII, only slightly over 500 of them applied for a Regular Army commission—which was a choice not possible for the women even if they had wanted it. In order for the military services to maintain Medical and Dental Corps of suitable size and quality, special provisions had to be made so that these doctors would have a standard of living close to those in civilian practice. The necessary legislation was passed 5 August 1947, and this authorized an increase in the pay of doctors of medicine by $100 per month and authorized the procurement of officers in all grades up to and including the grade of colonel.[36] Three years later, in 1950, only three women were recalled to the Korean War. Nevertheless, the Army influenced the career paths of many women doctors in two significant ways: exposing the women to the medical and psychological needs of veterans and pointing the way to specialization areas in civilian life.

Many former women Army doctors worked with state institutions after the war like psychiatrists, Poe-Eng Yu, de Aguiar, and Thomas. Although all four Army pathologists returned to their field, Khayat and Morris also worked for varying periods in state institutions. Other women made their way to VA facilities like Clara Raven who remained in the Reserves but started to work as Chief Pathologist for the Veterans Administration in Dayton, Ohio, leaving only after she was called up for the Korean War. She remained in the Army until her retirement and she was the first female physician promoted to full colonel in the Army Medical Corps in 1961. For a time, Margaret D. Craighill was hired as a VA consultant in 1945, and from 1948 until 1951, she was chief of the psychosomatic section at the Winter VA Hospital. In 1946, nine other women doctors including Marion Loizeaux, Jane M. Leibfried, and Angie Connor were the first to be named to VA posts across the country.[37] For the first two women, this exposure to veteran concerns influenced them so much that Loizeaux later became Chief, Long-Term and Geriat-

ric Medicine, with the VA Hospital in Albany, New York, and Leibfried, who was Board Certified in obstetrics and gynecology in 1950,
served as a consultant on the staff at the VA Hospital in Philadelphia
in 1975. Zdenka A. Hurianek Moore, a neuropsychiatrist, ended her
career working in VA Hospital in Phoenix, Arizona. Isabella Harrison, gave up surgery to become the director of a residency program
for the VA and Pauline Garber Clark, classified as a Medical Laboratory Officer, worked after her discharge as a pathologist in various
VA hospitals.

Since twenty-four women that we know of went on to accept positions with VA facilities in later years, this amounts to almost one-
third of the women medical officers who were commissioned in the
Army during WWII. Thus, if one is allowed to conjecture about the
impact of women doctors as far as veterans and their families are
concerned, it can be said that there was a strong correlation between
having served as medical officer and a willingness to work later at a
VA facility.

Some women doctors, who had learned the value of specialization
while they were in the Army applied this knowledge to their civilian
careers and completed residencies or pursued further studies after
the war. Such was the case for Katharine Jackson and Jean L. Dunham who had received special anesthesia training during the war,
while internist Jean Henley pursued a residency in anesthesiology,
later writing the first modern textbook of anesthesia to be published
in Germany. A handful of other women recognized the importance
of preventive medicine in the public sector and engaged in further
study in this field. Sally Bowditch received a Master of Public Health
degree from the Harvard School of Public Health in 1948, but she
never gave up on the Army. She became a civilian medical officer
at the Army Surgeon General's Office, Preventive Health Division,
in Washington, D.C. where she remained until 1953, and her last
position was as Chief of the Department of Health Data, Division
of Preventive Medicine at Water Reed Army Institute of Research

in Washington, D.C. Teresa T. Woo also went on to Harvard and completed her studies in 1955 in the same program as Bowditch, while Angie Connor received her Master's Degree in Public Health in 1952 from the University of California at Berkeley and remained active in this field in Hawaii until her retirement. Even though Agnes Hoeger had a specialty in tropical medicine, she was always looking for more ways to help the Lutheran community and she went to an institute in Denver, Colorado to study Public Health issues.

As the postwar period began After D-Day, the country faced the welcome transition to peace. In addition, the military and medical establishments as well as the public had grown aware of the number of psychiatric casualties that war could produce, and there was a growing awareness of the problems associated with mental illness which led to additional government funding for psychiatric training. After the National Mental Health Act of 1946 and the replacement of the Division of Mental Hygiene by the National Institute of Mental Health (NIMH), millions of dollars were appropriated for psychiatric research. One scholar noted that while there were approximately 4,000 psychiatrists in the United States in 1945, that number was close to 20,000 by 1993, and "between 1946 and 1951, 430 federally funded stipends were awarded."[38] Such changes impacted on the women medical officers who had served in WWII.

Margaret Criaghill once observed that the women psychiatrists seemed to fare the best in the Army, and she concluded that things would be just as good or better for them in civilian practice. She entered the Menninger School for training in psychiatry in 1946, and afterwards continued to practice in that field.[39] Adopting a similar course of action, among others, were Drs. Gutman, Seno, Hayes, Mills, and Holzberg. Miriam Mills, who had worked with Craighill as her assistant in the Surgeon General's Office seems to have been greatly influenced by her association with Craighill as she proceeded to complete a psychiatric residency at Vanderbilt in 1948.[40] Although Alcinda de Aguiar had been a psychiatrist before she volunteered, she honed her skills in WWII and Korea, and she became a prominent psychotherapist in Boston, Massachusetts. The same was true for Poe-Eng Yu, another psychiatrist, who had started out working as a contract surgeon with the WAAC/WAC, was finally promoted to captain, and after she was discharged in 1948 secured a post as senior psychiatric physician at the Connecticut State Hospital.

Women doctors, who had hospital or university affiliations, assumed the duties they had left before they volunteered, or else they advanced in their fields enough to engage in research or assumed teaching as professors or instructors. By 1959, Gladys H. Osborne, was at Vanderbilt where she worked in clinical and research applications of radioistotopes, and also worked on studies with air pollution and rats which was funded by the Public Health Commission.[41] Mila Pierce Rhoads, already a highly respected physician before the war, returned to Rush-Presbyterian St. Luke's Medical Center and served as a distinguished professor of pediatrics at the college associated with the Center. Some women physicians were associated with the WMCP at different times. Machteld Sano taught for two years for the WMCP starting in 1950, and then around 1957 she conducted research in cytology at Hahnemann Hospital in Philadelphia.[42] Jane M. Leibfried and Martha Howe, both graduates of the WMCP, also taught courses there after the war although Leibfried was a clinical associate professor of obstetrics and gynecology. Another doctor, Josephine Stephens, returned to her alma mater to teach as well, and she was an instructor in pediatrics at the University of Pittsburgh School of Medicine. In addition to assuming positions of increasing responsibility in the state medical bureaucracy in Hawaii, Angie Connor found time to teach in the psychology department at the University of Hawaii.

Women doctors were also committed to medical training. Melson Barfield Carter, a radiologist, went back home to be appointed first chair of the Department of Radiology at the University of Alabama, Birmingham, and she established a radiology residency-training program with the School of Radiological Technology. Elizabeth Khayat, a pathologist, became the director of laboratories and residency training in pathology at Jamaica Hospital in New York. Of course, more women doctors then are named here taught courses part-time, conducted seminars, consulted on hospitals and clinic staffs as well as with government agencies and medical centers. They also volunteered for local, national, and international organizations and agencies. Genia Sakin, a plastic surgeon, it will be recalled, donated her services in war torn countries in the 1950s.

While women physicians had volunteered as contract nurses or contract surgeons in previous wars, WWII was the first time that they were commissioned as medical officers in the Army, although it was only for the duration of the war plus six months. In performing new tasks and assuming different sets of responsibilities, women medical officers proved that they were up to the job. They had learned to work with others in the military setting with its administrative channels, regulations, and red tape, and they accepted the challenge even with all the frustrations and disappointments that went along with it.

In contrast to men medical officers, women doctors' wartime contributions did not advance their civilian careers although their Army service may have enhanced their skills and increased their knowledge. Like their male colleagues, however, many went to work at state institutions and VA facilities later on, and some studied or qualified in specialty areas like anesthesiology and psychiatry. When they returned home, women doctors were not hailed as conquering heroes, and they assumed their former medical places with no fanfare but with quiet dignity. Oftentimes people did not know they had served in WWII until it was printed in their obituaries, and then they wrote proudly of their association with them.

In the end, all the women doctors wanted was to serve their country and use their healing skills to provide medical care to those that needed them. It seems they did what they set out to do.

~ NOTES ~

1. Blanton and Cook, *Women Soldiers*, 205.

2. Kerber, "May All Our Citizens Be Soldiers," op. cit., 88. Black soldiers' quote, ibid. Also see her book, *No Constitutional Right to Be Ladies: Women and the Obligations of Citizenship*. She stresses that women's participation in citizenship has always been different from that of men. While women have related their struggle for equality to rights, she emphasizes that the history of citizens' obligations is also linked to gender—which has been less understood. She turns upside down the traditional paradigm of women's history as one of rights, as she maintains there is no "right" to be excused from the obligations of citizenship. This, in turn, brings up challenges to the gendered traditions of the military service.

3. In 1917, Congress struck Walker's name from the list of recipients for the Medal of Honor and asked that the Medal be returned on the grounds that her meritorious service was not combat-related. Although she was eighty-four years old at the time, she became infuriated at what she considered a great injustice, and she refused either to return the Medal or to stop wearing it. Noted in "Case Summary for Mary Edwards Walker," Ref, File No. 13.9, *Army Board for Correction of Military Records*, March 28, 1977. The Medal was restored to her posthumously in 1977. In *A Woman of Honor: Dr. Mary E. Walker and the Civil War*, Graf notes that the effects of her incarceration, such as anxiety, weight loss, and ensuing vision problems (all consistent with PTSD), made it difficult for her to practice medicine full-time in postwar years. As a result, Walker battled years for a pension and then a pension increase.

4. See Personal Data (PD) Cards of Spanish-American War Contract Nurses, 1898-1939, RG #112, Entry 149, NARA; Toland's PD Card, Box 6. Other handwritten notes on the PD card state that she "can speak Spanish." For more on her life, see Nize Fernandez, "Fifty Years of Irene Toland School," *The Methodist Woman*, November 1949; and Graf, *On the Field of Mercy*.

5. *Personnel in World War II*, 14. In December of 1942, women doctors numbered 42, in November 1944, they numbered 76, and on 30 June 1946, their number was 15.

6. *Personnel in World War II*, 436.

7. See Col. Russel V. Lee, M.C., "The Army Doctor," *California and Western Medicine*, January 1946, Vol. 64, No. 1, 10. This changed when Public Law 779 was passed 1 September 1950. This was commonly called the Doctors Draft Act, and it provided for the registration of all doctors fifty years old and under with induction eligibil-

ity to age fifty-one. It set out a priority of induction first with those doctors who had been students in the specialized training programs administered by the Army, Navy and the Air Force, but who had served for less than 90 days. The second category was for those who had served for more than 90 days; and third were those doctors who had no military service; and lastly those who had served since 16 September 1940, in inverse ratio to the length of their active service after that date.

8.   "Draining resources" in Personnel In World War II,

9.   Local recruiting, Ibid, 180; discussions, 184.

10. McNutt and quotes in *Personnel in World War II*, 189.

11. Ibid, 202.

12. Ibid, 204.

13. Apel, Otto F. *Mash: An Army Surgeon in Korea, 10.*

14. Walsh, *Doctors Wanted: No Women Need Apply*, 230.

15. Mr. F. D. Dobel to Maj. Margaret D. Craighill, letter, 2 October 1943; Box 18, MDC Coll. For more on Training and the 9-9-9 Plan, see *Personnel in World War II*, 192. For his part, The Surgeon General directed that the 9-month interns who entered the Army be given not only 6 weeks of basic military training, but an additional 6 weeks at a named general hospital. They were not to be sent overseas without having served a minimum of 60 days after completing their basic military training.

16. Craighill to F.D. Dobel, letter 6 October 1943; Memo to Colonel Raymond W. Bliss, 6 October 1943, both in Training, Box 18, MDC Coll.

17. Walsh, 233.

18. Walsh, 234, 231.

19. Advances in wartime medicine, *Personnel in World War II*, 500-501. Comments of women psychiatrists, all from their Questionnaires, Box 30.

20. Lee, "The Army Doctor," 9-13. Male gynecologists and obstetricians in McMinn, Personnel in World War II, 296.

21. Classification statistics in *Personnel in World War II*, 295.

22. Comments of all women doctors from their Questionnaires, Box, 30, MDC Coll.

23. See Harte, Henley, Mulloy, and Sano Questionnaires, Box 30, MDC Coll.

24. *Personnel in World War II*, age, 167; specialists, 193.

25. See McGregor, Questionnaire, Box 30. Wyckoff to Janeway, letter, Dated 6 January 1945; Janeway to Wyckoff, Dated 12 January 1945, letter, Histories, Box 29, MDC Coll.

26. Promotion and inequities, *Personnel in World War II*, 494-495; nurses, 467.

27. Numbers for women doctors were arrived at by taking a count from the list "Status of Women Commissioned in Army Medical Corps as of 1 September 1945 According to Initial Appointment and Present Rank," Histories, Box 29, MDC Coll. Craighill's promotion to Lt. Col. came when she was separated from service. Number of women overseas from *Personnel in World War II*, 155.

28. Discussion regarding pay and quote in *Personnel in World War II*, 451, 466-467.

29. *Personnel in World War II*, 497.

30. Statistics arrived at by a taking a simple count from the Questionnaires, Box 30.

31. *Personnel in World War II*, 381.

32. Overseas duty comments from Questionnaires, Box 30, Lt. Amar to Major Janeway, letter, Dated 12 March 1945, Official correspondence, Box 5; Poe-Eng Yu to Craighill, letter 20 February 1945, Craighill's Personal Papers, Box 1.

33. Comments of the women from their Questionnaires, Box 30.

34. See Besick's Questionnaire, Box 30.

35. Separation centers, *Personnel in World War II*, 493; Mulloy Questionnaire, Box 30.

36. Army Commissions, *Personnel in World War II*, 507.

37. See "Ten Women Doctors Named to VA Posts," *New York Times*, 28 November 1946, 47. Garber Clark had been in pediatrics before the war and remained in the Army until September 1946; notes on Dr. Garber Clark supplied by WIMSA.

38. See Menninger, Roy W. and Nemiah, John C., *American Psychiatry After World War II (1944-1994)* (American Psychiatric Press, Inc.: Washington, D.C.: 2000); quote 124-125.

39. Menninger and Nemiah noted that the postwar expansion of psychoanalysis resulted directly from wartime experience and from the prominent role played by many psychoanalysts as [male] leaders of military psychiatry. See preceding note, brackets mine. As chief of psychiatry for the Army, William Menninger had published manuals for military psychiatrists that partly reflected psychoanalytic theory. His acquaintance, no doubt, had an impact on Craighill's postwar career choices.

40. Notes on Mills, from Vanderbilt Medical Center.

41. Notes on Osborne's research provided by Duke University Medical Center Archives.

42. Sano's research in Koprowska, Irene, "Women in the Early Days of cytology: A Personal Recollection", *Diagnostic Cytopathology*, Vol. 10, No. 2.

MERCEDES GRAF

Appendix

Table A.
Status of Women Commissioned in Army Medical Corps as of 1 September 1945 According to Initial Appointment and Present Rank

Name	Age at Appt.	Rank at Appt.	Present Rank
Craighill	45	Major	Lt. Col.
Janeway	47	Major	Major
Carter	48	Major	Major
Loizeaux	39	Capt.	Major
Bowditch	38	Capt.	Major
Gutman	39	Capt.	Capt.
Garber, E*.	28	Lt.	Capt.
Dunham	24	Lt.	Capt.
Vohr	37	Lt.	Capt.
Olentine	28	Lt.	Capt.
Shedrovitch	37	Lt.	Capt.
Raven	38	Capt.	Capt.
Bill	27	Lt.	Capt.
Martin*	27	Lt.	Capt.
Reznick	45	Capt.	Capt.
Nersessian	41	Capt.	Capt.
Read	40	Capt.	Capt.
Adams	42	Capt.	Capt.
Holzberg	46	Capt.	Capt.

Jackson	43	Capt.	Capt.
Peck	36	Lt.	Capt.
Morris	39	Capt.	Capt.
Hamilton	41	Capt.	Capt.
Walters	50	Capt.	Capt.
Holmes	41	Capt.	Capt.
Bryan	46	Capt.	Capt.
Thomas	47	Capt.	Capt.
McGregor	53	Capt.	Capt.
Henley	34	Lt.	Capt.
Liebert	28	Capt.	Capt.
Ragus	49	Capt.	Capt.
Woo	33	Lt.	Capt.
Cone	33	Lt.	Lt.
Hayden*	36	Lt.	Lt.
Taylor	35	Lt.	Lt.
Bellaire	31	Lt.	Lt.
Shirlock	44	Capt.	Capt.
Harte	28	Lt.	Capt.
Hayes	27	Lt.	Capt.
Howe	41	Capt.	Capt.
Ross	44	Capt.	Capt.
Henderson	38	Capt.	Capt.
Yu	35	Capt.	Capt.
Mills	25	Lt.	Capt.
Mulloy	26	Lt.	Capt.
O'Donnell	34	Lt.	Capt.
Osborne	39	Capt.	Capt.
Kempker	40	Capt.	Capt.
Hoeger	33	Capt.	Capt.
Stephens	41	Capt.	Capt.

Pierce	42	Capt.	Capt.
Sano	40	Capt.	Capt.
Rost	45	Capt.	Capt.
Connor	31	Lt.	Capt.
Hurianek	42	Capt.	Capt.
Garber, P.	36	Lt.	Capt.
Hughes	31	Lt.	Lt.
Koppel	31	Lt.	Lt.
Amar	26	Lt.	Lt.
Seno	34	Lt.	Lt.
Patton	26	Lt.	Lt.
Kotrnetz	37	Lt.	Lt.
Wyckoff**	28	Lt.	Lt.*
Khayat	35	Lt.	Lt.
Besick	45	Lt.	Lt.
Sakin	41	Lt.	Lt.
Crandall	28	Lt.	Lt.
Rozov	40	Lt.	Lt.
Ramos	25	Lt.	Lt.
Reiley	?	Lt.	Lt.
de Aguiar	45	Lt.	Lt.
Leibfried	29	Lt.	Lt.
McNeel	26	Lt.	Lt.
Bremner	34	Lt.	Lt.
Harrison	30	Lt.	Lt.

*Name changes listed on records: *Wood/Martin; Hayden/ d'Orbessan; and Garber/Tate*

***Died in service*

Table B.
WWII Women Physicians Who
Graduated from Johns Hopkins

Name:	Rank When Commissioned
Margaret Craighill	Major
Sarah "Sally" Bowditch	Captain
Elizabeth L. Bryan	Captain
Marjorie Hayes	Lieutenant
Isabella Harrison	Lieutenant

Thanks to Johns Hopkins Medical Institutions, Alan Chesney Mason Medical Archives, for providing biographical materials.

Table C.
WWII Women Physicians Who Graduated from WMCP

Name	Rank When Commissioned
Delores Amar	Lieutenant
Angie Connor	Lieutenant
Martha E. Howe	Captain
Zdenka A. Hurianek	Captain
Adele Kempker	Captain
Jane Marshall Leibfried	Lieutenant
Anna Patton	Lieutenant
Margaret E. Shirlock	Captain

Thanks to Drexel University School of Medicine (DUCM) Archives and Special Collections (formerly WMCP) for providing biographical materials.

Table D.
Pioneer Women Doctors Abroad

Name	Status
Achsa Bean	RAMC; U. S. Naval appointment
Sarah Bowditch	AMC
Marion Loizeaux	AMC (contract surgeon)
Eleanor Peck	AMC (contract surgeon)
Mila Pierce (Rhoads)	AMC (contract surgeon)
Barbara Stimson	RAMC for the duration of the war
Josephine J. Stephens	AMC (contract surgeon)

Table E.
First Women Doctors Appointed to the VA in 1946

Name:	Branch Office Assignment:
Dr. Margaret Janeway	New York
Dr. Marion C. Loizeaux	Boston
Dr. Jane Leibfreid	Philadelphia
Dr. Gertrude R. Holmes	Atlanta
Dr. Grace Haskin*	Columbus, Ohio
Dr. Angie Connor	Chicago
Dr. Elizabeth Fletcher**	St. Louis
Dr. Eleanor B. Gutman	Seattle
Dr. Hulda Thelander***	San Francisco
Dr. Ruth Burgess****	Denver

Haskin: Not commissioned during WWII. She was a graduate of the medical school at Western Reserve University 1931, went to England under the Red Cross in 1943, and worked for the British Emergency Medical Service at a hospital which was "the center for head injuries." Quote from Marion Loizeaux, medical consultant, to Major Craighill, 17 April 1944, letter, Official Correspondence, Women Medial Officers, Box 5, MDC Coll.; also see WIMSA biographical card entry.

**Fletcher: Commissioned in the Navy during WWII. She graduated from the University of Alabama Medical School (UAMS) in 1934, and later married Dr. Howard Dishongh. She was board certified in psychiatry in 1948 and then graduated from the Arkansas Law School in 1960. See picture of her and biography at UAMS Library Digital Historical Collections.*

***Thelander: Commissioned in Navy during WWII. For more on her, see Women Doctors in War, pp. 97-98, 102-103, 114-115, 201. (She also has a picture in the book).*

****Burgess: Commissioned in Navy during WWII. She graduated from the University of Utah School of Medicine in 1944. In 1947, she married Reynold Cluff Merrill Jr. who later became a physician. For more see, "Obituary: Reynold Cluff Merrill Jr., Ph.D., MD.," Deseret News, Feb. 28, 2004. Also see, "In Memoriam: Classes of 1925-1950", Alumni Association, University of Utah School of Medicine, on-line.*

ABOUT THE AUTHOR

MERCEDES GRAF is a native of Chicago, Illinois, and she was formerly a professor of psychology at the Illinois School of Professional Psychology and Governors State University. She is now an independent scholar who resides in Highland Park, IL. Her articles on women medical workers, specifically nurses and physicians in American wars, have appeared in *Prologue* (the Quarterly of the National Archives), *Minerva Journal of Women and War, the Journal of Women's Civil War History, and the Journal of Army History*. She has also published books on these women: *On the Field of Mercy: Women Medical Volunteers in the Civil War to World War I; Women Doctors in War* (with coauthor Judith Bellafaire); *A Woman of Honor: Dr. Mary E. Walker and the Civil War;* and the *Introduction to "Hit: Essays on Women's Rights"* written by Mary E. Walker.

In this latest book, *To Heal and to Serve,* she discusses the role of women Army doctors in World War Two, an in-depth treatment that has not been previously undertaken in the literature.

MERCEDES GRAF

INDEX

Page locators in *italics* indicate photographs and tables.

nonmedical tasks, specialties and women's command assignments, 118, 121–22, 233

nonspecialists, general duty medical officers, 273–83, 288–91, 294–95

Norristown State Hospital, 146

North Africa, 49–50, 60, 149, 187–88

Northwestern University, 68

Northwestern University Medical School, 190

nursing: and anesthesiology, 203; Army Nurse Corps, *vii*, 41–42, 70; and gender identity stereotypes, 23; and nineteenth century medicine, 11–12, 14; and women doctors, 15–16, 20

nutrition and public health, 282–83

obstetrics and gynecology: Army doctors specializing in, 101, 117–18; Ida Holzberg, 255, 256–57, *272*; Jane Marshall Leibfried, 255, 257–59, 259, *272*; Jean Henderson, 255, 256, *272*; Margaret D. Craighill, 93–94, 95, 101, 255, *272*; Marion C. Loizeaux, 57

O.D. duties, 280

O'Donnell, Mae Josephine, 185–86, *222*

Olentine, Fred B., 148

Olentine, Julie Etta, 120, 148, *171*

On the Field of Mercy (Graf), 2

ophthalmology: Bronislava Z. Reznick, 251–52; Effie Ecklund, 87

orthopedics: Barbara B. Stimson, 43; as choice of specialty for women, 209; and military shoes for women, 58–59, 101; Trinidad Margarita Ramos, 209–10

Osborne, Gladys, 282–85, *300*, 320

overseas service: Achsa Bean, *42*, 43–48, 51; Barbara B. Stimson, 41–43, *42*, 44–51; desire of women doctors for military service, 39–41; Eleanor K. Peck, 46, 61–64; Josephine Stephens, 46, 68–70; Margaret D. Craighill, 56, 57–58, 60, 71; Marion C. Loizeaux, 46, 55–61; Mila Pierce, 46, 65–68; overseas service requests and postings, 17, 22–28, 41, 50, 315, *331*; Sarah "Sally" Bowditch, 46, 51–55

Parker, Caroline Pollard, 57

Parsons, Leonard, 65–66

pathology: Clara Raven, 189–96, *190*; Elizabeth Khayat, 175–76, 199–202, 211, 310, 321; Joyce Springer Morris, 202–3, 211; Machteld Sano, 196–99; Sophie Spitz, 83–85, *113*; women medical officers, 118

Patton, Anna M., 176, 248, 250–51, 259, *271*, *300*

Pay Readjustment Act of 1942, 286, 288

Peace Corps, 241

Peck, Eleanor K., 46, 61–64, 82, *113*, 294, *300*

pediatrics: Angie Connor, 177; Eleanor K. Peck, 61–62, 64; Elizabeth Garber Tate, 118; gender and medical specialties, 115; Mila Pierce, 46, 65–68, 80, 118, 320; Theresa T. Woo, 118, 235

Pierce, Mila, 46, 65–68, 80, 118, 320

plastic surgery, Genia Sakin, 242, 244–45, 246–48, 259, 310

Post-Traumatic Stress Disorder (PTSD), 304

postmortems, 198

postwar medical careers, 316–21

pregnancy: and honorable discharges, 97–98; WAC pregnancy rates, 58

prejudice: Aurelia Rozov on, 178; dependents of women medical officers, 131; Elizabeth Khayat on, 201; Elizabeth Lynn Bryan on, 144–45; Emily Dunning Barringer, 18; female doctors overcoming prejudice, *viii–ix*; gender and medical specialties, 115–116; Gertrude R. Holmes, 179; Gwendolyn Taylor on, 207; internships and residencies for women, 115–16, 308; and service rating scores, 126–27; and women doctors in the South, 200

Preston, Albert, Jr., 103

preventive medicine: Agnes Hoeger, 231, 236–41, *271*; communicable diseases and tropical medicine, 231, *271*; and military shoes for women, 59; Sally Bowditch, 53–55, 318; venereal disease and WAAC/WAC contract surgeons, 98–100; and venereal diseases, 53, 54

privacy, lack of privacy, 103–4

Procurement and Assignment Service, 305

Professional Service Division, Surgeon General's Office (SGO), 79

promotions: Achsa Bean, 49; Eleanor Peck, 62–63; gender and medical corps officer classifications, 118–19, 136, 148; Margaret D. Craighill, 93, 104; Marion C. Loizeaux, 56, 60; promotion and rank inequalities, 119, 135, 137, 144–45, 312–16; Sally Bowditch, 53

psychiatrists and psychiatry. *See* neuropsychiatrists and psychiatry

public health, 234–35, 239, 240; and nutrition, 282–83; and preventive medicine, 54

radiology: about, 223–25; Dorothy Bell, 225–26; Margaret Elizabeth Howe, 227–28, 230, 259; Melson Barfield-Carter, 226, *227*, 228–30, 259, 320–21

Ragus, Celia Ekelson, 252–53, 259, 315

rank: Achsa Bean, 49; Barbara B. Stimson, 49; Josephine Stephens, 70; promotion and rank inequalities, 119, 135, 137, 144–145, 312–316; rank of AMC-commissioned women as of September 1945, *327–329*

Raven, Bertram, 191

Raven, Clara, 133, 189–96, *190, 271*, 317

reasons for military service, 39–41, 43, 80, 102, 149–50, 152–53, 155, 235

Red Cross: and American women physicians serving in England, 20; blood banks, 245–46; and women doctors serving in World War, I, 15, 16, 39–40, 89

www.hellgatepress.com

DISCARD

CPSIA information can be obtained at www.ICGtesting.com
Printed in the USA
LVOW12s1208061213

364191LV00003B/9/P